KU-300-999

SIGHTHILL LIBRARY

NAPIER POLYTECHNIC LIBRARY

6042 00 27 5005

POSITIONING STRATEGY
IN
RETAILING

POSITIONING STRATEGY IN RETAILING

Gary Davies

MFI Professor of Retail Marketing,
Manchester Polytechnic

and

Janice Brooks

Market Research Analyst in the Mars Group

P·C·P

Paul Chapman
Publishing Ltd

658.87 DAV

Copyright © 1989 Gary Davies and Janice Brooks
All rights reserved.

First published 1989
Paul Chapman Publishing
144 Liverpool Road
London N1 1LA

No part of this book may be reproduced in any manner whatsoever without written
permission except in the case of brief quotations embodied in critical articles or
reviews.

Davies, Gary
  Positioning strategy in retailing
  1. Retailing. Marketing
  I. Title   II. Brooks, Janice
  658.8'7

ISBN 1-85396-050-0

Typeset by Burns & Smith, Derby
Printed by St. Edmundsbury Press, Bury St Edmunds
Bound by Hartnolls Ltd, Cornwall

Contents

Preface

A century ago the distribution of goods in many countries was controlled by wholesalers. The structure of the retail trade was evolving slowly from one dominated by open markets and fairs to one where most shopping was done in permanent premises, in high streets not too dissimilar to those in use today.

Fifty years ago most retailers sold mainly manufacturers' brands. The power of the wholesaler was in decline and that of the manufacturer was in the ascendancy. This change was aided by the growth of the mass media, which formed the channel for the manufacturer to promote to the consumer, over the head of the distribution system.

More recently the manufacturers' control over the market-place has been challenged by the ever-growing strength of the multiple retailers. Those multiples have also replaced much of the distribution role, traditionally held by the wholesaler, with their own warehousing and transport systems. Keen price negotiations at a central level, and the replacement of all but leading brands by the retailers' own-label merchandise are examples of the more proactive stance of the modern retailer and attract comment in the business press. But both are no more than symptoms of a shift in economic power away from both manufacturers and wholesalers to the modern multiples.

The first signs of change came in the 1960s following the lifting of resale price maintenance which made it illegal for retailers to discount from the manufacturers' recommended price. Even now such systems persist in other countries to protect the interests of the smaller retailers. The ending of price controls promoted price competition which, in the heyday of the brand, often meant the discounting of key national brands as loss leaders.

Retailers began to compete more and more on price. Profitability was determined by cost control and promoting high customer flow. Price competition became even more acute in the late 1970s and early 1980s because of high inflation and economic stagnation caused by two enormous rises in the price of crude oil. A number of retailers began seeking new ways to improve their abilities to compete on price; larger stores, limited product ranges, out-of-town locations, part-time staff and computerization were all used to a greater or lesser extent.

Some retailers had always resisted selling purely on price, recognizing that a price-led strategy could probably only succeed where it was based on a clear economic advantage. Such retailers included many of the 'niche' companies, particularly fashion retailers such as Benetton, NEXT and The Gap, but also some more mainstream companies such as Harrods and Habitat.

In the past decade in Britain it has become noticeable that more and more retailers, and in particular non-fashion retailers, are seeking factors other than price with which to attract and retain custom. The word 'image' is used frequently to encapsulate a number of non-price facets of a retail operation which combine to form, with the retailer's prices and merchandise, the overall offer to the customer. This emphasis on image in British retailing has its direct parallels in other countries but it appears to the authors that there are few countries where image-led strategies have been as successful. Certainly British retailers are, in many sectors, among the most profitable in the world in terms of net margin on sales. Yet the prices in British shops are still keen enough to attract day visitors on shopping trips from Continental Europe. There are also few restrictions on competition or on access to the market-place.

The objectives of this book are, therefore, to explore the relationship between the image of a retailer and its financial performance in order to try to explain the British retail phenomenon. The book draws on both marketing and strategic concepts for its academic context and structure, but the main content is devoted to a series of market research studies on various retail sectors. In many instances the authors provide commercial data on competing companies to demonstrate the potential value of 'a good image'.

What constitutes a good image is, therefore, of central concern to the book and each sector study has been selected to illustrate one or more aspects of retail image. Some of the studies have been published in varying form in the academic press and in one of the author's doctoral thesis, but this is the first time that the authors have been able to develop fully their ideas on image management. However, the book will doubtless raise as many issues as it ought help to solve. In particular the role of advertising in retail image formation and projection, severely questioned throughout the text, needs further investigation by both academics and practitioners.

Finally the authors wish to acknowledge the contributions made by colleagues to the development of their ideas, the undergraduate students who conducted much of the fieldwork under their supervision, and the financial support of Manchester Polytechnic and latterly of MFI for their work.

G. Davies
J. Brooks
Manchester, 1988

Acknowledgements

The authors are grateful to the following sources for permission to reproduce or quote from material which is their copyright.

Fig 2.3 p14 adapted with permission of the Free Press, a Division of Macmillan Inc. from *Competitive Strategy: Techniques for Analyzing Industries and Competitors* by Michael E. Porter, Copyright 1980 by the Free Press.

Market research data from NMRA on food retailer shares of packaged grocery purchases in Chapters 1 and 7.

Market research data from AGB and in particular Tables 4.1, 4.2 and 7.2.

Market research data and estimates from Mintel and in particular Tables 12.1, 12.3, 12.4 and 13.5.

Market research data from the Economist Intelligence Unit on the furniture and electrical market and in particular Table 10.1.

Market research data from Media Expenditure and Analysis Ltd on advertising expenditure in Chapters 5, 7, 8, 10, and 11.

Market research data from Harris International Marketing, in particular Table 7.5.

Market research data from Verdict Market Research on the furniture market in Chapter 10.

Price data on own labels from the *Financial Times* quoted in Table 7.4.

Quotations and data from *Retail and Distribution Management* published by Newman Publishing in particular the data on customers flows from Martin Simmons quoted in Chapters 10 and 11.

Quotation from Bob Tyrrel of the Henley Centre for Forecasting in Chapter 14.

Extracts from papers of J. D. Lindquist and L. L. Berry, previously published in the *Journal of Retailing*, and in particular Tables 6.1, 13.2, 13.3 and 13.4.

Extracts from *The Retailers* by E. Ornstein, published by Associated Business Programmes, an imprint of AGB Research PLC, in particular in Chapter 4.

Finally we would like to thank Brenda Oldfield for her work in the typing of the manuscript and the team at Paul Chapman Publishing for their invaluable help in producing the finished book.

Chapter 1

An Introduction

For centuries retailing has been a major economic sector. In recent estimates for Great Britain retailing accounts for over one-third of economic activity, employs 2.25 million people and offers the first employment area for 18 per cent of male and 26 per cent of female school leavers (McGee and Segal-Horn, 1985).

However, the size of retailing is currently less significant than the changing role of the typical retail company. Definitions of retailing as being concerned with the sale of goods and services to the public, or as an intermediary between the consumer and the manufacturer, have little relevance to the modern multiple retailer. Many retailers now have a high degree of control over their suppliers. In the main this has been achieved without vertical integration. A number of leading retailers sell only own-label products; many have a significant number of such lines. Others act as the main or the sole outlet for individual manufacturers. Retailers who rely on the resale of manufacturers' brands as their sole basis for business are now the exception rather than the rule.

It is not that the general public has become disillusioned with branded products or that the concept of branding has become redundant. There has not been a return to the pre-brand era where the retailer provided a packaging service for products bought in bulk. Rather the typical retailer seems to have acquired many of the attributes of the manufacturer's brand. Source loyalty to the retailer, has become as important a concept as brand loyalty to the manufacturer. Shoppers are being encouraged to form loyalties to stores for more reasons than just the price of merchandise and the convenience of the outlet.

SYSTEMS RETAILING

This change in role for the retailer has been facilitated by the growth in size and scale of the multiple and the trend towards centralized control. The so-called 'systems' retailers can boast a standard offering in each of their stores. Product range, pricing, display, recruitment policy, in fact virtually every aspect of store activity are controlled to a greater or lesser degree from the centre. Removing discretion from store level clearly removes some of the potential for local initiative, but it does appear that the more successful retail companies are those which have embraced the systems approach.

Food retailing offers a good example of the magnitude of both centralization and greater concentration of trade in the hands of the larger multiple (Davies, Gilligan and Sutton, 1985). Between 1970 and 1983 the number of buying points representing 80 per cent of grocery retailing fell from 750 to 220. Among the larger companies from 1970 to 1980, the number was reduced from 202 to 49. The three leading multiples, Sainsbury, Tesco and ASDA, increased their combined market share of packaged groceries from below 20 per cent in 1974 to nearly 40 per cent in 1983. In the key London market the first two held a 50 per cent share in 1985. In 1986 the Dee Corporation's acquisition of a number of food chains produced a combine large enough to rival Tesco in size. In 1987 Argyll's purchase of Safeway added to the list of food retailing giants. By that year the top five food multiples held a 68.5 per cent market share of packaged groceries (NMRA, 1987), and this figure ignored the share held by Marks and Spencer.

Significantly two of the leading three food retailers were exponents of the superstore approach, illustrating a general trend in a number of sectors towards ever-larger units. To survive, such retailers had to attract more than just the passing trade. While some retailers have continued to rely on the price promotion of manufacturers' brands to attract shoppers, the trend is towards offering the shopper something more than a cost saving in the battle for customer loyalty. Many have defined this trend as one towards promoting the image of a store. A good image, by definition, is capable of attracting custom and enhancing expenditure.

THE INDEPENDENT SECTOR

While the multiples have grown in most sectors at the expense of the small independent store, the more successful independents have often adopted the same strategy of benefiting from a coherent image. Some independents have formed voluntary chains; others, or at least their owners, have joined the franchise revolution.

In retailing, franchising is more likely to be concerned with retailing services, such as printing (Prontoprint) or fast food (Wimpy, Spudulike), than products, although product-based retail franchises do exist (Tandy, The Body Shop, Pronuptia). It may be significant that the franchise industry can claim success rates of the order of 90 per cent while the figures for small businsses as a whole indicate that the majority fail rather than succeed.

THE VALUE OF IMAGE

While franchising provides more than just the umbrella beneath which the independent retailer can trade, the franchise and the successful multiple have one thing in common – a coherent image. It follows that developing and maintaining a strong image are not only important in retailing, they could be a necessity. The larger multiple will develop an identity by centralizing control. It will promote an image to generate custom. Yet that image is by its very nature an intangible asset, something which cannot be costed or presented on the balance sheet.

If image is to be accepted as a viable tool in the retail business, rather than as a passing fashion, image and its value must be quantified. Image must be capable of being assessed. This book begins with the proposition that this is possible and, moreover, that image can be linked directly to commercial performance. It explores the potential for using image as a cornerstone in managing a retail organization at the strategic level and concludes that image is indeed such a vital factor. However, an early conclusion, drawn from current work in business strategy in general, is that it is not enough to have a coherent image. What matters equally is how an image compares with that projected by the competition.

We consider a successful image to be one which positions the retailer advantageously among the competing companies. The main challenge to the retailer is, therefore, one of positioning rather than merely image selection. Hence, this book refers to positioning strategy rather than image, marketing or business strategy.

We conclude that a favourable change in positioning will improve customer flow and expenditure per visit. In doing so, key financial indicators, particularly sales volume growth, net margin and return on assets employed, will also improve.

Positioning strategy is, therefore, likely to be of interest to the senior manager in retailing who has an input to corporate strategy and to managers at all levels who are responsible for implementing such strategies. The student of retailing and the practitioner could both benefit from the ideas being argued and the insights these may give into retailing as a business.

THE CONTENTS OF THIS BOOK

Chapters 2–5 of this book discuss retailing as a business, and identify the differences between retailing and other commercial activities.

We draw on aspects of marketing and corporate strategy to illustrate how a retailer can be regarded as equivalent to a branded product, and how relationships with the competition are generally more important to the retailer than to companies in other business sectors.

Chapter 5 is the first of a number of practical studies of various retail sectors. It deals with the menswear market in Britain in 1980–81, before the market-place became transformed as men bought fewer formal suits and more casual wear. There are clear links between the image of competing retailers and their commercial performance.

Chapter 6 explains the market research and image-mapping techniques used by the authors in enough detail for the reader who is interested in methodology.

Chapters 7–12 present a series of retail sector analyses, based largely on British companies but including one on West German department store retailing. These analyses illustrate the authors' earlier point that British retailers have often used image to better effect than their counterparts around the world. The final two chapters draw general conclusions on the value of image and on how to manage image as a part of retail strategy.

Each chapter concludes with a series of references for readers wishing to follow up specific issues and to acknowledge the original source of data. Also at the end of each chapter is a key point summary, designed to summarize the main points of that chapter.

Finally, a few words are needed on the selection of the various sector analyses for presentation in this text. The studies were conducted between 1980 and 1987. The most comprehensive is probably that of food retailers in Chapter 7, in that substantial amounts of commercial data on financial performance in particular are available for comparison. After 1987 the national food retail market in Britain became complicated by various takeovers. For example, two retailers were trading under two or more names and data were not freely available on the performance of individual operations.

Ideally, a study of the commercial significance of a retail image needs a well-defined sector in the mind of customers, nationally operating chains in the case of nationally based studies, and financial data specific to each individual retailer. In practice such an ideal situation rarely occurs, either at all, or for a long period of time. We do not claim that any of the studies offers a perfect analysis of any one retail sector, or that any provides insights relevant to the detailed performance of any one sector well into the future. Their value lies mainly in the general lessons which can be learned about retail strategy in the context of general views and theories about business.

In particular, we argue that while many of the concepts of marketing and business strategy are relevant to retailing, the single concept of differentiation holds the key to successful retailing. We consider that most methods of market segmentation in retailing, and the spectrum of options open to a retailer from price leadership to image leadership, are subordinate to the one key task for retail management: *to differentiate their offer in the eyes of the customer.*

References

Davies, K., Gilligan, C. and Sutton, C. (1985) Structural changes in grocery retailing: the implications for competition, *International Journal of Physical Distribution and Materials Management*, 15 February.

McGee, J. and Segal-Horn, S. (1985) Strategic issues in UK retailing, *Workshop on Retailing Strategy*, November, Arthur Young with the University of Aston.

NMRA (1987) Retail audit figures.

Chapter 2

A Strategic View of Business

The purpose of this chapter is to abstract the most relevant approaches to operating a business, and in particular a retail business, from the considerable volume of work published on corporate strategy. Inevitably the chapter is highly selective and focuses on those points of most value to later chapters in this book.

Corporate strategy is concerned with planning the long-term survival and success of a business. A strategy defines the direction for a business; it specifies where the business is going and determines how it will get there. A strategy guides the company towards its financial objectives. Figure 2.1 demonstrates how a strategy relates to the more straightforward idea of an objective and how both are given form further down the company hierarchy.

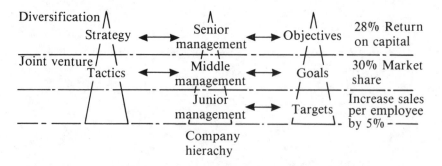

Figure 2.1 Strategy, objectives and the company hierarchy.

Most companies have an explicit or implicit set of financial objectives governing the operation of the business. Even if these objectives are not posted on the company notice board informing us that their organization aims for, say, a 25 per cent return on capital employed as its main business objective, a glance at the previous years' annual accounts will expose the implied financial objective. Quite simply, if the company has shown a certain financial performance over the past few years it is a safe assumption that it wishes to improve on this in the future.

Return on capital employed is one of the most common criteria used to express company objectives. This objective will be interpreted by key areas in the organization in terms of goals and then targets; for example, an increase to a 28 per cent return on capital employed might be interpreted by the marketing division as meaning the need to increase market share to 30 per cent as a goal. This will similarly be interpreted by store operations as meaning the need to improve sales per employee by 5 per cent in the next year as a target.

Clearly what is missing is any idea of how the last figure, the key to achieving both goal and objective, is to happen. Many line managers will be familiar with the exhortions of senior managers for greater shop-floor efficiency and effectiveness, without any accompanying explanation or guidance on how to achieve this. Inevitably many will have to interpret the sales per employee target increase not as an increase in total sales but as a reduction in the number of employees.

Objectives, goals and targets are often associated with financial control and cost cutting, rather than with expanding sales. Strategy and tactics, on the other hand, can often allow a company to improve its financial position through growth and, even with increased expenditure, produce an improvement in financial performance. For example, a strategy may involve diversification into a new area and an increase in expenditure. And here is where strategy and objectives may run into conflict. While the two must be in harmony in the long term, a valid strategy may involve a decline in financial performance in the short term because of the cost of implementation.

A strategy may involve numerous tactics. A shift up-market in a business might imply changes in products, people, advertising and many other elements. Tactics are, therefore, short-term changes in the business which are necessary to implement the strategy. A diversification strategy, for example, may involve the tactic of entering into a joint venture.

To understand the difference between a strictly financial approach to strategic planning and the more qualitative perspectives recommended by many authors, consider the hypothetical case of a retail organization which has, within its group of companies, a manufacturing unit and a mail-order business. Both these units make adequate financial returns in line with overall group performance. A purely financial approach would be likely to guide senior management towards retaining the manufacturing and mail-order businesses. However, the group may be better advised to divest itself of its peripheral activities and invest the proceeds in its retail operations. How can it gauge the future profit potential of each business area? How can it choose the right strategy?

Senior management will not suffer from lack of data nor lack of advice. The intellectual problem is to cut through the maze of conflicting data and reduce the tangle of seemingly unresolvable issues to a series of straightforward alternatives that can be understood by executives. This is not meant as a slight on the capabilities of executives. It merely recognizes that the typical group of functional specialists who comprise a board of directors cannot be expected to agree on an approach to business planning which is confused and confusing.

EARLY IDEAS ON STRATEGY

It is no surprise, therefore, that the earliest articles and books concerned with business strategy offered a series of methods of analysing business and of categorizing the types of actions management could choose. They simplified business problems into a number of categories and offered easily understood options to solve them.

In the 1960s the leading business writer of his era, Peter Drucker (1964), was telling managers that there were three kinds of business opportunity:

(1) additive;
(2) complementary;
(3) breakthrough.

The first develops the existing business, the second relies on synergy to expand the business in a new direction, and the third is virtually synonymous with diversification.

The same chapter in Drucker's book discusses in some depth the concepts 'build or buy decisions' and 'vertical and horizontal integration', illustrating the level of sophistication in such writings in the 1960s.

H. Igor Ansoff, another leading American writer of Drucker's era, produced one of the earliest books devoted entirely to strategy (Ansoff, 1965). The book introduced the idea of four basic strategies of 'sectors' for growth:

(1) market penetration;
(2) product development;
(3) market development;
(4) diversification.

Each was discussed in turn. Another whole chapter discussed synergy as a desirable concept in corporate development.

Business writings at about this time contained a number of concepts which have shaped management thinking ever since. One such concept was the product life cycle, the basic theory of which is that any product will progress through a number of phases in terms of sales volume. The most important are growth, maturity and decline. Decline may be due to a number of factors but is usually the result of products being replaced by others with a greater consumer appeal or technical advantage. Organizations as well as products are said to pass through similar cycles (Taylor, 1976). One of this book's authors has argued elsewhere that a company's involvement in managing its own distribution operations could well follow a life-cycle model (Davies, 1984).

Looking back over 20 years of developments in corporate strategy, and especially reading the work of Drucker and Ansoff, prompts two observations. First, the concepts being presented then seem, today, to be fairly basic. Second, the thinking of Drucker, Ansoff and others did at least attempt to shape the way managers should think when planning a business. Nevertheless, apart from some anecdotal case histories of US companies, little proof could be presented that the approaches they propounded would guarantee success to any company using them. Further, their advice was highly generalized and sometimes difficult to apply directly to the solution of real problems.

PLANNING GAP ANALYSIS

In the 1970s writings on corporate strategy continued in much the same vein, but with the addition of a number of specific techniques which could be used by managers as planning tools. For example, one leading consultancy used the concept of the planning gap as the basis for constructing a corporate plan for clients. Figure 2.2 shows the approach in outline.

The planning gap concept involves defining an objective for the company and comparing it with the expected position should management do little more than continue with its present policies. The difference between the two positions is the 'planning gap' that management must seek to fill with profit-making or cost-cutting ideas.

Using the technique involves defining both a financial objective and what is called a 'restatement of the business'. While the idea of a realistic financial objective is easy to grasp, redefining the business is a more difficult concept, but a more important one to deal with. Some examples will illustrate the idea.

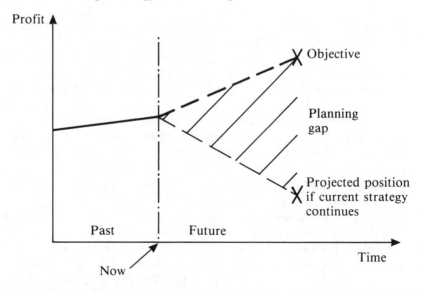

Figure 2.2   The planning gap approach to corporate strategy.

Redefining the business

A travel company specializing in the sale of package holidays to southern Europe from Britain decided that their existing market was becoming both saturated and overly price competitive. They redefined their business as being the 'sale of exotic destinations'. This apparently simple concept led the company to emphasize the more exotic destinations in their existing brochure, expand their packages to include new destinations and evolve a new and distinctive image in the market-place.

A company manufacturing cigarette lighters was concerned about the threats to their business from the anti-smoking lobby and from companies manufacturing disposable lighters. While their products relied on design and high technology, including the use of a novel crystal mechanism to produce a spark from mechanical contact, the company saw little future in their existing business. They redefined their business as 'the ignition business' and entered the market to supply ignition systems for products extending from domestic gas appliances to car and jet engines.

Managers from a large sugar-beet processor defined their existing business as the 'extraction of sugar from sugar beet and the sale of sugar to retailers and food manufacturers'. They selected a more desirable definition to help guide the future development of their company as 'agricultural management; the production of sugar and sugar-based products; the marketing of sugar and sugar-based products; the marketing of animal feeds'. The change led the company into considering how it could use its expertise in crops other than sugar beet, into vertical integration into sugar-based products, and into a more proactive marketing position to consumers. Finally it led them into seeing what had been viewed as by-products (sold off as animal feeds) as marketable and potentially highly profitable products in their own right.

Key result areas

Having redefined the business, the next stage is to identify the ideas to fill the planning gap. One approach is to divide the company and its activities into a number of key result areas. One method of doing so is to use the five Ms of business: money, marketing, manufacturing, materials and manpower. The company's strengths and weaknesses, the opportunities and threats it faces can be brainstormed in each key result area. Ideas for projects are the final output. Management will then assemble these into a coherent plan and assess whether the planning gap can be closed.

In the 1970s other similar planning techniques began to emerge, some based on research rather than the earlier, more intuitively based approaches. Two such techniques were product portfolio analysis and the concept of the experience curve.

THE EXPERIENCE CURVE

This is an important concept in understanding how a company can reduce its costs. Basically it is similar to a phenomenon established in early work study – the learning curve. In this, production workers, for example, will make the same quantum improvement in productivity each time the total volume they have produced in the past doubles. In other words, improvements in productivity become progressively more difficult to achieve, but such improvements will occur and can be predicted. The experience curve is the relationship between total costs, often of both manufacturing and marketing, and volume (Boston Consultancy Group, 1972). Real costs will reduce by the same quantum each time total historical volume doubles.

Cost advantage from the experience-curve effect is different from that from any economy of scale, although the high-volume company will benefit from both. Economies of scale can only be acquired by changing the size of a business operation. Experience-curve cost reductions can be achieved through experience or they can be bought by, for example, recruiting management with the relevant experience or entering into a joint venture with a company further down the experience curve.

PORTFOLIO ANALYSIS

Portfolio analysis is a family of techniques (Abell and Hammond, 1979) of which the most famous is the Boston Consultancy Group (BCG) technique. The BCG approach displays a company's individual products or business areas as a portfolio. Each product or area is categorized into one of four types of business depending on the relative market share of each and the growth rate of the market sector each occupies. The aptly named 'Cash Cows' generate large cash flows; 'the Dogs' represent products that are probably going nowhere; the 'Wild Cats' those that could develop into either 'Dogs' or 'Cash Cows' depending on how they are handled; 'the Stars', if handled well, will mature into the 'Cash Cows' of the future. 'Cash Cows' are low-growth rate businesses in mature markets with large market shares, while 'Dogs' are in similar markets but with low shares. 'Stars' have large shares of growing markets but could be displaced by 'Wild Cats' if the latter were heavily promoted. Portfolio analysis techniques allow companies, including multiple product manufacturers and retail groups, to define strategies for each product or retail chain.

The BCG technique can be thought of as a method of screening, identifying which products or business areas are likely to need which management action. Other business screens are more specific, for example the assessment of potential new products or business areas (see Rogers, 1975). In the main they have two points in common: they lead management to clear-cut decisions and they set the business into its market context.

The first point is relevant to an earlier comment made in this chapter about the intellectual challenge in business being to simplify the complex, so that clear-cut and correct decisions can be made. The techniques developed in the 1970s allowed this, and in doing so were a significant development over the more generalized approaches in the earlier decade. The second point, that the second generation of strategic planning techniques focused on the business in its market environment, needs further comment. In the 1960s and early 1970s (an era prior to oil crises, stagnation in international markets and inflation), sustained growth was taken for granted.

Markets grow for two reasons: through customers buying more or new customers entering the market. It is easier to compete with established competition, as the BCG approach highlights, when markets are growing. Customer loyalties, where they exist at all, are at a formative stage. New customers can be attracted to a new offering in the market without attacking the existing business base of established competition. A company can plan quite confidently by concentrating on the market, the consumer, with only the occasional glance over the corporate shoulder at the competition.

In the 1980s the situation changed dramatically. The response of the Western economies to the second oil price rise at the beginning of the decade contrasted starkly to the earlier strategy of inflating out of trouble adopted in the early 1970s. This time the response was monetarism, which if not synonymous with deflation certainly has much the same effect. World trade stagnated for three years or more. Demand in virtually every country declined as firms and individuals cut back on expenditure.

THE NEW COMPETITIVE ENVIRONMENT

Approaches to corporate planning which ignored the new, harsher economic environment were inadequate to meet a situation where competing firms were looking to survive in possibly declining markets. As costs continued to rise but buyers refused to pay more, survival came to mean survival at someone else's expense. A gain in market share meant a loss for someone else. The corporate planner had to consider not only the customer but also the competition, and place greater emphasis on the latter.

In the 1970s most corporate planning techniques and approaches had the company as the focal point. Planning consisted of building out from the status quo rather than first assessing the business within the overall market context. One exception was the BCG analysis, which depended on a measure of market dominance. But it is not always clear which competitors to include in such an analysis.

The second generation of strategic approaches in the 1970s were more useful as decision-making tools than the conceptualized ideas of the 1960s. However, there was a need in the 1980s for techniques which took more account of economic reality, where the influence of competition had to receive greater emphasis.

Competitive strategy

One recent approach which has proven popular in academic circles and capable of dealing with the current business conditions, is that of Michael Porter (1982). His definition of what he terms 'competitive strategy' is that it 'involves positioning a business to maximise the value of the capabilities that distinguish it from its competitors'. He lays great emphasis on analysing the market environment before attempting to construct a strategy, and was one of the first writers to emphasize the need to see competitive behaviour as the key determinant of strategy. The competitive forces Porter emphasizes are shown in Figure 2.3. Because the greater the competition the tighter margins become, Porter argues that firms should seek a position in the market where they hold a unique advantage. To define such a position he identifies three basic or generic strategies: cost leadership, differentiation and focus. The latter is close to the concept of market segmentation (see Chapter 3). Porter claims that a business *must* adopt one or more of these three generic strategies. However, before doing so the company must analyse its market by considering in turn each of the five structural components shown in Figure 2.3. Once selected, the generic strategy must be valued by the customer, should pervade the value chain, should be as different as possible, be immune to attack, and be sustainable.

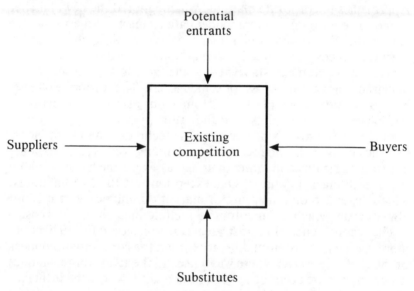

Figure 2.3   Porter's model of competitive forces.

Porter's approach is in many ways a tribute to the decades of work on corporate strategy. It encompasses many of the ideas first formulated in the 1960s and earlier, which can now be regarded as the 'common sense' of business. It encompasses some of the techniques developed in the 1970s. It sets the company in the entire complexity of its environment but at the same time offers the practising manager ways of reducing that complexity to manageable proportions.

Porter's approach is the one most relevant to the work we present in later chapters. In essence the market models of each retail sector represent the various competitors at the heart of Figure 2.3.

The development of corporate strategy serves, therefore, to offer direction to the business. Early work establishing the basic business truths can be used to avoid the fundamental errors that every business should seek to avoid. Later work offers the manager a number of techniques which can be used to simplify the complexity surrounding decision-making in large organizations. The most recent approaches place more emphasis on the need to include the current and potential actions of, first, competitors and then suppliers, customers, potential competitors and, in relevant circumstances, potential substitutes.

PROVIDING DIRECTION

All corporate strategy is aimed at providing direction for the business. One definition of corporate strategy recognizes the value of a clearly defined strategy: 'If a company has a clearly defined strategy, the entire senior management team can happily depart together on holiday knowing that the business will still be running smoothly on their return'. This somewhat tongue-in-cheek definition reminds us of the problems caused by telling a class of part-time students each to ask their managers for a copy of their company's main corporate strategy and objectives. Half returned to report none existed, a few returned with fairly meaningless, highly qualitative statements, and fewer with something which would allow the firm's employees to decide for themselves what to do in certain circumstances because the company had evolved a clearly stated strategy. Two companies had objected; one 'could not see why middle and junior managers need to be informed on corporate strategy'.

While data on tactics, goals and targets (market entry, acquisitions, etc.) are clearly confidential, it is not difficult to define any firm's implied corporate strategy. In retailing, as elsewhere, it is likely to be highly desirable that strategy is explicitly communicated at virtually all levels. On the basis of our work it could also be argued that it would be commercially desirable for a company to inform the competition of its own strategy, if that meant the competition would realize that it was in both parties' interests to avoid copying each other's initiatives.

In summary, businesses are normally managed to achieve financial objectives. Moving to meet these objectives has implications for many areas in the business, which can be described as goals and targets. A strategy works in concert with the objectives, explaining where the business is going. Strategies can be defined in a number of ways, guided by the basic ideas on strategy defined in the 1960s and by the more analytical techniques of the 1970s and beyond. Strategy is the key to achieving the company's commercial objectives. A successful strategy provides direction to management and employees; it tells them where they are going (for example, selling exotic destinations, into the ignition business) in simple but relevant terms.

KEY POINT SUMMARY

(1)   Corporate strategy defines the direction a business should take. A successful strategy produces the financial objectives sought by the company. However, strategies and objectives are not the same thing.

(2)   Early writings on strategy introduced basic concepts such as integration, synergy, life cycle and diversification, but such ideas were rarely supported by clear proof of their value and application.

(3)   In the 1970s the introduction of strategic planning techniques provided a better structure for the business strategist. They allowed the manager to simplify a complex business situation and identify the more desirable options.

(4)   In the 1980s, lower economic growth required the development of techniques in corporate strategy which emphasized the competitive environment.

References

Abell, D.F. and Hammond, J.S. (1979) *Strategic Market Planning: Problems and Analytical Approaches*, Prentice Hall, Englewood Cliffs, NJ.

Ansoff, H. Igor (1965) *Corporate Strategy*, McGraw Hill, London.

Boston Consulting Group (1972) *Perspectives and Experience*, BCG.

Davies, G. (1984) *Managing Export Distribution*, Heinemann, London, p.47.

Drucker, P. (1964) *Managing for Results*, Heinemann, London.

Porter, Michael E. (1982) *Competitive Strategy*, Macmillan, New York.
Rogers, D.C.D. (1975) The General Electric Business Screen in *Essentials of Business Policy*, Harper and Row, New York, p.52.
Taylor, B. (1976) Managing the process of corporate development, *Long Range Planning*, June.

Chapter 3

A Marketing Orientation Towards Business

Corporate and marketing strategy are sometimes used as virtual synonyms. Technically, corporate strategy defines the direction for the business, and marketing is one of the functions that puts strategy into practice by defining goals that give the corporate strategy real meaning. However, marketing is a business philosophy as well as a business function. A marketing orientation is then, arguably, a strategy itself. A marketing-orientated firm is often claimed to be intrinsically more capable of succeeding in the market-place. So what is marketing? More to the point, how can a marketing orientation contribute to business?

Our understanding of marketing has grown rapidly this century although that understanding had largely been in the context of the marketing of products by manufacturers rather than the marketing of a retail business. But many of the principles developed for selling products are equally valid for the retailer, although sometimes not so clearly. In this chapter, therefore, the main principles of marketing are defined and illustrated using mainly product-based examples.

Definitions of marketing tend to emphasize a customer orientation in running a business.

Selling goods that don't come back, to people who do.

Looking at the business through the customers' eyes.

Too many firms define a product first and seek a market second. By doing so they risk investing in something that no one will buy. The two approaches, market orientation and product orientation, are shown diagrammatically in Figure 3.1. Market orientation involves far more feedback from the customer, through market research but also through the orientation of its senior management and its employees. Market orientation does not appear merely through hiring a marketing department or changing someone's job title.

Perhaps the most extreme customer-orientated definitions of marketing are those such as: 'the customer is always right' and 'the

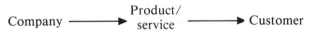

PRODUCT ORIENTATION

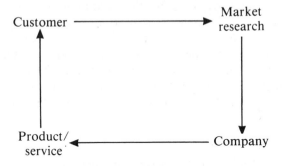

MARKET ORIENTATION

Figure 3.1   Market and product orientations towards business.

customer is king'. While such definitions may be valuable in exhorting employees to serve the customer there are real-life risks in taking customer orientation too far. Customers do not owe a living to those who provide them with goods and services. For example, if products and services are underpriced in the mistaken view that customers value keen price to the exclusion of all else, the rewards for the firm can include bankruptcy rather than profitable growth. Following blindly what customers tell you is not what marketing should be about.

A second theme can be identified in definitions of marketing that emphasizes profitability and the need to base marketing strategies on the strengths of the firm, as well as directing them towards the customers' desires.

ASSET-BASED MARKETING

Asset-based marketing has become popular in recent years as companies have counted the cost of ignoring the realities of their own businesses in endeavouring to offer what the customer wants. Creative marketing can build customer benefits onto a product or service that the customer needs. These benefits should, therefore, be those that the supplier can offer most cost effectively.

The danger of concentrating too much on the assets of the company was the main theme of Theodore Levitt's seminal article on marketing, 'Marketing myopia' (1960). Yet the actual article contained observations about the product orientation of major industries which are still valid today. Levitt criticized railroads for being overly concerned with the business of operating trains rather than conveying passengers. Flexible manning to tailor working hours to the hours when passengers wish to travel remains an issue in many railways. To be successful a marketing orientation must pervade an organization and be adopted by all its employees. It should be evident from the structure of the business that the company can meet the needs of the consumer, or that the consumer can be made to want that which the company is best at providing.

NEEDS AND WANTS

It is important to differentiate between what is essential to the customer in buying a product and what is desirable. A product is a package of benefits, some of which are tangible and some intangible (Figure 3.2).

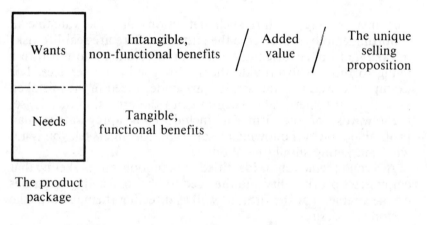

Figure 3.2   The product package of needs and wants.

A motor car offers its owner two types of benefit: the more tangible and functional benefit of transport and the less tangible and non-functional benefits of status and self-esteem. A problem facing the marketer is that the typical consumer is reluctant to acknowledge many of the more important intangible benefits. No one will readily admit to buying a car to impress others or to define status, yet anyone who has been involved in the allocation of cars in a company car system will recognize the importance to most of whether their car has a certain badge on its boot – especially if the person down the corridor has been given basically the same car but with a slightly different badge!

Car companies recognize this effect. The additional cost of the L-badged car over a basic model or an XL over an L, or a GL over an XL, is rarely commensurate with the additional equipment included in the price. In assessing the suitability or otherwise of the car allocated, managers will seem more concerned with the intangible elements in the car's benefits rather than whether the vehicle is functional for their work, or, for that matter, for their private use. The same effect is equally present when the typical customer is buying a car for domestic use.

The skill of the marketer therefore lies in identifying the non-functional benefits which can be associated with the company's product and which the customer will pay highly to acquire. But there is one other reason why a product should be enhanced in this way. Take the example of an automatic washing machine. It is difficult to sell one which is not white. The height and width are highly constrained. All machines have a round hole at the same level and an array of buttons. The customer is conscious of the need for an adequate spin speed but apart from that cannot be sure how to distinguish between various brands of machine. When was the last time a customer was allowed to try out even one machine before purchase?

The danger facing washing machine manufacturers is that if customers cannot distinguish between their various offerings in terms of performance and other benefits, they will select totally on the basis of price. Competing manufacturers therefore try to build on essentially non-functional benefits to justify a higher price and to differentiate their offering. Claims on reliability and the inclusion of special washing programmes for delicate articles (which are unlikely to be used frequently, if at all) are intangible benefits.

DIFFERENTIATION

Non-functional benefits offer the opportunity to build value in a product. They can also be used more easily to differentiate a product from any competition. This in turn helps avoid price competition. Differentiation is therefore frequently cited as a key element in marketing strategy.

Differentiation can be encapsulated in what Rosser Reeves first described as a 'unique selling proposition' (USP). USPs capture the essence of the main points of differentiation for the product. They are the labels consumers use to identify the product, almost in the same way as a Christian name and a surname help us to identify a person. Because these labels allow us to differentiate between products, they are often linked by marketers to 'positioning statements' – formal statements as to where a product is to be positioned in a market.

The USP for a product is how the company communicates its main points of difference to the consumer. The choice of media and the individuals portrayed in the advertisement focus the promotion onto the group most likely to be receptive to that message. For mass-market products, mass communication techniques seem essential in order to communicate the chosen image to the public.

Marketers talk in terms of brands rather than products. The distinction between a brand and a product was first written about in the 1950s (Gardner and Levy, 1955). The brand is the product plus the more intangible elements, or 'added value' as the enhancement of the basic product has been called. One writer referred to a brand of toilet tissue as having its own 'clear personality' (King, 1973). Taking this metaphor at face value, personality is a complex, multifaceted thing with many components. Similarly, there are a minimum of six elements that combine to form a brand, the six main elements of the marketing mix.

THE MARKETING MIX

The marketing mix is a combination of factors which contribute to the brand. In its simplest form it consists of the product, where it is sold, its price, its promotion, how it is sold and the attendant service elements (Figure 3.3). The mix provides an opportunity to emphasize that, unlike other disciplines or functions in a business, there is no prescribed list of best practice. Accountants and other functional managers conduct their roles within certain rules which have to be met. In contrast, while the mix is an important marketing concept, two similar products may have totally different mixes and still be equally successful.

In Britain in the 1970s a new brand of perfume, Charlie, marketed by Revlon, moved quickly to become the leading brand. Its marketing mix was fairly traditional, good-quality packaging, strong promotion of the brand name, distribution via high-street outlets and middle-of-the-road pricing. The product it superseded was marketed by Avon which sells through hundreds of self-employed agents working door to door. Their product benefited from Avon's umbrella promotion of its own name, but apart from that, was only featured in Avon's own literature.

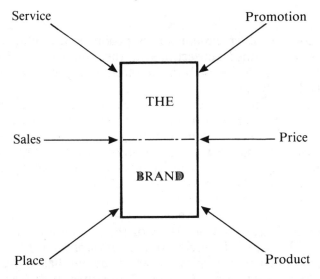

Figure 3.3 The marketing mix.

The marketing mix for each product was radically different, yet both brands had succeeded. One reason for this was that each element in both mixes combined to form a different but coherent whole. Products where individual elements of the mix do not blend, or even conflict, will probably not succeed, for example a high-priced brand sold through a down-market outlet.

One of the basic tenets of Gestalt psychology is that we perceive objects not as a sum of their parts but as a single entity. When we view products, we seem to see them holistically. Too low a price on a product which seems to have a strong branded appeal makes us suspicious, because the low price seems incompatible with the total offering. In psychological parlance we probably experience what Leon Festinger referred to as a 'cognitive dissonance' (cited in Chisnall, 1978), that uneasy feeling, perhaps when things are 'not quite right'. A company must, therefore, be capable of co-ordinating each element in the marketing mix. Organizationally this can be solved either by excellent communication or by appointing one person, a brand manager, to oversee the development of the brand as a whole.

MARKET SEGMENTATION

Brands such as Cadbury's chocolate and Heinz baked beans have a broad enough appeal to be desired by almost everyone. Some companies have the resources to market to all members of a population. In other circumstances products are better directed towards well-defined subsections of the population. Marketing expenditure can be focused on the target group or segment most likely to buy the product.

Market segmentation depends to an extent on the availability of specialist media so that promotional expenditure in particular can be directed at a predetermined group. In fact the main impetus behind targeted marketing came from the identification of socio-economic groups in work originally funded by newspaper publishers. The work established six groupings – A, B, C1, C2, D and E – dependent on the occupation of the head of the household. Frequently these six groups were aggregated in practice to just three, each representing about one-third of the population – ABC1, C2 and DE. The use of the socioeconomic groupings as the basis for segmentation came into question when the purchasing pattern of two of the largest groups – C1 and C2, the supervisory/clerical and skilled manual groups – seemed to be merging. For example, many people, in particular the retired and the partially-employed, could not easily be allocated to any group.

The basis for the A–E classification system – the occupation of the head of the household – became a contentious measure in an era when more married women are working full-time. A new method based on the type of housing and neighbourhood offers a potentially more objective measure of socioeconomic grouping. ACORN (A Classification of Residential Neighbourhoods) is already used by mail-order companies and others as the basis for their market segmentation.

If newspapers, magazines, television channels and other media are read or viewed by the same target group which the business is endeavouring to reach, then advertising through such selective media is likely to be more cost effective. However, as society becomes more homogeneous, the whole basis of segmentation using social class and apparent household income as the main determinants of purchasing behaviour, is questionable.

Take, for example, the young married couple, neither of whom is well qualified but who both work and receive middle of the range salaries. They have, like many of their peers, a desire to move up in the world and show this by using their high disposable income to buy products and services normally associated with households in a higher socioeconomic group. In the jargon they have a higher reference group than the one to which they actually belong. The antithesis of this couple would be the apparently upper socio-economic household who have rejected many of the values of the consumer society, who own neither a car nor a television set but still live in a middle-class neighbourhood.

Both these stereotypes could be ignored if they represented small sections of society. But a large section of the population can be described better by their attitudes than by their income or even their housing. The use of attitude or lifestyle as an alternative basis for segmentation is growing, but its application is limited because of the problems of classification and measurement. Housewives, for example, can be classified by their attitude to housework. This can be correlated with their purchases of labour-saving products. But if their attitudes do not also correlate with media exposure, the value of segmentation based on attitude is questionable. Thus a product or service which relies on promotion should select methods of segmentation that are relevant to the available media.

Market segmentation as a concept is still valid but the problem is selecting a method of segmentation which divides a market into clearly defined and identifiable segments in a useful way.

Segmentation appears to have three or four main benefits to the marketing company. There are the straightforward economic advantages of specialization in certain products, customers or ways of doing business. Then there are the benefits of clarifying to employees and customers alike to whom the product package is being directed. The advantage of clear segmentation in helping to guide and focus a business has a synergy with the direction that good strategy can offer. Segmentation is, therefore, a strategic tool. Segmentation also makes for easier control of a business, as it should allow the marketer to calculate in financial terms the size of the chosen sector at which the product is being aimed. Calculation and monitoring of market share provide a useful measure of performance. Segmentation is all the more powerful if there are useful links to the media, which can be used to promote the product. The more specialist the product, the greater the need for specialist media, focused on the same target group, to keep promotional costs within reasonable bounds.

In Chapter 4 we list and review the methods used by retailers in market segmentation. The list is a very long one and few approaches seem to guarantee the advantages that segmentation should bring to the business. As society becomes more socially homogeneous, identifying clear traits which distinguish one group from another becomes more difficult. There is a danger that in practice segmentation involves far too much generalization.

UNBRANDED MARKETING

The main theme of this chapter is the advantage of branding. A strong, differentiated image for a product or service is desirable if not essential in business. The consequences of ignoring the branded approach to product management could be that the product is seen as inferior to other, more branded offerings in the same market.

An unbranded product is often seen as a pale copy of a brand. Such copies are referred to as 'me too' products. In the Boston Consultancy Group terminology (see Chapter 2) they are likely to be in the 'Dogs' category, dominated by the branded, market leader and only marginally profitable.

The strategy adopted by the 'me too' product is merely to follow the success of the brand leader. Normally the logic behind the 'me too' is to try to share in that success. Typically, an innovative organization has developed a new and profitable market or market sector. Quite rightly competitors seek to benefit from this development but, possibly because they are moving too fast, they copy the innovator rather than developing the new market by seeking a novel niche within it.

The reaction of the consumers is crucial to the 'me too' product. If the new arrivals are seen as merely aping the brand leader, consumers do not buy, at least not in the quantities required to establish a profitable product. Why this is so has never been adequately explained. What happens next is easier to understand; retailers are reluctant to give shelf space to slow-selling lines competing with market leaders and delist them.

In a more established market the situation can arise where a number of products are competing but with little or no real differentiation between them. This is often the case in industrial markets and is commonplace in the commodity sectors. The temptation is to seek advantage by price promotion rather than image promotion. Unless one of the players in the market has a real technical or other advantage to be able to offer a lower price than the competition (Porter's cost-leadership generic strategy – see Chapter 2), companies are reduced to cutting prices and margins in a price-led competition that can have no ultimate winner.

There is substantial evidence (Pecham, 1973) that price promotion of a brand, a temptation when the brand is towards the end of its maturity phase, merely accelerates the decline phase in a product's life cycle. It seems that price promotion should be used as a tactic, to encourage trial or repurchase, and not generally as a strategy. It is no coincidence that brand leaders are rarely towards the low price end of their sector. By definition a brand has some intrinsic quality for which consumers will pay a premium above the price of a generic product.

Trial and repeat purchase rate, the objectives of price and non-price promotion, are crucial elements in marketing strategy. Parfitt (1972) has demonstrated how the penetration of a new brand settles down some 20 weeks after launch, and the rate of repeat purchase even faster. Together market penetration and the repeat purchase rate define the brand's sales volume and market share. It is likely that a new brand needs to establish itself within the first six months of life to guarantee a long-term future. Price promotion, at launch, to encourage trial is therefore a perfectly valid approach.

MARKETING PRODUCTS AND SERVICES

So far in this chapter we have discussed marketing theory with the implied assumption that the same concepts have equal validity when applied to products and services. The purpose of the chapter is to identify the main tenets of marketing which can be applied to the positioning strategy of retailers later in the book. But is a retailer offering products or a service? Superficially, at least, retailing is a prime example of a service industry (although the growth in own-label products offers grounds to argue quite differently).

Academic thought is somewhat divided as to whether distinctions between product and service marketing are valid or indeed useful. Certainly services are themselves hardly a homogeneous group and distinctions between service and product marketing are unlikely to be clear cut. Nevertheless there are a number of points from the growing literature on services marketing which could be relevant in applying marketing to the retail sector.

The first observation, admittedly from a survey in 1974, is that service companies tend to have less of a marketing orientation (George and Barksdale, 1974). This is despite the fact that, by definition, service companies have greater day-to-day contact with customers than do many manufacturers. The survey of 1,000 companies revealed that marketing activities in service organizations were less structured and that less money was spent on them. It found a general lack of market analysis in service companies, a point commented on by Wilson (1972), the author of one of the few books on services marketing. He stated that 'knowledge of and attitudes to clients may be formed on impressionistic evidence'. Although written in the context of the marketing of professional services, Wilson's comment is not irrelevant to those retailers whose marketing consists of 'seeing how it sells' rather than being able to predict that 'it will sell' because of prior research and market knowledge.

A number of writers have commented on the different interaction between the customer and the service and product providers. An interesting idea is that with services the interaction is shaped to a considerable extent by the customer. How the customer uses the service will define the service that is actually purchased. Consequently the service supplier has less control over what is perceived as being purchased. Any values added to the basic service by service marketers will be somewhat ethereal. They will be difficult to define and difficult to communicate to the customer.

Shostack (1977) has advised companies marketing services to use tangible factors in their promotion, and companies marketing more tangible objects (i.e.products) to concentrate on intangible elements. A transport service, for example, should be promoted by featuring tangible aspects such as trucks or photographs of senior management, while a product such as perfume must rely on the imagery of male infatuation rather than a list of ingredients. Other writers have commented on the search by consumers of services for tangible 'cues', which may be taken as evidence of the capabilities of the firm providing the intangible offering.

Guseman (1981) pointed to the need for service companies to create a mood in their premises 'which is consistent with the image the firm wants to create'. Another tangible – the personnel of the seller company – can be vital (Boom and Nyquist, 1977; Dutch and Ash, 1981); by having a careless, impersonal manner towards customers staff can destroy the image the company has striven to create. Gronroos (1978) remarked that 'in a service company, almost every employee belongs to the marketing department' – a sentence which is certainly relevant to every retail store.

MODELS OF BUYER BEHAVIOUR

Apart from the many concepts which form what we describe collectively as 'marketing principles', the development of marketing as a discipline has encompassed a range of approaches to solving marketing issues. The largest single area associated with marketing is market research, which is discussed in a retail context in Chapter 6. Probably the next most important area is buyer behaviour. Understanding why people buy and, therefore, how they can be encouraged to buy has been the objective of both theorist and practitioner. The practitioner tends to use the ideas of the theorist in market research or, more directly, in developing new approaches which can be tried in the market-place.

Theorists have developed a number of different approaches to modelling customer behaviour. These fall broadly into two groups: behavioural and cognitive. Behavioural models describe human behaviour in terms of our responses to a set of stimuli, such as basic needs for food, the persuasive advertisement, social needs and so on, in a preconditioned way. The work of Pavlov is typical of studies which have contributed to our understanding of behaviour when seen from this perspective. Psychologists and psychiatrists such as Freud and Jung have given us explanations of motives that drive us to respond to our environment. These, and more recent workers such as Maslow, have had their ideas on motivation applied to many aspects of business but none more so than marketing.

The cognitive model argues that human beings are more logical in their decision-making; they evaluate and make conscious decisions rather than being driven by reactions. Theorists such as Engel, Kollat and Miniard (1986) have devised flow models describing buyer behaviour as a series of steps. Darden (1983) found a model first proposed by Fishbein to explain four purchase situations in retailing. The model involved measures of social compliance, past experience and, interestingly, beliefs about individual stores.

In a review of the various approaches to modelling consumer behaviour, Fletcher (1987) argues that models divide into those that imply high involvement and those that imply low involvement in the decision-making and buying process. He and others claim that certain psychological models are more useful in describing certain types of purchase. An impulse purchase could be argued to be purely behavioural in nature, while a house purchase involves a considerable degree of evaluation and involvement. For more routine purchases there seems to be agreement that we 'satisfice', telling ourselves subconsciously that 'it will do' – a modified behavioural response. For non-routine purchases, on the other hand, we are forced to think even though we still employ our emotions – a modified cognitive response.

Models are useful in helping us to understand behaviour but they are only really useful if they can reliably predict behaviour. Unfortunately no single approach developed thus far can even claim to describe all consumer behaviour.

MARKETING IN PRACTICE

The concepts of branding, differentiation, marketing segmentation and the marketing mix are well established and widely accepted as being essential to the success of most consumer product companies. However, many companies seem to pay lip service to marketing as a philosophy in running their businesses. One recent British study (Heidrick, 1985) showed the senior marketing executive becoming progressively more involved in critical strategic and policy decision-making. Marketing had moved from being a service function to more of a central driving force in many companies. However, the survey implied that despite the attention given to marketing by business, it was still seen as a specialism rather than as a central part of business activity.

Many managers and consumer groups view marketing with suspicion. It is difficult to prove that marketing orientation works. The reasons why customers prefer particular brands are still unclear, although the branded product seems to offer a greater guarantee of quality, reliability and value.

Much of what we have discussed in this chapter can be regarded as compatible with ideas proposed by the business strategists and reviewed in Chapter 2. In Chapter 4 we apply both sets of ideas to retailing.

KEY POINT SUMMARY

(1)   Marketing is a business philosophy closely aligned in its ideas to corporate strategy.

(2)   Products and services are sold on the basis of tangible and intangible benefits, the latter appealing at a psychological level. The appeal is a blend of the many aspects of the marketing mix.

(3)   Markets for products can often be segmented by the income, social group or attitude of consumers and by many other factors. While segmentation is a powerful tool in theory, in practice it is often difficult to identify clear market segments.

(4)   Unbranded products, particularly those designed to copy the success of another product, are generally less successful.

(5)   Branded goods are rarely successfully promoted on price in the long term. Price promotion is better seen as a tactic than a strategy.

(6)   The marketing of services, of which retailing is arguably a part, could present different challenges to the marketing of a product. An emphasis in promotion on the tangible aspects of the service is advised. The attitude of any service organization's personnel to customers is also emphasized.

(7)   The behaviour of customers can be modelled. However, no model can reliably predict customer behaviour in all circumstances.

(8)   Many organizations still seem to do little more than pay lip service to marketing in managing their business at the strategic level.

References

Boom, B.H. and Nyquist, J.L. (1977) Analysing the customer/firm communication component of the service marketing, *Journal of Marketing*, April.

Darden, W.R., Erdem, O. and Darden, D.K. (1983) A comparison and test of three causal models of patronage intentions, in *Patronage Behaviour and Retail Management*, ed. Darden, W.R. and Lusch, R.F., North Holland, N.Y.

Dutch, J.A. and Ash, S.B. (1981) Consumer satisfaction with professional services, in *Proceedings of a Special Conference on Services Marketing*, Orlando, Florida, 1981, American Marketing Association.

Engel, J., Blackwell, D. and Miniard, P., (1986) *Consumer Behaviour*, 5th ed. Dryden Press, New York.

Festinger, L. as cited in Chisnall, P. (1978) *Marketing a Behavioural Analysis*, McGraw Hill, London.

Fletcher, K. (1987) Evaluation and choice as a satisficing process, *Journal of Marketing Management*, Vol. 3, no. 1.

Gardner, B.B. and Levy, S.J. (1955) The product and the brand, *Harvard Business Review*, Mar-Apr.

George, W.R. and Barksdale, H.C. (1974) Marketing activity in the service industries, Marketing Notes and Communications, *Journal of Marketing*, October.

Gronroos, C. (1978) A service orientated approach to the marketing of services, *European Journal of Marketing*, Vol. 12, no. 8.

Guseman, D. (1981) Risk perception and risk reductions in consumer services, in *Proceedings of a Special Conference on Services Marketing*, Orlando, Florida, 1981, American Marketing Association.

Heidrick, Struggles (1985) The chief marketing executive, *Institute of Marketing Journal*, January.

King, S. (1973) *Developing New Brands*, Times Management Library, Pitman, London.

Levitt, T. (1960) Marketing myopia, *Harvard Business Review*, July-August.

Parfitt, J. (1972) Panel research, in R.M. Worcester (ed.) *Consumer Market Research Handbook*, McGraw Hill, London.

Pecham, J.O. (1973) *The Wheel of Marketing*, A.C. Nielsen.

Shostack, G.L. (1977) Breaking free from product marketing, *Journal of Marketing*, April.

Wilson, A. (1972) *The Marketing of Professional Services*, McGraw Hill, London.

Chapter 4

Strategy and Marketing in Retailing

In this chapter we take the main ideas identified in the previous two chapters on corporate strategy and on marketing and show how they apply to retailing. But how relevant is it to give similar weight to both approaches? One view of marketing is that it is a subsidiary task to corporate strategy, a method of delivering rather than of shaping a strategy. However, many of the concepts central to both approaches to business are similar if not identical, such as, for example, differentiation and segmentation. The point was also made earlier that marketing is a business philosophy as much as a business function.

Although whole businesses have been 'marketed' in sometimes substantial corporate-image promotions, can a business be viewed at all realistically as if it were a product? More specifically, can you market a retail chain using much the same principles as when marketing a packaged grocery? We believe that you can. Viewing a retail chain as a product is not an entirely novel idea. One of the few texts devoted to retailing strategy (Knee and Walters, 1985) talks of the 'retailing product package' and uses the concept to refer to a retail company and to link to standard product marketing theory. Practitioners also talk in terms of marketing retailers as if they were brands (Street, 1986). Many ideas in consumer marketing have direct parallels in retailing.

The marketing concept of the product life cycle is very similar to that of the wheel of retailing theory. The wheel theory (McNair and May, 1978) argues that retail operations grow from essentially price-led operations into higher-cost, higher-margin operations. They then fall prey to newer, more competitive retailing concepts as they near the end of their life cycle.

The concept of the marketing mix is closely paralleled by that of the retailing mix, where a number of essentially retail variables are considered to contribute to the corporate whole (Lewison and DeLozier, 1986) (Figure 4.1). The concept uses much the same elements as the marketing mix discussed in Chapter 3.

Retailers in Britain and elsewhere have made good use of the idea

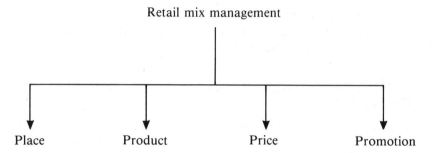

The 4Ps of the retail mix, identical to the
4Ps of the marketing mix.

Figure 4.1 The retail mix.

of market segmentation, whether on traditional demographic lines such as Mothercare on age and Sainsbury on socioeconomic group, or on attitude such as NEXT. However, these few examples also demonstrate that segmentation by product type (children's goods, food and fashion) is probably more important. The challenge of segmentation in retailing seems to be whether, for example, the food market itself can be segmented, and if so, how?

If segmentation is a relevant concept in retailing and if there are parallels between the marketing mix and the retailing mix, the product life cycle and the wheel of retailing, what of the concepts of added value and differentiation? The relevance of added value is the easiest to identify because most retailers clearly do not survive by acting merely in their basic function as an intermediary between manufacturer and consumer. Most add value in some form or other – lower price, better service, more choice, higher quality or whatever – each provides the basis for differentiation.

In retailing a more difficult test of the relevance of marketing in practice might be whether there is much evidence of problems when marketing principles are ignored. Issues of differentiation are discussed later, but a clear example of product orientation in retailing, rather than market orientation, could be seen in many of the smaller specialist computer shops that sprang up in the 1970s. Their owners were often enthusiasts, nearly always users of the most confusing jargon and, most important, concerned to sell computer hardware rather than solutions to business problems. Their lack of understanding of business problems was evident in the little or no advice they offered to a commercial market (which was eager enough to buy), and in their inevitable liquidation as retail businesses. Such firms are directly comparable with the railroads in Levitt's 'Marketing myopia' (see p.20).

PRICE AND IMAGE: THE EXAMPLE OF PETROL RETAILING

In Chapter 2 we saw that when products are undifferentiated they tend to compete on price. Petrol stations are an unusual example of retailing but they allow us to examine the effect of branded retailers becoming undifferentiated and to study retailers which are synonymous with the brands they sell.

Until the 1960s motorists in Britain would drive long distances to fill up with a specific brand of petrol. They would pass by one retail outlet believing that someone else's 'Extra' was a better product than the 'Super' on offer more locally. The reality of the petrol business was, and still is, that a limited number of refineries supply a large number of different petrol retailers from the same source. Moreover, the technical differences between petrols *have* to be small to meet the design specifications of motor car engines which cannot be retuned each time a motorist chooses to switch petrol brands.

Government legislation introduced in the 1960s not only defined just four types or grades of petrol, based on octane ratings, but also prevented the petrol companies from claiming or implying that their 'four star' was better than someone else's, unless clear proof could be offered that this was true. As a result it became increasingly difficult for marketers to differentiate one brand of petrol from another. The product became more like a commodity to be bought on price.

By 1984 petrol prices in Britain had risen steeply to a point where 196 pence per gallon was the benchmark for four-star petrol, the highest octane and most popular product.

British motorists fall into two groups: those who own their own vehicles and pay for their own petrol, and those who use vehicles owned by their employers and who are likely to have their petrol paid for them. The proportion of company car drivers on the road and their share of petrol sales are not clear. But a substantial number of petrol buyers could be less than totally price sensitive in petrol purchasing, given that someone else would be paying for it. In 1984 a project was undertaken, under the authors' supervision, to assess the price sensitivity of petrol retailing. The number of cars visiting each petrol station on a main road into Manchester were counted during one day and for two hours in both the morning and the evening peak commuter times. On a 13-km stretch of road there were nineteen petrol stations representing nine different brands. Prices varied between brands and even between stations selling the same brand.

A number of pointers emerged from the work. The most startling was the traffic flow generated by one station, poorly sited near a main intersection and with a small, crowded forecourt. The station, an independent, selling a less well-known brand, had always discounted its petrol and at the time of the study was selling four-star petrol at 192 pence per gallon with a further discount of 1 penny for members of their 'club'. As 'members' were rarely, if ever, asked to show their membership cards and membership was free, the extra discount was probably automatic. The vehicle count revealed a traffic flow into this station four times higher than the average for any local competitor. A 2 or 3 per cent price advantage, against the benchmark of 196 pence, had produced a substantial increase in custom, despite the presence in the market of company car owners who might not be price sensitive.

The extent of price sensitivity in the market proved to be the major constraint on petrol retailers in their pricing and marketing at the time. Numerous attempts at differentiation through enhancing the quality of forecourts, games and free gifts were quickly matched by the main competitors. Inevitably the presence of discounters drove prices down in the 1980s as the oil price fell, despite the attempts of companies to take it in turn to lead on price rises. By 1986 it was being claimed that price was no longer the key issue in petrol retailing (Fox, 1986). The garage identified in the Manchester study had by then been taken over by one of the leading companies. It retained some of its price leadership locally but the forecourt did not appear to be so crowded.

There are two ways of interpreting these results in the context of retailing as a whole. First, the way to retail petrol is clearly to sell on price. If a small price reduction causes such an increase in demand then such logic seems difficult to fault, until the overall effect on profitability for all petrol retailers is considered. Price promotion merely resulted in competitors matching the lower prices of the discounter, and, with each firm buying from the same source, the inevitable effect is to see margins reduced for all concerned.

The second way of interpreting the results is to realize that price promotion can be self-defeating unless a retailer has a real cost advantage over its rivals. Realizing this, petrol companies have eventually turned again to non-price factors to differentiate themselves. With the change in legislation towards standardized products, differentiation is no easy task, but it offers the only realistic way to profitability.

Before it was taken over by one of the major oil companies, the petrol station with the low-price strategy probably had an inbuilt cost advantage over its local rivals that enabled it to succeed. Being an independent it could wheel and deal in a market-place where petrol was often in over-supply from the refineries. Oil companies seemed to have the strategy of making profits from extraction and refining but not from retailing, and discounting excess petrol at the refinery, despite the effect on its own retailing arm, could have made sense.

Differentiation, in the absense of cost advantage, is, therefore, a central theme in corporate strategy and also in marketing. It appears to be valuable in retailing.

PRACTITIONER OPINION

Further evidence for the value of drawing on both strategic and marketing perspectives simultaneously in managing a retail business, comes from practitioners and those closely associated with them. Referring to food retailing, Altman (1986) commented on the shift to an image-led approach by food retailers in the 1980s:

> There also appears to be a tacit agreement among market leaders that the days when competitiveness focused on price alone are gone. In the absence of price wars, fierce competition has led to a considerable sharpening up of marketing structures and strategies.

A leading practitioner of image-led retailing, Ralph Halpern, was even more specific (Halpern, 1985):

> Think of Marks and Spencer. It stands for something. Burton stands for something. Or NEXT. Now think of Debenhams. If you've got a blank in your mind it's because the retailers have not successfully stamped a position and an image on the store.

These comments were made in the context of a takeover of the Debenhams department store chain by the Burton Group. Burtons had promised during the takeover battle to sharpen up the Debenhams image. Halpern commented further at the time: 'The retailers who survive in the future will be those who offer a clear cut definition of what they're trying to do to a clearly targeted audience'.

The Burton Group offered a good example of this philosophy with outlets such as Top Shop, Top Man, Dorothy Perkins, Evans, Principles and Burtons, each with a clear market position. It is tempting to draw direct parallels with the marketing philosophies of leading consumer goods manufacturers, who aim to develop a portfolio of leading brands. The Burton Group's portfolio of brands merely happened to be retail outlets. The marketing principles of segmentation and differentiation are being followed in both instances.

Terrence Conran described the 'birth of Habitat' in the 1960s and its development through the 1970s and 1980s (Conran, 1984). His first of fourteen principles, established after opening his first outlet in 1964, was:

> Choose products that will appeal to the customer identified as our target, thus giving the collection a homogeneity that is not found in those shops that try to offer a little of everything to everybody.

Later in the same article Conran refers to the 'Habitat formula', summarizing in this phrase an orientation towards retailing that goes beyond the systems concept of retailing identified in Chapter 2. Whereas the systems approach emphasizes the need for a systematic approach to operating a retail business, the word 'formula' seems to offer more in strategic terms. The implication is that retailers should each be looking for a unique formula to give direction to their business.

These anecdotal comments and specific examples seem to imply that there are basic rules for running a retail business and that these rules draw from both corporate strategy and marketing thought.

ANALYSING RETAILING FROM A STRATEGIC PERSPECTIVE

Chapter 2, on strategy, ended with reference to Porter's approach to the area as an example of the latest thinking. His approach emphasizes the need to plan a business not in isolation but as a small part of a larger environment. His message is that a company must understand how 'the contending currents... affect the company in its particular situation' (Porter, 1979). He advises starting by analysing the market structure and the competitive position before defining a strategy for the business.

What generalizations can we make about retailing as a business which could shape the strategy of any retailer? Porter models any market-place in terms of five competitive forces (see Figure 2.3): potential entrants, suppliers, buyers, substitutes, and existing competition. Using this approach, what can be said under these headings about virtually any retail business?

Potential substitutes

Traditional retailing has some existing threats from substitution by mail order, direct door-to-door selling, possibly by manufacturers, and catalogue shops. None of these has had more than a peripheral effect on most sectors of mainstream British retailing. However, the rise of mail order in Britain in the 1960s at a time of low postal charges, and the price advantage of catalogue shops, indicate that there is no room for complacency when considering these alternatives.

A greater threat in the future could come from home shopping aided by modern electronics. The technology exists already, not only for using home computers to examine retail offerings, but also for three-dimensional (holographic) image projection which, if perfected at a reasonable cost, will allow customers to examine products even more realistically at home than via a two-dimensional television screen. Nevertheless the present cost of establishing a database and linking it to enough homes to provide sensible competition to the more sensory-based end of retailing, fashion for example, is prohibitive. Food retailers might feel more threatened and experiments are already underway to test the concept of home shopping, to date largely unaided by the most sophisticated technology. Even here the costs of picking, packing and delivering orders make home shopping relatively unprofitable.

In summary, the threat of substitution in retailing is far less than, say, for the manufacturer of mechanical clocks faced by the electronics industry or the railways threatened by road transport.

Retail customers

A retailer's customers have little power as individuals. Collectively they may be able to exercise influence through consumer groups, but the lack of importance of any one customer to a given retailer lies behind the indifference to customer service of many retail employees. This indifference would not be tolerated by, for example, the retailer's *own* buyers when dealing with a supplier. The retailer's customers are, therefore, in a reactive rather than a proactive role. They will vote with their feet if dissatisfied but can rarely shape the retailer's business directly. Again, compared to other businesses, retailers will not be so dependent on the whim of a limited number of large buyers as, for example, in many industrial product companies. Although customers are vitally important to any retailer they do not enjoy any collective or cohesive power that can be used to exert pressure on the typical retail business.

Potential entrants

Potential, as well as actual, competitors offer a real threat in certain sectors. Even this threat is lower than that for most manufacturers because of the difficulty of obtaining good retail sites in Britain. The constraint of new development in Britain is very noticeable in contrast with many parts of the USA where land is relatively freely available. The retailer who needs large, possibly out-of-town, units might not see its frustration in obtaining sites as a strategic advantage, but it does reduce the risk of new entrants. Elsewhere in the world, planning restrictions and a protectionist concern for the smaller shopkeeper make the building of new, larger units very difficult, adding to the problems of potential entrants.

Porter lists a number of barriers to entry into a given market. The most relevant to retailing are capital requirements, customer switching costs and economies of scale. Even these are no absolute deterrent to entry by, say, a tobacco company diversifying into retailing, as in BAT's acquisition of a number of retail interests in Europe and North America.

As the size of retail multiples increases year by year, this raises the cost of entry for new aspirants. But the targeting tactics in the fashion sector make some retailers more exposed to competition. Even the largest multiple can feel the effect of a well-positioned newcomer, as was the case with Marks and Spencer and NEXT. Marks and Spencer management tended to dismiss the NEXT operation by pointing out that their Marble Arch store had a larger turnover that the entire NEXT operation, or more disparagingly, that their sales of yoghurt were more than NEXT's turnover in fashion! Perhaps such comments merely show that even the best of retailers can feel threatened by new entrants who choose well their ground to launch an attack.

New entrants into many manufacturing sectors find it hard to establish themselves because customers are unwilling to accept the costs and risks associated with switching suppliers. This issue is almost irrelevant in retailing. Customer loyalty is one of the more fickle assets for a retailer. Efforts to build loyalty through trading stamps, dividend stamps in the Co-op movement, charge accounts and, more recently, credit and charge cards have had some effect, but the fact remains that to the typical customer the switching costs of going next door are minimal.

The effects of economies of scale and the experience curve (see Chapter 2) are relatively new phenomena in retailing. The rise of the large multiple, the application of modern technology and the growth in expertise of management teams have produced real cost advantages for many retailers. For example, one food retailer saved at least a six-figure sum by computerizing the ordering of its more perishable merchandise. Traditionally, each store had been telephoned daily by three suppliers to obtain reorder quantities. This system was replaced by stores placing orders using a computer system linked to the suppliers via the retailer's head office. The retailer calculated the saving to the supplier in telesales time, and demanded a proportionate discount.

Many retailers have decided to handle their own physical distribution (McKennon, 1985). This again builds expertise that would be difficult for a new entrant to acquire as the established companies gain experience and move down the experience curve. One low-cost way of moving down an experience curve is to buy expertise, usually in the form of an experienced manager or two. For example, ASDA's move into own label in a significant way in 1985, and the acceleration of that development in 1986, were accompanied by at least one acquisition of a senior manager from a competitor (Altman, 1986).

Porter also cites differentiation as a way of building barriers against new entrants. He argues that entrants need to spend heavily to overcome the existing customer loyalties created by previous expenditure by the existing competitors.

In summary, companies must seek to build barriers to deter potential competition from entering their market. They must leave the competitor in no doubt that any aggressive action will provoke retaliation, thus reducing the newcomer's potential profits if the entry is made. Potential entrants are an issue in retailing as in any business. Many sectors are dominated by well-organized and very large multiples: this means that entry is no easy matter.

Retail suppliers

By far the most significant trend in retailing in the 1970s (which continued into the 1980s) was the shift in power between the suppliers to the retail trade, the manufacturers, and the retailers themselves. Traditionally, manufacturers' brands had dominated. Retailers merely formed the delivery system which reacted to the decisions of their suppliers. Increased power but also increased competition between the new food giants led initially to a price war at the expense of declining margins in both manufacturing and retailing. Between 1971-72 and 1979-80 average profit margins halved in food manufacturing, and food retailers fared little better (Davies, Gilligan and Sutton, 1985). In the early 1970s the market share of brands became eroded by a growth in own label. Table 4.1 shows how the own-label sales continued to increase their share of the market into the 1980s. Table 4.2 shows within this overall trend the wide variation in the percentage of turnover accounted for by own-label sales. Between 1980 and 1986, J. Sainsbury was the only retailer to announce a decreased emphasis on own label. ASDA announced a target of 2,500 lines by 1987, Tesco an increase to 2,200 from 1986, and Argyll increases in certain key product sectors to between 20 and 40 per cent of volume (Altman, 1986). In 1986, Mintel predicted that the trend in own-label products would continue into the foreseeable future.

Table 4.1 Own-label share of packaged grocery sales, 1975–85

Year	% Value
1975	20.5
1979	22.1
1980	22.5
1981	23.4
1982	24.9
1983	27.1
1984	27.4
1985 (est.)	28.0

Source: AGB/TCA, Mintel (1985–86).

Table 4.2 Shares of retailers' private labels in the UK (1980)

Retail organization	%	Retail organization	%
Co-operative societies	31	Fine Fare	20
J. Sainsbury	56	Allied Suppliers	16
Tesco	19	Kwik Save	0
ASDA	7	Safeway	27
Marks and Spencer	100	Key Markets	25
International	19	Waitrose	41

Source: Audits of Great Britain. Copyright AGB/TCA.

Food retailers were still novices by comparison with many retailers in their emphasis on own label. Marks and Spencer have traditionally sold 100 per cent own-label products. Sixty-five per cent of Habitat products were exclusive to them in the 1980s. The target was 85 per cent, leaving 15 per cent 'to be easily recognised products where price comparisons can be made between Habitat and other retailers' (Altman, 1986). MFI stocked products under a number of brand names, but almost all exclusive to them. C & A was one of several fashion retailers which offered the customer a number of house brands while the clothes on sale were virtually exclusive to them.

The balance of power in the market-place had shifted from manufacturer to retailer. However, in food retailing retailers did not capitalize on their more proactive role. In the 1970s and early 1980s margins in food retailing fell almost as fast as in their suppliers. The temptation to promote price, without the benefit of real cost advantage, eventually gave way in the mid-1980s to greater emphasis on image promotion. Retailers increasingly recognized that their main corporate issues centred on their relationship with competitors in the market-place, rather than on their relationships with suppliers, customers, substitutes and new entrants.

In summary, retailers are now generally well placed in their relationships with suppliers. This change in power structure has done much to shape retail strategy.

Existing competition

By comparison with other business sectors, from a strategic perspective, suppliers, customers, potential entrants and substitutes are less important than the competition that exists within any one particular sector. Consequently a retailer's business strategy is likely to be market driven.

The point was made in Chapter 2 that a strategy devised by concentrating on the company somewhat in isolation had its value, but was likely to be inferior to a strategy which looked outside the company and viewed the potential for the company in the context of its market. This competitor-based approach to strategy is likely to be even more relevant in times of limited economic growth, where growth in sales volume has to come from competitors losing their share of existing business, rather than from the firm achieving growth in its customers' expenditure or attracting new customers into the market.

Within any market, the type of business undertaken will shape the nature of competition. For example, as Porter points out, if a market is typified by both low value-added and high fixed costs, price competition is the inevitable consequence as competitors seek to get or maintain volume. Many retail sectors suffer from low value-added. The high fixed costs of the newer and larger sites will promote price competition, the traditional method of competition in retailing. Few retailers have been able to base such a strategy on a cost structure which allows them to compete profitably on price. In later chapters the ability of Kwik Save and MFI to compete successfully on price because of the way each has organized itself will stand as two rare examples where retailers have successfully adopted a cost-led approach.

As mentioned earlier, Porter argues that there are only three generic corporate strategies: cost leadership, differentiation and focus. Focus is best described as segmentation, and as segmentation and differentiation are often associated strategies in retailing, it can be argued that cost leadership and segmentation/differentiation are the two alternatives for retailers to consider. A shorthand for segmentation/differentiation as a strategy would be the term 'positioning' used in Chapter 3. Positioning a product, or in this case a retail organization, involves defining both a target market and a unique image.

It is also possible to consider cost leadership as a positioning strategy. Companies like Kwik Save and MFI have clear positions in their respective markets (in fact Kwik Save has one of the best-defined market positions of any retailer). Cost leadership can, therefore, have its own associated positioning strategy. There is no reason why a retailer cannot adopt elements of both types of generic strategy, although there is a danger in attempting a strategic approach that is too broadly based.

A successful business strategy is coherent; it affects every element of the business so that each element can add to one coherent direction for the business. Too many retailers seem to try to adopt weak cost-led approaches alongside a more image-based strategy. Customers clearly need reassuring as to the value for money they will receive when patronizing a store, but their perception of value could even be undermined by a retailer trying to 'bolt on' cost-led claims to a basically image-led approach. The up-market or well-targeted retailer could even alienate customers by overtly price-based promotions. For example, Harrods can benefit from a sale, but would never benefit in the long term by promoting discounted lines in its windows throughout the rest of the year.

MARKET RESEARCH IN RETAILING

In Chapter 2 we saw that market orientation was associated with the use of market research to ensure that the company's business is in touch with, and based on, market needs. With their direct contact with the customer, retailers have a unique advantage over the manufacturer. The added sophistication of EPOS (electronic point of sale) enhances many retailers' views that in the words of one retailer interviewed by Ornstein (1976) 'the ring on the till is our main form of market research'. Ornstein himself argues that market research can 'rarely initiate innovation' and that 'it is a blunt tool in evaluating the influence of store character because the public's awareness of character is subconscious'. His list of uses for market research by practising retailers contains eleven items divided equally between the operational and strategic, but the emphasis in the comments by those interviewed was very much on the operational level. Retailers, it seems, are so much in contact with their market that their business is constantly providing them with data on market trends. The problem is very often the need to step back and analyse the same data from a strategic perspective.

MARKET SEGMENTATION IN RETAILING

Knee and Walters (1985) suggest three advantages of specialization through segmentation and differentiation in retailing:

(1) A coherent range with acceptable width, depth and availability at acceptable cost.
(2) Cost optimization due to similarity of product and customer characteristics.
(3) Control over strategy by narrowing the alternatives to be considered.

They also saw certain risks in specialization; these include the cost of investment, loss of flexibility and the inherent risks in misreading the market. Finally they argue that segmentation and positioning are closely related concepts in the field of retailing. Segmentation, in turn, has been defined by William Wilkie (1986) as

> a management strategy that adapts a firm's marketing mix to best fit the various consumer differences that exist in a given market.

and by Walters and White (1987) in the context of retailing as

> a set of customers with common expectations and perceptions towards particular combinations of merchandise and trading formats.

It follows that retailers should be looking to describe their target market in ways that differentiate between groups of shoppers. The problem is that there are a large range of methods available and few appear to be universally valid. Socioeconomic grouping, as mentioned in Chapter 3, has declined in its usefulness because of the social changes which continue to blur traditional distinctions. It is becoming increasingly difficult to relate purchasing behaviour to socioeconomic groups.

Segmentation on the basis of neighbourhood has provided a partial answer to the problems of methods based on social grouping. The approach pioneered by CACI, based on the British national Census, and known by its acronym of ACORN, is a widely recognized method. The value to retailers in general appears to be less than to mail-order businesses, but the method has been used by practitioners to locate new stores and to target promotional material. Mail-order companies have also seen the potential of marketing their customer lists, analysed on somewhat different bases to ACORN, but derived from the same principle of linking our major purchase – the home – to the statement we make about ourselves in selecting a neighbourhood and thus to our overall lifestyle.

Lifestyle is a major source of segmentation/differentiation for a number of retailers such as Habitat, Conran in the USA, Harrods, Laura Ashley, IKEA and NEXT. Lifestyle is the retailer's equivalent of attitudinal segmentation in product marketing. Such retailers assemble products and create an environment which allows them to sell a wide range of products with a common theme or look. While the idea of lifestyle is easily understood and acts as the focus for many retail businesses, it has two weaknesses. The first is that few people will buy solely from the one retailer to create the same look in their own homes as in the retailer's store. The idea of becoming a retail clone is the antithesis of the individuality projected by the retailer. The customer is more likely to buy a selection from a number of lifestyle retailers, rather than to become totally loyal to one source. The second problem is to find a means of promotion which links to the target group most likely to value the retailer's lifestyle offer. The retailer is usually forced back on more traditional demographic methods of describing its market in selecting a promotional channel.

As a method of segmentation age is not relevant to all types of retailing, but has been useful in targeting fashion stores, for example Dunns, Burton and Fosters. It will be interesting to see what retail concepts emerge to cater for the growing market aged 55 to 75, or even if such a segment can be targeted.

Credit is another method not generally thought of as a valid basis for segmentation. In practice it has been used for over a century. These days an individual's credit rating determines *how* large purchases can be made and even *if* they can be made. Even food retailers have very different policies on how they accept credit cards and cheques. Some allow a cheque to be written at the checkout, or a credit card to be used at the till. Others force shoppers to queue to have cheques or cards validated by less than welcoming scrutineers.

The sex of a customer is another traditional method of segmentation, an obvious one in fashion. But even here unisex outlets have demonstrated that clothing for men and women does not have to be sold in separate stores. Women used to account for 80 per cent or more of all retail sales. The emancipation of the female and the domestication of the male have seen a blurring of traditional roles leading some food retailers to cater more and more for the needs of the male shopper by emphasizing non-food items and wines.

Pricing level offers the retailer a clear opportunity to specialize. Many retailers use the expressions 'up-market' and 'down-market' in the context of different price levels and margins. In the authors' experience such concepts are often misleading. Two retailers who have successfully competed on price, MFI and Kwik Save, appeal to a very broad spectrum when measured by socioeconomic group. The problem here is that market research will often identify customer support for 'low prices' when what is desired is 'value for money'. Really low prices can often only be attained by offering poor quality. Such retailers may find themselves appealing only to those who cannot afford more. The real opportunities lie in appealing with a combination of price and quality. Discounting of branded merchandise, as shown by the off-price boom in the USA, is a safe method of achieving this, but the risks are clear in that such a strategy is easily copied.

Berry and Barnes (1987) identified four trends in American retailer strategies, each offering a basis for segmentation and differentiation. These were the already mentioned off-price approaches in a number of sectors; time-efficient retailing, recognizing that some consumers had in effect become buyers of time as well as merchandise; high contact retailing with increased personal service; and sensory retailing where the store uses sight, sound and smell to appeal to the consumer.

The list of bases on which a retailer can found a segmentation strategy is already long, but by no means complete. Some retailers rely on the physical size of their customer (Evans, High and Mighty, Long Tall Sally), others use location (city centre or out of town), still others convenience (Sunday traders, convenience stores, weekly markets). Some rely on co-ownership or co-purchase (Bejam selling freezers and frozen food, Thomas Cook selling holidays, insurance and foreign currency). Some appeal more to the family shopper (ASDA in food, Littlewoods in clothing) and some even to different ethnic and religious groups.

Thus far we have identified fifteen different methods of segmentation which have been used to some extent by retailers. Even so this list is not exhaustive. The most obvious method of segmentation – product type – has been ignored, but the message seems to be that *how* one segments within a market for a product area is more important than using the type of product as the basis of segmentation.

In practice retailers and product marketers have used combinations of various methods of segmentation and have often discovered their major segment after launching the concept. The type of customer segment profiling achieved in practice is illustrated by Ornstein (1976) in reporting a series of interviews with retail executives. Spar, a voluntary chain, described its profile thus:

> 72% of Spar shoppers shop daily or every two days. 48% live within five minutes of the store. There is a bias towards C2DE in socio-economic group. Shoppers tend to live in small homes with limited storage space. They are hand to mouth buyers. 71% have children, many under school age.

The Spar profile uses six different dimensions in describing the typical shopper. The profile is detailed enough to be quite specific and general enough to be understood.

If a profile is comprehensive enough it is possible to go further and define quite small, highly homogeneous groups of people, tending towards what Kotler (1988) refers to as 'customised marketing', where it is possible to tailor a retail offer to the needs of an individual shopper. Kotler quotes examples of men's tailoring and furnishing stores in Japan that follow this idea. In both instances the product is only defined after the customer has entered the store. Profiling can achieve many of the objectives of segmentation. But the more complex the description, the less likely it is to be capable of describing what is different about the segment by comparison with other segments or the customers of specific retailers, notably the given retailer's nearest competitors. However, this is a minor problem by comparison with the two anomalies present in almost all segmentation analyses: the ability of most retailers to compete successfully in quite different geographical markets where the geographical mix differs greatly, and the fact that individual shoppers will patronize a very wide range of competing outlets. The first observation indicates that retailers do not appeal to as tight a segment as might be implied by their profiles. A segment profile at best can only present a generalization. The second observation indicates that customers can and do move from one segment to another, altering their purchasing behaviour to suit a purchasing occasion, a short-term change in financial circumstances, or a change in mood.

These problems in segmenting a retail market, by comparison with a product market, stem from the basic differences between the two types of situation. To experience a physical product or service the consumer has to make a definite commitment by purchasing. To experience much of the retailer's offer, a customer can merely enter a store. There is no charge for doing so and little commitment is asked from the customer. Generalization rather than specification is a feature of many product segmentation methods, but it appears that generalization may be the norm in retail market segmentation. That is not to say that segmentation is irrelevant. Segmentation is just as relevant in retailing as in product marketing and strategy. The problem is to find methods that aid retail management to be as specific about who buys from them, as their colleagues are in manufacturing. We argue in the remainder of this book for a simpler method of market segmentation in retailing, based solely on differentiation at a strategic level and needing only profiling at an operational level to ensure the retailer can communicate to the most appropriate customers.

CONCLUSION

Basic product marketing theory appears to be relevant to the management of the more complex phenomenon of a retail business. In particular, consumer market segmentation and the differentiation of the total retail offer from that of competition would appear to be particularly important. Practitioners use such concepts when describing the operation of a retail business at a strategic level. It would appear, therefore, that marketing can be central to the strategic management of a retail business. It can be argued that marketing and strategy will overlap far more in the management of a retail business than in the management of a non-retail business.

In the following chapters the various sector studies highlight the importance of differentiation for the strategic management of a retail business. Even cost leadership contains its own element of differentiation. In other words, a retailer with a cost-led strategy needs not only an economic advantage, as far as the customer is concerned, but it needs also to differentiate itself from its competition along the price dimension in image terms.

KEY POINT SUMMARY

(1)   Retail practitioners use marketing and strategic concepts interchangeably.

(2)   Petrol retailing provides an example where the retailer is synonymous with the brand. The dangers of price promotion, where no competitor holds a real economic advantage, are also shown.

(3)   Relationships with other retailers are probably more important in strategy formulation than relationships with customers and suppliers, or the threats posed by new entrants and substitutes.

(4)   Cost leadership and differentiation/segmentation appear to be the two main strategic alternatives for retail organizations. Differentiation, from the consumer's viewpoint, is shown in the following chapters to be the more crucial issue.

References

Altman, W. (1986) Image: the supermarket giants' new weapon in the battle for supremacy, *Campaign*, 22 August.

Berry, L.L. and Barnes, J.A. (1987) Retail positioning strategies in the U.S.A., in G. Johnson (ed.) *Business Strategy and Retail*, Wiley, New York.

Conran, T. (1984) A learning experience - the birth of Habitat, *GDI Conference*.

Davies, G.J. *et al.* (1985) SITPRO Systems Evaluation Project for SITPRO, London.

Davies, K., Gilligan, C. and Sutton, C. (1985) Structural change in grocery retailing: the implications for competition, *International Journal of Physical Distribution and Materials Management*, 15 February.

Fox, M. (1986) Petrol firms bid for refinement, *Marketing*, 18 September.

Halpern, P. (1985) *Report to Employees*, Burton Group and Debenhams.

Knee, D. and Walters, D. (1985) *Strategy in Retailing*, Philip Allan, Oxford.

Kotler, P. (1988) *Marketing Management* (6th edn), Prentice Hall, Englewood Cliffs, NJ.

Lewison, D.M. and DeLozier, M.W. (1986) *Retailing* (2nd edn.) Merrill Publishing Co., New York, p. 386.

McKennon, G. (1985) *Workshop on Retail Strategy*, November 1985, Arthur Young with the University of Aston.

McNair, M.P. and May, E. (1978) The next revolution of the retailing wheel, *Harvard Business Review*, Sept./Oct.

Mintel (1985-86) *Own Brands*, Mintel Retail Intelligence, Winter 1985–86.

Ornstein, E.J. (1976) *The Retailers*, Associated Business Programmes.

Porter, M.E. (1979) How competitive forces shape strategy, *Harvard Business Review*, March–April.

Street, G. (1986) Changes in grocery retailing: the ASDA story, *Admap*, December, p.36.

Walters, D. and White, D. (1987) *Retail Marketing Management*, Macmillan, London.

Wilkie, W. (1986) *Consumer Behaviour*, Wiley, New York.

Chapter 5

Men's Clothiers 1980–81: the Value of Being Different

In this chapter we introduce our method used to analyse positioning strategy in different retail sectors, by presenting an analysis of menswear retailing in 1980–81. The analytical technique used, multidimensional scaling (MDS), and the market research methods employed are explained more fully in Chapter 6. While this may appear to be putting the cart before the horse, experience has shown us that most people are more interested in the results and value of research rather than the techniques used. The techniques only become relevant once the results appear to be interesting, and possibly only then to check whether the results are significant.

First, what should any technique offer the practitioner seeking to define strategy, or the observer wishing to understand a retail market? Work on business strategy has demonstrated the value of focusing management attention on clear goals, uncluttered by the 'noise' of conflicting data. The most recent work on strategy suggests the context for analysis should be the company in its competitive environment. Profitability can largely depend on being different from competition. It follows that a valuable approach would be one able to present a simple analysis of a market showing which retailers were seen by their customers as similar, and which as different. To be useful in formulating strategy it would be important to include reasons *why* customers perceive these differences and *what* these differences are. Then retail managers could deduce how to change their positioning with respect to competition in order to maximize their own profitability.

Finally it will be recalled that, in the authors' opinion, retail organizations can be marketed in the same way as consumer products. Customers are therefore capable of describing intrinsically complex stores in simple terms using descriptions or concepts such as traditional, hygienic, fashionable, etc. For example, the reader is asked to accept the notion that there can be a fashionable sector in a clothing retail market-place which can be labelled as 'fashionable', and possibly a 'traditional' sector which will be some distance from it.

Figure 5.1 depicts a model of a retail market. Stores 1, 2 and 3 represent the traditional sector, while stores 4 and 5 represent the fashionable sector. Stores 1, 2 and 3 are seen by customers as differentiated from stores 4 and 5. They will be used by different groups of people or for different purchase situations.

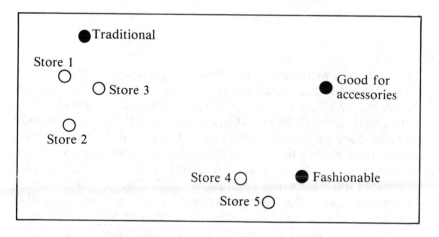

Figure 5.1   Model of a retail market.

Of all the stores, store 2 is the worst placed. Its positioning strategy is apparently to promote a traditional image, but stores 1 and 2 seem to do this better. The concept of 'good for accessories' is not associated with any store, at least not one included in this model. Store 2 could be advised to reposition itself against that concept. To do so would involve a number of changes, but at present the store is neither one thing nor the other.

Figure 5.2 illustrates how store 2 could be repositioned and how the market would then appear. We believe positioning and repositioning strategy in retailing can be modelled in these quite simple terms. Anything simple runs the danger of being simplistic. The selection of concepts to describe a market is vitally important. They must be the most salient in that market. The choice of stores can also be important but this is often a matter of selecting the main players in the market.

For the time being the reader is asked to take on trust the market research techniques used in the preparation of the book. Too detailed an analysis of technique will detract from the main messages which the various case studies can offer to retail managers to help them understand their competitive environments and for strategic

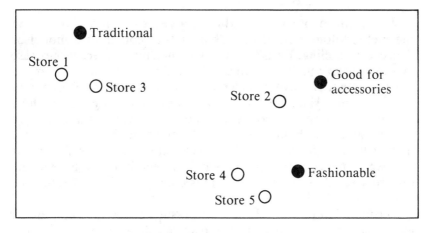

Figure 5.2 Revised model of a retail market.

planning. Multi-dimensional scaling (MDS) as a method of producing market models is merely a means to that end. MDS is a widely used technique. Understanding MDS is not vital to an understanding of this book and the reader who wishes to skim most of Chapter 6 may do so without missing anything needed to benefit from subsequent chapters.

MEN'S CLOTHIERS

In the early 1980s menswear retailing in Britain offered a good example of the problems and opportunities facing retailers in differentiating themselves when several are competing for one market.

Menswear sales had been affected by the recession in the early 1980s. Total sales of menswear were down, measured by the volume of traditional purchases of suiting. However, despite the recession the market was already changing. The 'Sunday' suit was no longer a key purchase item and casual wear had become more important. Although some retailers, in particular Burton, had moved more into this market, menswear retailing was still associated with the traditional 'high-street tailor'. The major companies in this sector were Burtons, Hepworth, Hornes, UDS (with the names of Collier and Alexandre) and Dunns. Menswear was also important for department stores and mail-order companies but the specialist retailers seemed to form a homogeneous group in the market.

Within this context we conducted a series of surveys following the methodology outlined in Chapter 6 to construct a model of menswear retailing. By asking men who had made a recent purchase in a menswear outlet to compare the main retailers in the market, it is possible to discover which companies are seen as different and which are most similar. It is also possible to gather opinion on how customers associate concepts such as 'well-trained staff', 'fashionable' or 'boutique', with different retailers. Finally, we include the idea of the 'ideal' menswear retailer as a reference point for people participating in the market research to compare to the different retailers and to the various concepts, and as a reference point in the final model.

The model in Figure 5.3 shows the results of research conducted at the end of 1980 (the market research data are shown in the Appendix at the end of the chapter). Each dot represents the position

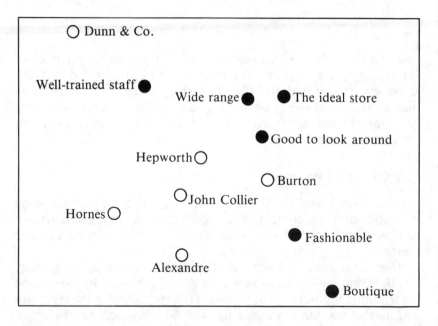

Figure 5.3　MDS model of menswear retailing, 1980.

of a retailer or a concept in the opinion of customers at the time. Figure 5.3 has no axes; in other words the fact that Dunn and Co. are 'higher' than, say, Hornes on the map has no meaning. What is relevant is that Dunn and Co. are close to 'well-trained staff' and far away from 'boutique'. In other words Dunn's image or position in the market-place is best described as a store with well-trained staff. Dunn's is also some distance from the ideal menswear store indicating that it is not universally popular. But it is also isolated from the other four stores on the model. In strategic terms Dunns had positioned itself away from competition in its appeal to the slightly older, more conservative male.

In contrast, the other four competitors are closely bunched, with Burton and Hepworth being closest to the ideal menswear store. John Collier, Alexandre and Hornes are somewhat in their shadow. None, with the possibility of Hornes, appears to be at all significantly differentiated. Of the two companies nearest to the ideal store, Burtons could be argued to be best positioned in that it is associated more with the concept of 'fashionable' and would appeal more to that market segment. If the ideas on marketing and strategy cited in previous chapters have any practical value or relevance, then the better positioning of one store compared to another should be manifest in improved financial performance. Unfortunately Dunn and Co. had a possibly unique financial structure and did not produce published accounts, which made a direct comparison with the other retailers impractical. Even so, the comparisons that are possible between the more mainstream companies are quite revealing.

Figure 5.4 shows the percentage net margin on menswear sales for each of the four closely competing companies. Alexandre, which with John Collier formed part of UDS, is included in the John Collier figure. The two best-placed retailers in terms of image have the best margins on sales in and around the time of the image analysis at the end of 1980.

Table 5.1 offers more commercial data: sales per employee; market share of both made-to-measure (MTM) and ready-to-wear (RTW) suits; return on capital employed (ROCE) averaged over 1978–81, and the actual turnover in menswear (allowances have been made for other business activities) in 1980. On sales per employee and return on capital employed, Burton and Hepworth are again prominent. The market-share figures show that John Collier was unable to produce good financial results despite a sizeable share of the traditional market for men's suiting. Hornes' share of the market was too small to be recorded; as the turnover figures indicate, they were small by comparison with the other three. Interestingly John Collier, which is the same size as Burton and Hepworth, cannot offer small size as an explanation for its weak image and poor financial performance.

While similar data on Dunn and Co. are not available, enquiries by the authors of informed sources in the trade indicated that Dunns

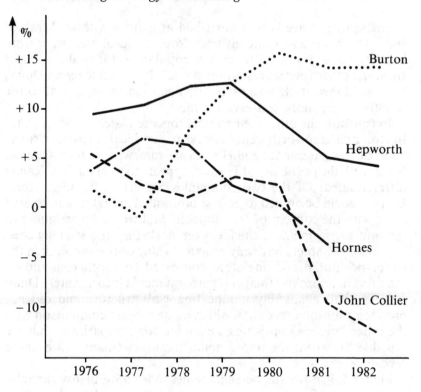

Source: Annual Reports/MBS/LBS.

Figure 5.4   UK menswear retailing: percentage net margin on menswear.

was about the same size as Burton and Hepworth in 1980–81. However, while the mainstream retailers were suffering declining margins and falling profits in 1980–81, Dunns was enjoying 'its best year ever'. Margins, while calculated in a different way from the method used to produce the data in Figure 5.4, appeared to be far higher than any displayed by the other companies.

Figure 5.5 is an attempt to investigate if there is a simple explanation of retail image, by charting total monitored advertising expenditure figures around the time of the analysis. Burton's and Hepworth's advertising figures had slumped from quite substantial levels, representing significant percentages of company turnover in the late 1970s, to what must be regarded as potentially subliminal levels of advertising in the early 1980s. In 1980, the year of the image analysis study, only Hepworth spent significantly on advertising.

Table 5.1 Commercial data menswear retailing, 1980

	Sales per employee	% Market share suits		Return on capital employed	Turnover
	1980 (£000)	RTW	MTM	Average 1978–81	1980 (£m)
Burton	18.8	9	13	9.2	77
Hepworth	14.4	6	16	6.6	62
Hornes	13.6	?	?	2.7	14
John Collier	12.6	5	12	− 7.3	52

Source: Annual accounts (analysed by Manchester and London Business Schools).

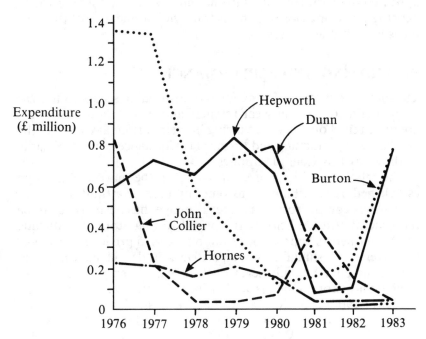

Source: MEAL

Figure 5.5 UK menswear retailing: advertising expenditure.

Advertising does have a longer-term effect than just in the year it appears. There is a cumulative effect over many years from a sustained presentation of an image to the public, but this accumulated benefit is eroded once advertising is stopped. How long this process of 'wear-out' takes depends on many factors. Both Burton and Hepworth had spent more in previous years than Hornes and Collier, so there may be a link between advertising and image. However, on the available evidence we cannot support the view that there is any direct link between the two.

Dunns' advertising had followed the rest of the market and was not outstanding enough in expenditure terms to explain their apparently strong position. While expenditure is not the only measure of advertising effectiveness, creativity being at least as important, Dunn's position cannot be ascribed solely to its direct promotion.

In summary Dunns had a highly differentiated image and appeared to profit from it. Burton, and to some extent Hepworth, benefited by being closer to the average view at the time of the ideal menswear retailer.

POSITIONING AND PERFORMANCE

The match between performance and positioning seems quite clear in the mainstream menswear retailers and, if the data on Dunn's are to be relied on, very convincing in their particular case. Yet the link between positioning and financial performance is not necessarily as direct as this example implies.

The relative positions of each retailer in the market-place were established by ascertaining customer opinion or attitudes towards the various competitors. A retailer's 'image' has been argued to be the general attitude held by the public to that store. An attitude can be defined as 'a predisposition to react in a predetermined way to a given set of stimuli'. Thus a positive attitude will make me enter a store and buy. A totally negative attitude might ensure that I never even enter a store. One researcher into the way we treat products (Stefflre, 1964) claimed that we behave in similar ways to things that we perceive as being similar. Significantly, Stefflre was one of the first to use MDS to model the way customers perceive competing products (Stefflre, 1971). Applying Stefflre's concept of human behaviour to store patronage, we would predict that stores perceived as similar will be used by customers in the same way, and will therefore compete directly for patronage for those purchases that the customer perceives they will be best at offering.

Thus the lack of differentiation between the mainstream menswear retailers in 1980–81 ensured that each mainstream company would have to compete for the same customers. Meanwhile Dunns was left free to attract those customers who valued its type of offering, or who were looking for the purchasing experience promised exclusively by Dunns.

What happens when retailers are undifferentiated and are seen as followers rather than leaders in their sector of the market? John Collier and Alexandre fell into this category. They were second choice to Burton and Hepworth. They were described as 'a middle market store aimed at the 18–45-year-old age group' (Centre for Business Research, 1985) – in other words with no distinctive positioning in a market full of similar offerings. Their reaction was to try to attract custom by lowering prices, the typical reaction in similar circumstances in other sectors. This merely prompted a similar and inevitable competitive response and as a result margins on menswear fell generally because the competition realized they could not offer the customer a reason for paying more for their similar offering. Because of their positioning Dunns was immune to this price competition.

A poor market position will therefore mean two things: poor patronage and the temptation or need to promote price in order to generate sales. The consequence will be static or declining sales volume and pressure on both gross and net margins as prices are cut and sales cannot meet overheads. Sales per employee, overall profit and, ultimately, return on capital employed (ROCE) will suffer. What could be unusual in the example of menswear retailing is that comparative financial performance reflects relative image. For example, Burton's ROCE is higher than that of UDS. Firms can affect financial indicators such as ROCE by the way they manage their assets. For example, a company leasing retail premises will often have a higher ROCE than a similar-size competitor which owns its premises. Margins and sales volume should be the indicators most susceptible to image, with financial measures such as ROCE following the same trend, as long as any image change is not accompanied by a change in strategy with respect to asset management, for example by investing in refurbishment.

ADVERTISING AND IMAGE

How is a chosen image or position achieved? This case study cannot be used to argue a direct link between advertising and image. In fact, what has happened to Hepworth since 1980–81 suggests that advertising may not be as important in the retailing mix as it is in the marketing mix for consumer products.

A number of Hepworth menswear shops were converted to NEXT outlets, initially specializing in women's fashion targeted at 18-40-year-olds. By 1985 NEXT had grown to dominate the

Hepworth accounts and had widened its merchandising to include menswear (NEXT for Men), soft furnishings (NEXT Interiors) and other product groups. The innovation was hailed as the success it most surely was. Margins on sales rose to nearly 15 per cent in 1985 from the 5 per cent recorded in 1982. Share prices doubled between 1983 and 1984.

This phoenix-like transformation was launched with an expenditure of only £140,000 on advertising placed entirely in *Vogue* magazine (Davies, 1986). Chief Executive George Davies chose instead to spend heavily on shop refitting. Typical costs for the generally small outlets were around £70,000 for each unit. Typical changes in resulting turnover were from £10,000 per week before refitting to £30,000 per week thereafter.

A major image change had been achieved without substantial advertising, although the company achieved wide coverage through an effective PR campaign. We return to the issue of how to achieve a chosen positioning strategy at various stages in this book (see also Chapter 4). At this stage it is enough to say that creating an image is unlikely to be achieved merely by changing advertising strategy.

USING THE MARKET MODELS

As well as offering a potentially valuable insight into the structure of a retail market, the MDS model can be used to define directions for future strategy. For example, Dunns would have been well advised to emphasize its differential advantage. Instead, its advertising at the time seemed to emphasize the trendier aspects of visiting Dunns by showing first a football team buying suits, and then a fashionable young woman visiting the outlet for a deerstalker hat. A third theme of a rather overbearing wife shopping with her husband and refusing to like virtually everything her spouse tried on, while the sales assistant maintained his demeanour, seemed more likely to complement Dunns' position.

In using market models it must be emphasized that the positions of stores and concepts represent the average views of all people researched. Dunns is seen by the whole market as somewhat less than the ideal menswear store but this did not stop it succeeding. The Dunns shopper will see the store as being closer to the ideal or, more precisely, the positions of the shopper's ideal store will be closer to Dunns. As we see in Chapter 6 the market maps can vary depending on the sample chosen, and the main variance is for the ideal store to be seen to be closer to the one patronized by the respondent.

By 1986 Dunns appeared to have lost its way somewhat in the

market-place. The perceptions of menswear buyers might have changed in six years, emphasizing the need to take regular measurements of any market-place. More probably, Dunns reluctance to re-emphasize its market position resulted in the company's image losing its clarity and possibly its appeal to the traditional Dunns customer. Meanwhile, Burton had moved towards the fashionable boutique end of the market. 1979 had seen a change in ownership, with the Burton family giving control to a new group, which in 1982 was headed by Ralph Halpern. 1981 saw a return to profitability for the first time in a decade (Johnson, 1986). Hepworth did not follow Burton but instead metamorphosed into NEXT. John Collier, as part of UDS, continued to struggle despite numerous attempts to rejuvenate its image (Green, 1987). In effect it remained unassociated with any differentiated position in the market-place. Eventually the Collier name became absorbed into the Burton portfolio. Conceivably either Hepworth or Collier could have repositioned itself against the concept of wide range in between Burton and Dunns, a difficult position to occupy with the limited size of their stores. Alternatively they could have sought a totally new direction for their business. Or, they could have joined Burton in its move towards a more overtly fashionable image and sought a niche there.

CONCLUSIONS

The menswear model suggests that being different pays dividends, as Dunns and Burtons demonstrated at a time when menswear retailing was in the doldrums. Hepworth's decision to abandon the sector was a good one, since repositioning in the market would have been difficult. Burtons was not only differentiated from other mainstream retailers but was close to the ideal store position. In many ways this was an enviable position but not one on which the group could capitalize. This was because of the burgeoning effect of a loss-making manufacturing element at the time, but also because Burton was not differentiated enough from its mainstream competitors to justify higher prices. Only Dunns was immune to price competition at the time.

In this example the links between positioning strategy and a number of measures of financial performance are remarkably clear, even though a direct relationship to ROCE might not have been expected. Later chapters examine which financial and commercial measures are affected most often by image, irrespective of the capital structure of a retail business.

Theory and practice

In 1980 each menswear retailer appealed to the market-place in different ways. Burtons appealed to the younger age-group, Dunns to the older and more conservative male. Age and attitude were being used as methods of market segmentation, but both were accommodated in the MDS image map that relied on difference as its main method of positioning each retailer. The concepts acted as labels or miniature positioning statements in explaining why each retailer was seen as it was, but concepts were less important than the degree of differentiation in determining whether the retailer held a good market position. Second in importance was proximity to the ideal, which favoured Burton and Hepworth. The significance of the ideal and how it is described is explained in Chapter 6.

These two apparent rules in positioning strategy – differentiation and proximity to the ideal – are relevant to all the sector studies presented in this book.

KEY POINT SUMMARY

(1)   As shown by Dunns, being different in a retail market-place can prove more profitable than being positioned close to the average view of the ideal store.

(2)   In an undifferentiated market, the retailers in the shadow of those closest to the average view of the ideal store will suffer.

(3)   There is no obvious link between a successful retail image and advertising.

(4)   A wide range of commercial criteria could be linked to a successful market position.

(5)   Men's clothiers are just one type of retailing operation. It is too early to draw firm conclusions on the value of positioning strategy.

References

Centre for Business Research Retail Strategy Analysis Series, *Retail Reference Book 1985*, Part 1, (1985) Manchester Business School.
Davies, G. W. (1986) 'Young Businessman of the Year', Presentation at Manchester Business School, 5 March.

Green, S. (1987) From riches to rags: the John Collier story, in G. Johnson (ed.) *Business Strategy and Retailing*, John Wiley, New York.

Johnson, G. (1986) *The Burton Group A & B*, Case Studies, Manchester Business School.

Lester, I. (1980) The retailoring of Burton, *Management Today*, February, pp.43–130.

Stefflre, V. (1964) in *Maxwell House Division (A) Case Study*, Harvard Business School.

Stefflre, V. (1971) New products and new enterprises. A report on an experiment in applied social science. PhD Thesis, University of California.

APPENDIX: MARKET RESEARCH DATA USED TO BUILD THE MDS MODEL

Each figure represents the average score given by menswear customers in comparing stores and concepts one with another.

MDS input matrix – Average all interviews

1		7
totally similar		totally dissimilar

	Alexandre	Dunn & Co.	Burton	Hepworth	John Collier	Hornes	Good to look around	Well-trained staff	Boutique	Wide range of clothes	Fashionable	Ideal
Alexandre	1.00											
Dunn & Co.	4.85	1.00										
Burton	3.15	4.85	1.00									
Hepworth	3.45	4.65	2.90	1.00								
John Collier	3.10	4.65	3.70	3.00	1.00							
Hornes	3.95	4.45	3.80	3.70	3.70	1.00						
Good to look around	3.95	4.70	2.75	3.15	3.45	3.80	1.00					
Well-trained staff	3.60	2.30	3.90	3.20	3.30	4.15	4.00	1.00				
Boutique	4.85	6.30	3.65	4.55	4.60	4.30	4.25	4.90	1.00			
Wide range of clothes	3.85	4.25	2.85	3.50	3.40	3.70	2.65	4.00	5.25	1.00		
Fashionable	3.55	5.70	3.10	3.50	3.50	3.95	3.45	5.00	2.00	3.65	1.00	
Ideal	4.55	4.90	3.10	3.70	3.75	4.60	2.10	2.85	4.50	2.10	3.35	1.00

Chapter 6

Modelling Retail Markets

In Chapter 5 we introduced the type of marketing model that we use to analyse retail markets. In this chapter we explain the mechanics of the necessary market research and the computer technique employed to analyse the research data to produce a multi-dimensional scaling (MDS) map. The nature and use of MDS maps are also explained and appraised.

MEASURING STORE IMAGE

The image of a store can be measured in a number of ways. The most frequently used method is to ask customers to rate the store, and possibly its competitors, against a number of criteria or concepts. Selecting the right criteria and ensuring that the list is comprehensive are clearly important. There are a number of essentially qualitative market research techniques that can be used to generate criteria, but no technique can ensure that the list thus generated is comprehensive.

The position is further complicated by the fact that many criteria overlap. Sometimes such potential duplication is obvious. In the context of a food store the criteria 'hygienic' and 'clean' are close enough in everyday use for any pragmatist to accept that measuring a retail outlet on both criteria invites duplication. Such judgements can be supplemented or even replaced by statistical techniques such as factor analysis (Harman, 1967). Essentially factor analysis examines the pattern of responses to various criteria for each object being assessed in a market research survey. Thus if respondents gave similar ratings for 'hygienic' and 'clean' (not necessarily agreeing always as to which stores could be rated highly, but that a high rating on one was generally accompanied by a high rating on the other and a low with a low) then a factor analysis would conclude that the two criteria were not separate but in fact formed one underlying factor. This technique is not always totally convincing. In research conducted on Spanish food outlets (Rivas and Grijalba, 1986), the criteria 'cleanliness', 'product quality' and 'assortment' were found to be closely associated in a factor analysis. While some subtlety of meaning could have been lost in translation, it is difficult to see what underlying factor is represented by a combination of such concepts.

Defining criteria is, therefore, less than straightforward. Some guidance which offers the researcher a structure at least to check a list of criteria for completeness, comes from work by Lindquist in 1974. Table 6.1 is a summary of Lindquist's review of nineteen earlier retail image studies. Lindquist's purpose was to identify the main attributes or types of criteria which had been used in earlier image analysis. He grouped some thirty-two individual elements into nine groups or major attributes.

Table 6.1 Lindquist's nine store image attributes

Attribute	Contributing factors/components
Merchandise	Quality; selection/assortment; styling/fashion; guarantees; pricing
Service	Service general; sales clerk service; self-service; ease of merchandise return; delivery service; credit policies
Clientele	Social class appeal; self-image congruency; store personnel
Physical facilities	Physical facilities, e.g. air-conditioning, washrooms; store layout; shopping ease, e.g. width of aisles; architecture
Convenience	Convenience general; locational convenience; parking
Promotion	Sales promotions; advertising; displays; trading stamps; symbols and colour
Store atmosphere	Atmosphere congeniality, i.e. feelings of warmth and acceptance
Institutional factors	Conservative vs modern projection of store; reputation and reliability
Post-transaction satisfaction	Merchandise in use; returns; adjustments

Lindquist concluded that merchandise, service and convenience were the three dominant areas. Berry (1969) concluded that the quality and assortment of merchandise were the two most important image components, followed by sales personnel and store atmosphere. It follows that any qualitative work to define criteria should probe at least these key areas, if not all nine of those defined by Lindquist, so that the criteria identified cover all the areas.

Further work on store image has identified that images of particular stores vary between different groups in the population. These groups do not always conform to the traditional demographic characteristics of age, sex, social class and marital status. Factors such as attitude to types of merchandise and overall lifestyle are frequently more important (Martineau, 1958; Weale, 1961). Not surprisingly, another researcher has concluded that frequent shoppers at a store generally hold more favourable images of that store (Arons, 1961).

Finally there is a word of warning from work on West German department store retailing by Lenzen and Reisner (1980). In analysing previous image research they identified two major problems: first, researchers had tended to use image dimensions that were too general and were consequently difficult to relate to strategic action; second, the strategic implications of differences between image areas tended to be ignored.

Any methodology used with credibility to analyse a retail market-place has to address the key points identified so far:

(1) The need to be able to make strategic decisions from the data generated.

(2) The need to encompass a broad cross-section of the population in any research.

(3) The need to include a range of image factors in any analysis.

The second and third points are essentially methodological in nature and can be taken into account in designing the research. Point (1) is more difficult to meet and can conflict with (3) in that the more complex the analysis, the more difficult it will be to make sense of it. Furthermore, as we have seen in earlier chapters, it is clear that strategy should not be based solely on an analysis of the firm itself, but on an analysis of where the firm stands in relation to competition. Only then is it possible to position the business to enhance those features that distinguish it from its competitors.

We believe that the process of market mapping, as demonstrated for menswear retailing in Chapter 5, is capable of meeting this point. However, it has to be pointed out that our technique can limit the number of image factors that can be included in the analysis of most retail sectors.

DEFINING AND REFINING THE IMAGE CRITERIA

The definition and selection of the criteria that can be used to assess retail positioning or image are a major issue. The techniques used in all the models presented in this book to generate criteria are group discussion, word association and analysis of retailer advertising. A group discussion, or 'focus group' as it is sometimes called, is probably the most efficient way of generating criteria. Some eight or so 'members of the public' are asked to sit with a researcher and to take part in a free discussion of shopping in the chosen sector. A number of topics are introduced, selected to channel the group's deliberations in each of the main areas defined by Lindquist, but without leading the discussion. The comments of the group are later interpreted to define some thirty or more criteria which may be supplemented by further group discussion or some other technique. For example, comments on the professionalism (or lack of it) of sales assistants in menswear outfitters led to the 'well-trained staff' concept in the menswear retailer map in Chapter 5.

MDS cannot cope easily with a very large number of criteria and it is convenient to use a screening method to reduce the number to more manageable proportions. Factor analysis can be valuable, particularly in eliminating duplication. A method we have found particularly effective is to ask shoppers to compare their perception of the 'ideal' retail outlet in the sector under study, with each criterion. This approach identifies three main types of criterion: those that shoppers rate as describing their 'ideal' store; those they cannot agree on largely because the concepts are ambiguous, or even meaningless; and those concepts which, like 'well-trained staff', are not synonymous with the ideal store but which have some value in the market-place.

The 'ideal' concepts can be assumed to be subsumed within the composite concept of the 'ideal' store. In the case of menswear retailing the ideal was described by the concepts 'wide range of sizes', 'large selection' and 'accessories in stock'. In some sectors as many as ten concepts have been found to describe the 'ideal' store. If they had been included on the model they would merely cluster around the ideal position. As the authors' preferred technique is limited in the number of points that can be used, ideal concepts are not included separately in the next stage of the model building.

BUILDING A MARKET MODEL

The final stage in our methodology is to compare all the chosen retailers and all the chosen concepts in a market research survey structured to represent the known characteristics of the market-place. Typically respondents to the survey are asked to compare two retailers, two concepts or a concept and a retailer, and to rate their similarity. The gradings given are averaged for all respondents to produce a semi-matrix as in the Appendix to Chapter 5. This semi-matrix is the final market research data. The MDS analysis that follows is designed only to represent those data in such a way that the hidden structure in the data, the market structure, can be seen more easily. The map or model produced is not a theoretical model as described in Chapter 3 but a representation of data in a form that can be used to describe and predict customer behaviour.

The traditional way of explaining how MDS analysis uses the semi-matrix data is to refer to a semi-matrix familiar to most readers: the mileage chart in a road atlas. The different mileages between a number of selected towns and cities are displayed next to a map showing the positions of those towns and cities. If the mileage chart were to be used as the input to a MDS computer program, the output from that program would be very similar to the map beside the mileage chart. The main practical difference between the MDS map and the atlas map is that the MDS chart does not specify any axis; in other words there will be no way of telling from the MDS map which way is north or south. The term 'map' is often used to refer to the typical two-dimensional output from an MDS program.

Multidimensional scaling

Multidimensional scaling (MDS) dates from the discovery in the 1960s of suitable algorithms to allow the construction of models from data consisting of measures of similarity (Kruskal, 1978). Since then a number of subtly or radically different approaches to the analysis of similarity data have been published so that the term 'MDS' is now used to refer to a family of techniques. A number of variants have been published (Coxon, 1982).

The most popular type of MDS is the one we have used throughout this book – MINISSA (Roskam, undated). A number of other researchers have used the same or similar programs to analyse retail issues (Doyle and Fenwick, 1974–75; Jain and Etgar, 1976–77; Ring, 1979; Arora, 1982; Korgaonkar and El Sheshai, 1982; Hooley and Cook, 1983). The main distinguishing feature of MINISSA is that it is a non-metric MDS program. This means that it uses the rank order of differences in similarities rather than their absolute value. Thus on a model the greatest dissimilarity should be represented by the longest distance between two points on the resulting map, the smallest by the shortest distance and so on. The discrepancies in rank order between the real data and their representation in the MDS model contribute to the main measure of the precision of the model, the so-called stress figure.

It has been claimed (Kruskal, 1978) that a stress figure of 0.1 or less indicates that the MDS model provides a good representation of the data. We have found in practice that any model should be checked back to the semi-matrix, particularly when drawing conclusions. Thus the assertion that Burtons is closest to the ideal menswear retailer, as is apparent from the MDS map in Chapter 5, needs to be checked with the input data, the semi-matrix in the Appendix. The computer has no way of knowing that its human partners place more importance on the position of the ideal than on other points in the model!

INTERPRETING MODELS

MDS models are a representation of market research data, albeit data gathered in a way best suited to that technique, rather than any original source of information. Nevertheless they allow an easily assimilable picture of a market, which can be used to assess the relative positioning of one's retail organization with respect to the competition.

Retailers can be repositioned in one of two ways: moving towards the ideal to broaden appeal, or moving away from competition to emphasize differential advantage. Sometimes both options are available, usually only one. The concepts in the model act as pointers for the strategist to use to guide such moves.

For example, consider the hypothetical model in Figure 6.1. Five stores A, B, C, D and E compete in the chosen sector. A map has been produced from market research data which asked shoppers to say how similar or different each retailer was in their opinion. Stores A, B and D were seen as similar, with stores C and E somewhat differentiated from these. Potentially, stores C and E could be well positioned in that they are seen as distinctly different from the rest.

The problem is that the model contains no reference point to guide such a judgement. The main reference point used by the authors is the opinion of the average shopper of the position of the 'ideal' retail store in that sector. In Figure 6.2 the 'ideal' is also included, changing our impression of the market situation. Store C now seems the only really well-placed store in that it is not only differentiated but, because it is placed close if not closest to the ideal, it has the widest appeal. Store C has adopted the best possible positioning strategy. Store D is also fairly well placed – being close to the ideal

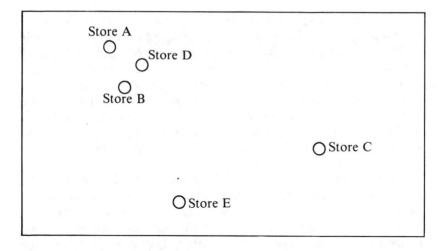

Figure 6.1 Hypothetical model of a retail market.

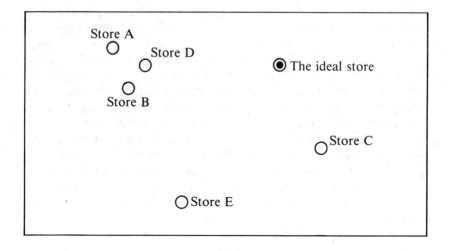

Figure 6.2 Hypothetical model of a retail market, including the position of the 'ideal' store.

store, it has broad appeal. However, stores A and B compete with store D for the particular shopping experience associated by the shopper with all three stores. Stores A and B are worse off in that they appear to be second choices to store D. All things being equal, the shopper will visit store D first and will be better disposed to buying similar merchandise there rather than at store A or B.

As the reader will discover, where the market structure is similar to that modelled in Figure 6.2, stores A and B may try to compete by lowering prices, by cutting margins and by offering low-quality merchandise. Unless either store A or B has an inbuilt advantage allowing it to offer low prices and still make an adequate margin, in our experience such cost-cutting strategies will *never* succeed. Indeed they will serve merely to provoke the retailer in store D's position to respond, generating the kind of price-led competitive spiral which will result in reduced profitability for all.

The inclusion of the 'ideal' store as a reference point in Figure 6.2 makes store E's position look highly undesirable. Although the retailer is differentiated it cannot be said to have a broad appeal being so far from the 'ideal'. In some instances the store E position is indicative of a low level of appeal, which will mean low traffic flows and low purchase rates. In other instances, however, the positioning can be viewed more favourably and these circumstances are often associated with a successful price-led appeal. One outstanding example of this can be seen in Chapter 7 in Kwik Save's positioning in food retailing. An example of the opposite consequences of such a market position can be seen in the same case study in the position of the Co-op. The retailer perceived as being far from the average view of the 'ideal' store must have a clear-cut point of difference which appeals to a minority.

To be successful without an image-led strategy, it seems a retailer must have a well-founded, price-led strategy so that, bluntly, people will shop there whatever they think of the store because it clearly saves them significant sums of money. To be able to deliver a coherent and valid price-led strategy in the long term means that the method of operation has inbuilt economies. These will allow the retailer to offer low prices profitably, and will be difficult to imitate. Virtually every retailer will claim to offer low prices at some stage or other (far too often for their own good in the authors' opinion). Being convincing and correct in offering the lowest cost to the customer is a different matter entirely. While all retailers will have an element of price leading in their strategy, very few can sustain it as their only strategy.

Therefore, what is needed in Figure 6.2 is some indication of why each retailer is perceived or positioned as it is and where any one might reposition. This is where the concepts generated and screened in the market research process have their greatest value, and Figure 6.3 offers a hypothetical example of their inclusion. It seems that store E is in fact the price-led competitor in the market-place. Because it is out on its own it is highly likely to be successful (with the assumption that it can maintain its cost structure). Store B is

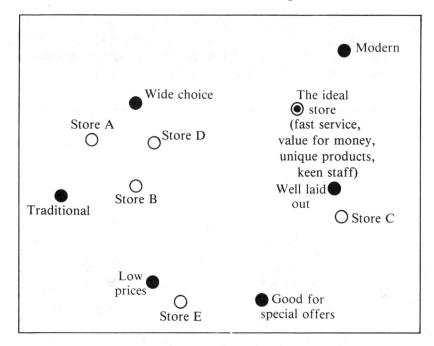

Figure 6.3 Hypothetical model of a retail market, including the 'ideal' store and concepts.

close to low prices but is anchored in the 'traditional' sector of the market-place, which is typified by offering a 'wide choice'. Store C, seen more clearly now as likely to be the market leader, has positioned itself as 'well laid out' and more 'modern' than its competitors, with store D, its main rival, also associated with the latter concept but very weakly.

The ideal store position can be described as having 'fast service', 'unique products', 'young staff' and offering 'value for money'. Although this is a hypothetical example, 'value for money' and 'low prices' are deliberately shown as separate concepts because that is our experience in most retail sectors. They mean different things to the shopper and allow a retailer to promote a price component (value for money) without having to indulge in overt price competition and thus be associated with 'low prices'.

The market model is generally identical for all groups of shoppers, with one significant exception. The shoppers who prefer a more 'traditional' offering will see that concept, and the stores associated with it, as being closer to the 'ideal'. The preferred stores will, in their opinion, genuinely offer faster service, more unique products and so on. The shoppers at store E will in turn see their store as closer to the 'ideal'; likewise those whose first choice is store C will see their preference closer to the 'ideal'. Figure 6.4 illustrates this by presenting the hypothetical model for the more traditionally orientated shopper whose first-choice store is store D.

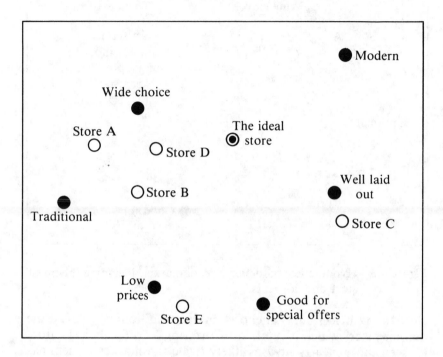

Figure 6.4   Hypothetical model of a retail market for the traditionally minded shopper who patronizes store D.

USING MODELS TO REPOSITION

So far we have discussed the use of models to describe retail sectors. To be of full value they must also be capable of guiding future strategy. To explore this potential, let us return to Figure 6.3 and examine it from store A's perspective.

There may be little potential in continuing to compete with stores D and B, and store A might well decide to reposition. Clearly any such move must not bring it up against another competitor, especially store C. The obvious choice is to move between 'wide choice' and 'modern' by adopting a more 'modern' image and at the same time adopting more of what the majority of shoppers perceive as the 'ideal' store attributes.

Further market research may be necessary to identify how this can be achieved. The work of the authors and others on the relationship between department and store image is presented in Chapter 13. An image change may involve a substantial change in the operation of a small number of key departments in the store. How more dramatic changes can be implemented is discussed at length in Chapter 14.

Once repositioned the new market structure will appear as shown in Figure 6.5. Stores D and B could also benefit from store A's move.

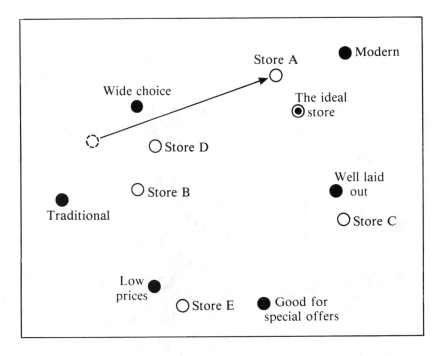

Figure 6.5 Hypothetical model of a retail market with store A repositioned.

This is not so far-fetched an idea as it might seem. What can well happen is that the entire market will grow because the shopper is offered a better and wider choice. Store A's more traditional customers will patronize stores B and D more, and store A will gain new customers and/or a greater share of its existing customers' disposable income, because of their moving to satisfy a previously unfulfilled need. Two examples, in electrical and furniture retailing, are presented in Chapters 10 and 11 to illustrate this potential.

ISSUES IN USING PERCEPTUAL MODELS

In our experience some people find it difficult to accept the perceptual maps being used here to model markets. Often this is due to lack of familiarity in seeing market research data presented in this way. A more traditional method of presenting such data would be as shown in Figure 6.6, which contains much the same data used to construct the model of menswear retailing in Chapter 5. We feel that such a method is not a great deal of help in visualizing

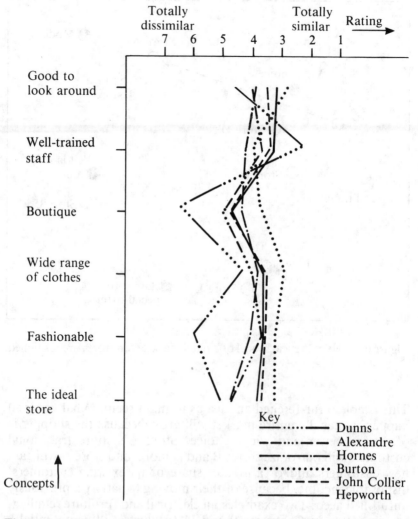

Figure 6.6 Menswear data from Chapter 5 in traditional presentation.

a market as a whole, although such a presentation can add another dimension to understanding the market, as it offers a profile of each competitor.

A more valid issue is that of the choice and number of points on each model. In practice this is likely to be limited to fourteen points to allow a fair representation of the market research data as a two-dimensional map. It is possible to produce a three-dimensional model using MDS. These are more difficult to interpret and intrinsically difficult to represent in an essentially two-dimensional book.

In most retail markets there are about four or five prominent competitors. The number of concepts that can be useful in segmenting a retail market is unlikely, according to Lindquist (1974–75), to exceed nine. The 'ideal' store is also a useful way of aggregating a number of concepts which, while important, would not add to an understanding of market structure if presented separately. In practice, therefore, twelve or fourteen points are often adequate to model a retail market.

Where this is unlikely to be valid, an alternative method of analysing and presenting concept data is to superimpose a series of concept vectors onto a map of stores only (Hooley and Cook, 1983). Such a model is shown in Figure 6.7. Instead of being identified as points, concepts are presented as vectors indicating a growing tendency for a retailer to be associated with the concept in the direction of the vector. In Figure 6.7 store E has the image of low prices and good for special offers. Store A has a wide choice, is traditional and is not seen as well laid out. It could improve by being seen as better laid out, which would bring it closer to the ideal, or it could concentrate on appealing more to perhaps a smaller market by emphasizing choice and tradition.

For the sake of simplicity almost all the models in this book use concepts as points. Some people find the absence of axes in the typical MDS map confusing and are happier with the vector style of presentation. In practice, unless the market is complex, we find vectors more difficult to use to analyse positioning strategy and always prefer to gain an understanding of market structure using the non-vector technique first.

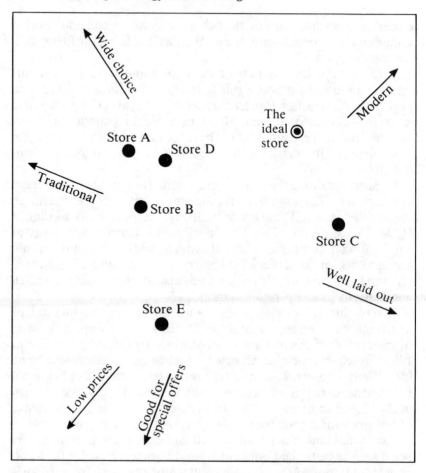

Figure 6.7 An alternative method of market mapping for more complex markets.

THE STRENGTHS AND WEAKNESSES OF THE APPROACH

To summarize, our methodology involves a number of stages:

(1)   The selection of the main stores that define a market sector.

(2)   Qualitative market research to identify a number of potential concepts (guided by Lindquist's checklist of concepts).

(3)   The screening of the output of the qualitative research (normally thirty to forty concepts) to identify those which describe the ideal store, and those which can be used to define

the market structure. A third group of concepts, which are invalid, are eliminated. This screening is done by asking a random sample of about 100 shoppers to rate each potential concept against their idea of the ideal store.

(4) Comparison of each store and concept on a differential scale (1 indicating total similarity, 7 indicating total dissimilarity) with a survey of a structured sample of shoppers (normally 150).

(5) The averaging of all ratings for each comparison to produce a semi-matrix that is both the final reference data and the input to the MDS computer program.

(6) The production of the MDS model, its interpretation and the comparison of the market structure with commercial and other data on the competing retailers.

MDS as a technique is still relatively new, although it has been applied by a number of workers to both product and retail research. One issue is the absence of any known way of assessing the statistical validity of the market maps which form the main output of the work. In later chapters we present two sector studies where a series of measures have been taken over a number of years. In each case the overall market structure is consistent between studies. The various models also appear to reflect real changes in the market-place. This implies some stability in the technique.

The technique also appears to be fairly robust. The average perception of as few as 30 or 40 respondents is often enough to produce a stable picture of any retail market. However, the position of the ideal store does seem to vary depending on the nature of the sample, leading the authors to use larger sample sizes of around 150 respondents.

Nevertheless we know of no method to define a statistical confidence level for the market models produced. The stress measure normally produced by an MDS analysis appears to have no absolute value, other than as a guide to whether the rank order of similarities is similar in the model to that in the input data. The MDS technique is arguably somewhat more than a qualitative method. It has the value of reducing a complex market situation to a simple representation which can be used to make strategic decisions. We endeavour to demonstrate that such models, taken together, allow us to propose approaches in positioning strategy which are relevant to all retailing.

KEY POINT SUMMARY

(1) Market models include a mixture of stores and concepts. Selecting concepts is an important part of our methodology. Concepts can be used in models to describe the 'ideal' store or to help understand the market structure. The 'ideal' is a useful marker in a model and a vital reference point.

(2) Earlier work on retail image suggests there may be as many as nine types of image criteria relevant to retailing which can be used as a checklist to guide the generation of concepts.

(3) Individual shoppers generally agree on the structure of a retail market with the exception of where each perceives the 'ideal' store to be. The shopper sees the ideal as being closest to their preferred store.

(4) A good market position is to be seen as different as possible from the competition, close to the average view of the ideal store, and closely associated with one or more concepts.

(5) We use one variant of multidimensional scaling (MDS). One other, which can incorporate more data, uses vectors rather than points for concepts.

References

Arons, L. (1961) Does television viewing influence store image and shopping frequency, *Journal of Retailing*, Vol. 37, pp. 1, 13.

Arora, R. (1982) Consumer involvement in retail store positioning, *Journal of the Academy of Marketing Science*, Vol. 10, pp. 109–124.

Berry, L.L. (1969) The components of department store image: a theoretical and empirical analysis, *Journal of Retailing*, Vol. 45, pp. 3–20.

Coxon, A.P.M. (1982) *The Users Guide to Multidimensional Scaling*, Heinemann, London.

Doyle, P. and Fenwick, I. (1974–75) How store image affects shopping habits in grocery chains, *Journal of Retailing*, Vol. 50, pp. 39–52.

Harman, H.H. (1967) Foundation of factor analysis, *Modern Factor Analysis* (2nd edn), University of Chicago Press.

Hooley, G. and Cook, D. (1983) Measuring retail store images through perceptual mapping techniques, European Marketing Academy Paper, Grenoble, France, 1983.

Jain, A.K. and Etgar, M. (1976–77) Measuring store image through multidimensional scaling of free response data, *Journal of Retailing*, Vol. 52, pp. 61–70.

Korgaonkar, P.K. and El Sheshai, K.M. (1982) Assessing retail competition with multidimensional scaling, *Business USA*, Vol. 32, pp. 30-33.

Kruskal, J.V. and Wish, M. (1978) *Multi Dimensional Scaling*, Sage Publications, Beverley Hills, Ca.

Lenzen, W. and Reisner, H. (1980) Kundenorientierung im Handel - Ein Imageanalytischer Ansatz zur Erfassung, *FFH Mitteilungen*, July, pp. 1-7.

Lindquist, J.D. (1974-75) Meaning of image, *Journal of Retailing*, Vol. 50, pp. 29-38.

Martineau, P. (1958) The personality of the retail store, *Harvard Business Review*, Vol 36, pp. 47-55.

Ring, L.J. (1979) Retail positioning: a multiple discriminant analysis approach, *Journal of Retailing*, Vol. 50, pp. 25-36.

Rivas, J. and Grijalba, J.M.M. (1986) Customer store image in Spain: an empirical study on food stores, *International Journal of Retailing*, Vol. 1, no. 2.

Roskam, E.E. (undated) MINISSA In *MDS(X) Programs*, MDS(X) Project Program, Library Unit, University of Edinburgh.

Weale, W.B. (1961) Measuring the customers' image of a department store, *Journal of Retailing*, Vol. 37, pp. 40-848.

Chapter 7

Food Retailing: Clear Positioning on Price, or Image, Can Pay

In this chapter we examine the effect of an image change on retailer performance. Three measures are presented of the British food retailing sector between 1983 and 1985. The dates coincided with a dramatic change in image for the Tesco organization, once identified with the 'pile it high, sell it cheap' maxim of its founder Sir John Cohen, but subsequently with considerable innovation in own-label branding. A final section presents a wider picture of food retailing, in 1987, incorporating the effects of the takeovers by the Dee and Argyll groups.

This chapter examines in greater depth the links between image and commercial performance. This is made easier because of the wealth of data available on food retailing, by comparison with non-food retailing, and the comparative homogeneity of the market sector, at least at the time of the studies reported here. It is therefore one of the longer chapters containing some of the strongest evidence offered by us in arguing the importance of positioning in retail strategy.

Food retailing also affords an insight into the structural changes occurring in the British economy since the halcyon days, for the manufacturer that is, of the brand. Even earlier, the first food retailers had packeted foodstuffs for their customers. They also sold semi-manufactured products that they made themselves. They may have specialized in one food type or other. In their packeting function, food retailers and their customers did not rely on the food manufacturer to any great extent.

By the late 1960s virtually every foodstuff, even including fresh food, was branded. The retailer represented the supplier's distribution system. Source loyalty to the retailer was far less important than brand loyalty to the manufacturer. Many customers would leave a retail outlet rather than forgo the purchase of their regular brand if that line was out of stock (Christopher, Walters and Wills, 1978). For example, 48 per cent of those questioned in one study would have gone to another store for their brand of tea if it was out of stock in the retailer visited.

The temptation for retailers to compete by offering the keenest prices on leading brands was (and still is to some extent) very high. The abolition of resale price maintenance and the high inflation levels in the 1960s and 1970s both conspired to ensure that price promotion was a common strategy in food retailing. Only a few shops – the specialist delicatessen, the 'open all hours' corner shop and shops like Fortnum and Mason – selected non-price strategies as their basis for competition.

THE MAJOR FOOD RETAILERS

Sainsbury

The first of the major food retailers to break the price-led mould was probably Sainsbury. J. Sainsbury plc grew from a single outlet in London's Drury Lane in 1869 to become the largest food retailer in Britain by 1983. Perhaps significantly, the company had turned its back on trading stamps and free gifts in the 1960s and had based its approach instead on 'good value and quality' products retailed in tidy, clean, hygienic and gimmick-free shops (Channon, 1985a). The company had traditionally retailed a range of own-label products which by 1986 accounted for 60 per cent of turnover (AGB, 1986). This share was achieved apparently from a minority shelf space (Channon, 1985a) even though the shelf space given to own label sometimes swamped that devoted to brands (Themistoclik & Associates, 1986).

The company was well represented in the high street and had been one of the earliest to take up the supermarket concept. A combination of moving off the high street to larger sites and closing older, smaller outlets gave the average Sainsbury store a sales area of over 16,000 sq. ft by 1984.

Kwik Save

Although Sainsbury was normally quoted as a market leader in food retailing, when assessed in terms of return on capital employed, a somewhat smaller retailer, Kwik Save Discount, could boast a comparable or even better performance. In many ways, Kwik Save could be regarded as the antithesis of Sainsbury. While Sainsbury's strength was in the South of England, Kwik Save was concentrated in the North. The typical Kwik Save store, until the 1980s at least, was likely to be a redundant cinema or church. Kwik Save retailed only manufacturer's brands and a limited range at that. The company's approach in many ways reflected the orientation of the original owner. Albert Gubay had disregarded business precedent in the way he had operated his first food store in the North Wales resort of Rhyl, discounting despite resale price maintenance and remaining open until 9 pm on Fridays, despite local restrictions (Channon, 1985b).

The typical Kwik Save was located in an urban centre, had limited car parking and a spartan interior. Kwik Save's advertising, making heavy use of television, was overtly price based with slogans such as 'No need to ask the price, she went to Kwik Save'. In the early 1980s the advertising generally featured a leading national brand in a jointly funded promotion.

Kwik Save handled its own physical distribution and bought only in bulk. Its staffing costs were considerably below those of its competitors, achieved through operating a simple, no frills system by not price marking goods and by using the manufacturers' cardboard boxes as the means of displaying goods.

Kwik Save aimed to stock the brand leader in any sector but if the manufacturer concerned refused to discount sufficiently, the company would delist it and carry the number two or three brand.

ASDA

Just ahead of Kwik Save in market share in the 1980s was ASDA, the largest part of Associated Dairies plc. ASDA's origins were as the retail outlets for the original organization's farm products. The company's later attitude to food retailing, however, was shaped by the purchase of two (at the time comparatively large) superstores in 1965. During the 1970s ASDA pioneered the superstore (Channon, 1985c) selecting mainly out-of-town sites, with ample car parking and around 40,000 sq. ft of selling space. The stores stocked a wide range of essentially branded food products, fresh foods and a range of non-foods.

ASDA's promotional platform, evident from its television advertising, was again overtly price led with the slogan 'ASDA price' featuring strongly throughout the early 1980s. Following the merger with furniture retailers MFI in 1985 a switch to own labelling was given more prominence. The objective was to reach a total of 2,500 lines under the 'ASDA brand' by December 1987, out of some 20,000 food and non-food lines. A new design concept was launched and a new corporate logo based around a distinctive yet controversial selection of pastel colours. A move into car retailing and estate agency, and an expansion of franchises adjacent to the ASDA stores themselves but within the ASDA enclave, was offered as evidence of achieving the company's objective of offering the customer 'one-stop shopping'.

Tesco

These later changes at ASDA are only partly relevant to even the last map presented in this chapter (see Figure 7.22). The major developments in Tesco in the 1980s are somewhat more relevant. Tesco had been a reluctant follower into the trading stamp promotions of the 1960s (Channon, 1985d), offering Green Shield stamps at a reported equivalent cost of 2.5 per cent on prices. In 1977 Tesco dropped trading stamps and launched one of the most successful retail price promotions, under the banner of 'Operation Checkout'. The 3 per cent price cut and the associated promotion saw sales leap from 1.7 million units/month to 2.4 million in just four months (Davies, Gilligan and Sutton, 1985).

Despite this success Tesco's net margin continued to decline from nearly 6 per cent in the early 1970s to barely above 2 per cent by 1981. Although margins had been falling generally in food retailing in the early 1970s, Tesco was alone among the majors in seeing a continuing fall in the late 1970s.

In the 1980s food retailers seemed to have moved the focus of their marketing away from price, with the exception of Kwik Save. The Marketing Director of ASDA offered the explanation that in the inflationary 1970s, price was a dominant factor in determining store choice, and quoted research showing price to have dropped from first to sixth position in consumer ratings between 1980 and 1984 (Street, 1986). Other factors such as 'convenience, quality, range and store environment' had become more important. Other observers explained the same apparent trend in slightly different ways by suggesting that consumers had grown to expect keen prices, because of the price theme inherent in most food retail promotion in the 1970s, and were now looking for other benefits. However, this view of a changing market-place was not universally held. A spokesman for the Co-operative Wholesale Society was quoted in 1980 as predicting a continuation of price-led competition into the following decade, although in the same article (Gayfer, 1980) another industry source referred to an 'obsession with price' causing some to lose ground in the race to outprice everybody else.

A price-sensitive era?

The 1970s in Britain saw high levels of inflation (29 per cent between July 1975 and July 1976, for example), the beginnings of economic stagnation and an era of high unemployment. It would be expected that customers would be very price-sensitive. Yet it was no easy matter comparing prices objectively from one outlet to another. *Which* consumer magazine published regular price checks on what were held to be two typical 'shopping baskets' of basic grocery items, one of leading brands, one of cheapest brands (Consumer Association, 1976, 1979, 1982). In 1976, 1979 and 1982 four of the leading six food retailers featured in both surveys. Kwik Save was included in the 1979 and 1982 surveys only, and Marks and Spencer in 1982. The two slightly different baskets are compared in Table 7.1. The comparison is made on a rank order basis and where the difference found by *Which* was marginal the stores are ranked the same. Also for comparison the rank order of percentage net profit margin before tax is shown for the business year in which the shopping basket was selected.

The differences between prices found by *Which* were sometimes quite startling. In the 1982 survey, the cheapest well-known branded basket (from ASDA) was exactly 10 per cent cheaper than that from the Co-op. Kwik Save was not included by *Which* in any of the top-brand basket studies, presumably because of its policy not to offer the leading brand unless it could obtain a significant price advantage. It implies that Kwik Save specialized, in practice, far more in the number two or three brand. When the baskets for any brand are compared, Kwik Save was the cheapest in each study. In 1982 the difference was 7.7 per cent cheaper than the Co-op. Despite offering such low prices Kwik Save led on net margin in each of the three years.

There are a number of points that should be noted about the data in Table 7.1. The shopping basket approach is not an entirely reliable measure of relative selling prices. Prices fluctuate and retailers can justifiably adopt very different approaches to pricing what they believe their customers regard as a realistic shopping basket. However, the main point to be drawn here is that despite the success of Tesco's Operation Checkout in generating customer flow and their consequent increase in market share, the net effect was not to increase Tesco's relative position with respect to net margin (Figure 7.1). On the other hand Sainsbury had improved both its net margin position and the relative price of its shopping basket. Kwik Save seems to have fared less well in relative terms although in overall profitability it was still doing well.

Marks and Spencer

The last two retailers to be included in the studies in this chapter are Marks and Spencer and the Co-op. Marks and Spencer were

Table 7.1 Profit margin and relative price of a shopping basket, 1976–77

Retailer	1976 rank order		Net margin rank order	1979 rank order		Net margin rank order	1982 rank order		Net margin rank order
	Brands	Any		Brands	Any		Brands	Any	
Tesco	3	1	3	2	4	4	2	3	4
Sainsbury	4	4	4	3	3	3	2	3	1
ASDA	1	3	2	1	2	1	1	2	3
Co-op	2	1	—	4	5	—	4	4	—
Kwik Save	—	—	1	—	1	1	—	1	1

Sources: Consumer Association (1976, 1979, 1982); Davies, Gilligan and Sutton (1985).

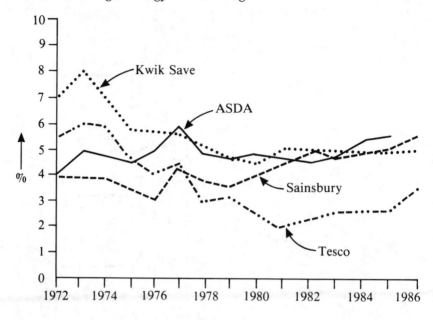

Figure 7.1   Net profit margin (%) (before tax).

added in the second of the four studies because of their growth rate in food sales, achieved using very different tactics from those of their competitors, but ones which had brought them into the top half-dozen food retailers. Marks and Spencer traded mainly in the high street. Few stores had parking spaces. The company had a 100 per cent own-label policy coupled with the approach that each product line, be it food or non-food, should be judged primarily on its gross margin contribution. In practice this meant Marks and Spencer did not offer branded foodstuffs and that margins on food had to be considerably higher than those expected generally by food retailers. Marks and Spencer consequently offered a limited range of products often ignoring staples such as baked beans where they could not achieve their target margin. They concentrated on pre-prepared dishes, snacks, wines and confectionery, in producing an offering that was described as concentrating on 'treats'. Being 100 per cent own label, their range was not extended by offering competing products within a line. Their pricing policy was on the high side. Because it is difficult to compare Marks and Spencer directly with other retailers they are generally excluded from shopping basket studies. However, the 1982 *Which* survey did include them in a survey of shopping basket essentials for 'cheapest brands'. Marks and Spencer ranked 38 out of the 39 stores surveyed, some 22 per cent more expensive than the leader, Kwik Save.

Marks and Spencer found that food made a better return for them on the basis of store space, than much of their traditional merchandise. In 1985, 40.4 per cent of Marks and Spencer turnover was from food, making them Britain's third largest grocer, even though food was allocated only some 25 per cent of floorspace.

The Co-op

The last retailer to be considered is the Co-op. Opinions differ as to whether it is reasonable to consider the Co-op as a single, homogeneous entity. The Co-op is more than a complex retail organization. Its origins as a social as well as an economic organization continued to shape its business operations in the 1980s. Essentially, a co-operative is run for the benefit of its members, who share in any profits. Not so long ago shoppers 'joined' their local Co-op and received a dividend each year based on their total purchase. This concept was replaced by offering trading stamps as part of an attempt to co-ordinate the activities of the Co-op nationally. The familiar blue and white logo dated from the same era.

In terms of numbers, the Co-op dominated British food retailing with over 6,000 outlets, and until the 1980s it held prime position in food retailing. The outlets ranged from modern stores to traditional corner shops. The Co-op movement consisted of a number of independent societies. Some societies operated as few as two or three outlets, others ranked in the top twenty food retailers in their own right. Each society retained at least something of its own individuality.

The Co-op had been innovators in own label, largely through its wholesale society, the CWS. However, each individual society could choose whether to accept the CWS Co-op own-brand, or to market its own under its society name, or to concentrate on brands. Establishing a coherent corporate identity in such circumstances is always going to be difficult, as the studies presented later in this chapter will illustrate.

The main market trend, measured as the share of packaged groceries, is shown in Table 7.2. The independents and the Co-op were losing market share to the leading multiples.

MARKET STUDIES 1983–85

Five food retailers, Tesco, Sainsbury, ASDA, the Co-op and Kwik Save, were included in each of three studies between 1983 and 1985.

Table 7.2   Food retailer market shares

| | Market share (%) | | | | | | | | | |
	1973	1974	1975	1976	1977	1978	1979	1980	1981	1982
Sainsbury	7.8	7.8	8.6	8.4	8.4	10.4	10.7	12.2	13.5	15.0
Tesco	7.2	7.7	7.8	7.7	9.8	12.2	13.3	14.0	13.7	13.8
ASDA	2.9	3.3	4.1	5.0	5.6	5.9	6.2	7.7	7.8	8.5
Kwik Save	n/a	2.1	2.6	2.7	3.4	3.8	4.6	5.2	5.5	5.4
Co-op	21.1	21.9	21.5	21.7	20.3	19.2	18.9	17.7	17.0	15.9

Source: Audits of Great Britain 1983. Copyright AGB/TCA.

Marks and Spencer were added in the 1984 and 1985 studies. Slightly different concepts were used to describe the market in each study (although some are clearly close enough to be considered as synonyms). The retailers and concepts used in each model are shown in Table 7.3, together with the concepts found in each study to describe the ideal food retailer. Two points emerge: first, that some concepts found to be less important one year were included in the general view of an 'ideal' food retailer the next ('convenient', 'value for money', 'good for fresh foods'). One interpretation of this is that food retailers had been emphasizing such concepts in their strategy and promotion, thus changing people's ideas on what was desirable in food retailing. Whatever the interpretation, the marketplace was changing quite rapidly in many respects. Certainly customers seemed to have had their expectations of food retailing changed over a fairly short period. The second point to emerge is that certain concepts seemed to remain important in segmenting the food retailing market, namely 'wide product range' and 'well laid out', and others in describing the ideal food retailer, namely 'clean'.

Figures 7.2–7.4 record the results of the 1983 survey showing the results of the matrix comparisons, a model of stores only, and a full model including concepts. Sainsbury was clearly well positioned, being close to the 'ideal' food retailer and appealing differentially on reliability and service factors. ASDA and Tesco shared a second sector described by the concepts 'wide range' and 'organized'. However, ASDA's position closer to the 'ideal' compared to Tesco, must be weighed against Sainsbury's good scores against just those concepts which appear to differentiate ASDA. The sheer presence of a larger organization (Tesco) in the same sector would also detract from ASDA's position, although ASDA's concentration in the North and Tesco's in the South at the time would have reduced their mutual impact. ASDA's close association with 'value for money' in 1983 would also motivate the price-conscious shopper.

Table 7.3 Food retailer studies, concepts and retailers included

	1983	1984	1985
Food retailers	ASDA Tesco Co-op Kwik Save Sainsbury	ASDA Tesco Co-op Kwik Save Sainsbury Marks & Spencer	ASDA Tesco Co-op Kwik Save Sainsbury Marks & Spencer

Concepts used	Good standard
	
	Value for money
	
	Good service
	
	Organized
	
	Wide range
	
	Convenient
		Quality products
		
		Good for fresh
		  foods
		Wide product
		  range
		Well laid out
		
		Competitive
		  prices
		Good customer
		  relations
			Good for
			  specialist food
			Good for basic
			  products
			Wide product
			  range
			Well laid out
			
			Well-trained
			  staff
			Steady prices

Concepts found to describe the ideal food retailer	Clean
	Fresh
	Hygienic
	High standards
	Good quality
	  products
		Clean
		Convenient
		Value for money
		Fast checkouts
			Fast till service
			Polite staff
			Quality products
			Value for money
			Good for fresh
			  foods
			Clean
			Long opening
			  hours

The Co-op was ranked furthest from the ideal and close to only one concept – 'convenient'. This concept did not, however, differentiate strongly between retailers (see the market research data in Figure 7.2) and was unlikely to be valid as the basis for any strategy based on differentiation. Kwik Save occupied the 'value for money' sector and it was differentiated strongly from all the other mainstream food retailers. Nationally some other retailers seemed to be operating a similar approach to Kwik Save – Shoppers' Paradise, Lo-Cost and, soon, the Tesco subsidiary Victor Value. However, none could compare to Kwik Save in its scale of operation and promotional expenditure. In the 1982 *Which* survey only Shoppers' Paradise competed on actual prices charged.

Figure 7.5 shows the market research matrix for the 1985 study, including Marks and Spencer for the first time. The data and models

	Co-op	Tesco	ASDA	Sainsbury	Kwik Save	Ideal foodstore	Convenient	Organized	Wide range	Good service	Value for money	Good standard
Co-op	1											
Tesco	5.40	1										
ASDA	5.58	4.54	1									
Sainsbury	7.63	6.01	4.54	1								
Kwik Save	5.73	5.67	6.39	7.95	1							
Ideal foodstore	8.41	5.31	4.24	3.75	6.71	1						
Convenient	5.31	5.71	5.65	5.95	5.38	2.46	1					
Organized	5.41	4.16	3.21	2.85	5.68	2.35	6.55	1				
Wide range	5.18	3.92	2.76	2.67	6.73	2.14	6.47	5.50	1			
Good service	5.00	4.50	3.61	2.69	6.05	2.08	6.84	4.35	5.56	1		
Value for money	5.30	3.98	3.15	3.71	3.34	1.79	6.80	6.65	6.75	6.10	1	
Good standard	5.54	4.24	3.22	2.24	5.24	1.71	6.92	5.12	5.67	4.39	4.78	1

Figure 7.2 1983 matrix data. Average ratings: 1 = totally similar, 10 = totally dissimilar.

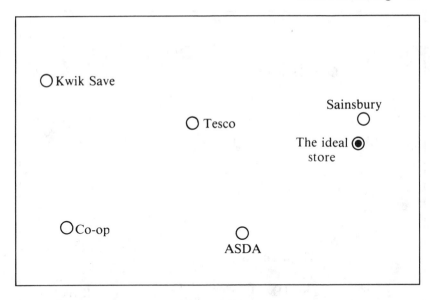

Figure 7.3 Food retailers: stores only, 1983.

for 1984 do not differ from those for 1983, so they are not presented or discussed here. However, by 1985 some significant changes could be seen in the position of Tesco. The results of the 1985 study are shown in Figures 7.5–7.7.

The concepts 'good for specialist food', 'interesting place to shop', 'well-trained staff' and 'well-laid out' form a closely associated group. Sainsbury and Marks and Spencer are the only two retailers occupying the sector, with Sainsbury being the dominant retailer (Figure 7.7). Sainsbury, however, was also still associated with the concepts 'wide product range', 'good for basic products' and 'steady prices'. Marks and Spencer were not associated with the last three, indicating some differentiation from Sainsbury and still more from the other retailers being considered. Marks and Spencer would probably have argued that theirs was a very different food shopping experience from that of the more mainstream food retailers. They were more likely to attract the casual, even selective food purchase, rather than the weekly family shop. They could expect to appeal strongly to the working shopper, male or female, for convenience foods. Marks and Spencer clearly did not see the mainstream food retailer as a threat. By this time they had formed a partnership with Tesco in searching for suitable out-of-town locations, a strategy

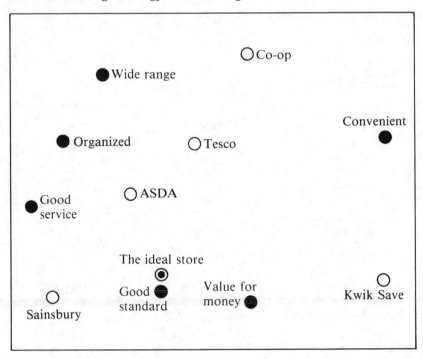

Figure 7.4   Food retailers: stores and concepts, 1983

which may raise a few eyebrows when the reader assesses Tesco's apparent repositioning strategy.

In 1985 Tesco and ASDA were still in very much the same position as in 1983, although their association with the concepts 'wide product range', 'good for basic products' and 'steady prices' was shared somewhat by Sainsbury. However, Tesco had moved closer to the 'ideal' than ASDA.

Kwik Save remained the sole occupant of the price-led end of the market and remained far from the 'ideal'. But it was still highly differentiated from the other leading retailers. A weak association with 'stocks well-known brands' emphasized the reality that Kwik Save's strategy did not always allow it to carry the number one brand. However, Kwik Save continued to use the slogan 'top brands at rock bottom prices' in its promotion.

By 1985 the Co-op was not strongly associated with any concept. The concept 'convenient' had become subsumed within the ideal store position in 1984. In our experience it is also a difficult concept

	ASDA	Tesco	Sainsbury	Kwik Save	Marks & Spencer	Co-op	The ideal store	Well-trained staff	Wide product range	Good for specialist food	Good for basic products	Steady prices	Interesting place to shop	Well laid out
ASDA	1													
Tesco	3.77	1												
Sainsbury	4.38	3.80	1											
Kwik Save	4.56	4.49	5.58	1										
Marks & Spencer	5.53	5.12	3.88	5.94	1									
Co-op	4.19	3.95	4.93	3.70	4.75	1								
The ideal store	4.13	3.80	2.88	5.00	3.80	4.57	1							
Well-trained staff	3.91	3.90	2.65	4.65	2.82	4.29	2.46	1						
Wide product range	2.37	3.20	2.56	5.10	3.85	3.55	2.26	4.36	1					
Good for specialist food	4.03	3.58	2.43	5.60	2.68	4.72	2.85	3.81	2.97	1				
Good for basic products	2.43	2.46	2.97	2.70	4.30	2.56	2.00	4.74	2.96	5.20	1			
Steady prices	2.72	2.87	3.56	2.38	4.19	3.00	2.17	4.77	4.16	4.76	2.84	1		
Interesting place to shop	4.25	4.05	2.84	5.42	2.78	4.69	2.59	3.40	2.70	2.89	4.64	4.82	1	
Well laid out	3.59	3.57	2.63	3.95	3.27	3.78	1.97	3.76	3.17	3.97	4.05	5.14	2.87	1

Figure 7.5 1985 matrix data. Average ratings: 1 = totally similar, 7 = totally dissimilar.

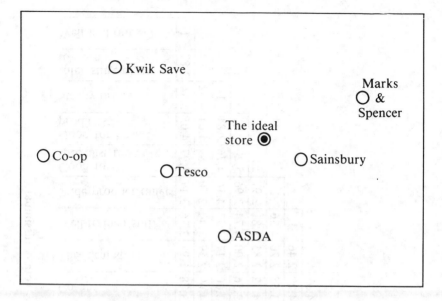

Figure 7.6   Food retailers: stores only, 1985.

on which to base positioning, because convenience means different things to different people.

The changes in image from 1983 to 1985 can be tracked by examining the rank order of stores against certain key concepts in the matrix data. The advantage that ASDA held over Tesco in 1983 and 1984 against the service-related concepts had been eroded by 1985. Tesco had also improved in terms of the ambience-related concepts. Between 1984 and 1985 Tesco had moved from fourth to third place against the concept 'well laid out', and was rated above ASDA as an 'interesting place to shop' in 1985. The obvious conclusion is that Tesco had strengthened its image considerably between 1983 and 1985, somewhat at ASDA's expense. Tesco's general direction was towards the more image-led sector occupied in 1985 by Sainsbury and Marks and Spencer.

In the context of this book it is then particularly interesting to examine what Tesco was doing and to assess the effect of this on both its financial performance and that of its competitors, particularly ASDA. In essence, Tesco seemed to have realized that its basically price-led promotional strategy, a cornerstone of the business since the days of its founder, had increased market share but not profitability. A change in strategy was marked by the

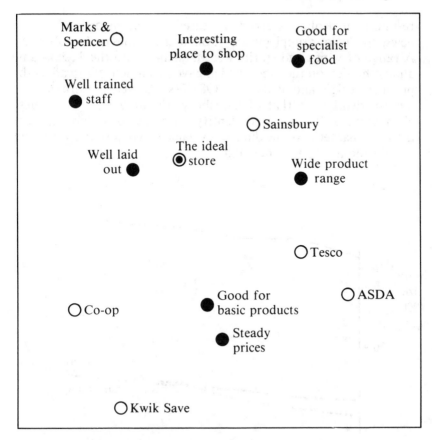

Figure 7.7 Food retailers: stores and concepts, 1985.

introduction of a new promotional appeal based on the theme 'Tomorrow's Tesco Today'.

From 1982 a number of the smaller Tesco stores were renamed as Victor Value and carried a limited range of products concentrating on low-priced, generic lines. In 1986 these were sold to Bejam. The management structure became more centralized, particularly in dealing with suppliers. A strategy group was formed with wide-ranging responsibilities including image and own-label products. Like other retailers Tesco had made an earlier move into own labelling, concentrating on the price differential this offered the consumer. The promotional emphasis on price advantage was subsequently switched to a quality platform. Tesco pioneered nutritional labelling of packaged groceries. Leading chef and restaurateur Robert Carrier appeared on television and in the newspaper colour supplements, extolling the virtues of Tesco's meat. A range of wines and spirits were launched with the Tesco name almost hidden on the label, which gave prominence instead to the products' origin and quality. By 1983 Tesco's average store size was almost identical to that of Sainsbury (Figure 7.8). For all these changes it is still difficult to identify where Tesco was going, other than 'up-market'. As one director explained: 'We just know we want to lose the image we once had'.

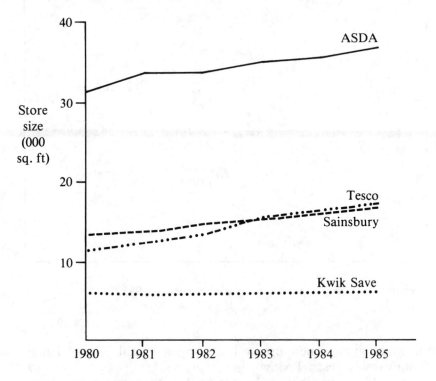

Figure 7.8   Average store size (000 sq. ft), 1980–85.

FINANCIAL ANALYSIS

It is difficult to obtain data on Marks and Spencer's food retailing as a separate entity, and aggregate data on the Co-op's food retailing are not only equally difficult to obtain but are generally not comparable to those of the mainstream food retailers. It is possible to conclude that many Co-ops returned a low financial performance by comparison with the other retailers considered here.

Figures 7.8 and 7.9 give data on average store size and total sales area between 1980 and 1985. Figure 7.10 shows total sales value. Sales per square foot are shown in Figure 7.11. Total profit before tax is shown in Figure 7.12 and profits per square foot in Figure 7.13. Profit and sales per employee are shown in Figures 7.14 and 7.15.

Kwik Save's price-led strategy shows through in its very low manning costs and consequently high sales and profit per employee performance. Tesco had held its sales area but had increased its sales value and profits. In particular its sales per square foot had increased significantly; only Sainsbury could claim the same.

Possibly the most relevant summary of performance is the somewhat complex Figure 7.16 showing the deflated growth rates of sales. Sainsbury had maintained a consistent growth rate between 1980 and 1985 of around 12 per cent per annum, while that of the Co-op had declined by around 2 per cent. Marks and Spencer performed as well as Sainsbury. Tesco and ASDA both suffered in 1982 but the most significant feature is the change in their relative fortunes from 1983 to 1985, with Tesco increasing its rate of sales volume growth and ASDA showing an opposite trend. Tesco's margins were also exhibiting a healthy growth (see Figure 7.1).

POSITIONING AND FINANCIAL PERFORMANCE

Figure 7.17 is an attempt to summarize the various strengths and weaknesses, in terms of image, of the retailers included in the food retailing models in 1985. It has been argued in earlier chapters that proximity to the ideal and degree of differentiation are the most salient factors in positioning strategy. The Co-op can be seen to have been consistently far from the ideal, and poorly differentiated in that it had no distinctive factors distinguishing it from competition. It had no coherent positioning and lacked broad appeal. Consequently its market share and general financial performance both suffered.

Marks and Spencer and Kwik Save are both clearly differentiated, the latter slightly more so than the former. Both offer a coherent image to the market-place and also to their employees. While it is not possible to separate Marks and Spencer's performance in food totally from its other business, its overall performance (see Chapter 8) exceeded that of any of its food competitors on most criteria. Sales and profit per employee, for example, were considerably higher than those of Kwik Save, the best performing specialist food retailer.

Tesco's and ASDA's relative movements in positioning are indicated by the 1983 situation being shown in brackets in Figure

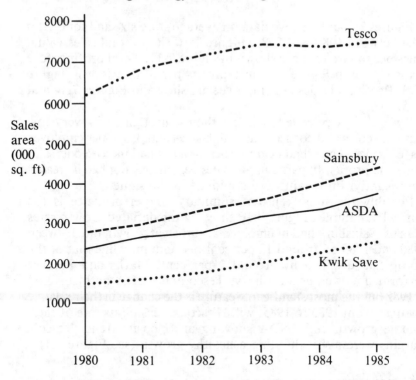

Figure 7.9　Sales area (000 sq. ft), 1980–85.

7.17. Tesco had overtaken ASDA in terms of positioning, by moving closer to the ideal and by becoming better associated with a range of image factors. This had been accompanied by an improvement in most financial criteria, the most notable being a strong relative increase in real growth rate (despite no increase in footage). However, both Tesco and ASDA had no single coherent positioning strategy. In their promotion they both appeared to be aiming for the concept of one-stop shopping emphasizing non-food lines, with ASDA more able to justify this in the majority of their stores, but Tesco able to match them in their newer, larger, out-of-town sites. Tesco's main advantage at the time could have lain in their highly successful range of own brand products, a strategy that ASDA was hurrying to emulate in 1985 but which would not have shown through in the models presented here.

The lack of a strong, clear and uncluttered image for both companies and the fact that they were seen as similar by shoppers, must have been cause for concern as ASDA moved South and Tesco

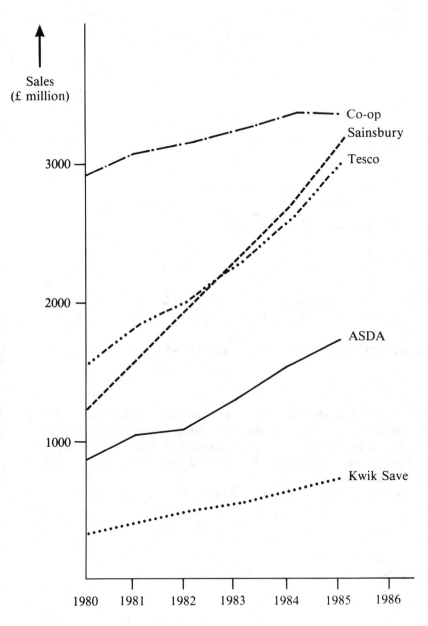

Figure 7.10 Sales value (£ million), 1980–85.

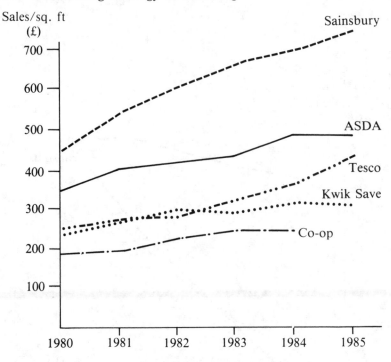

Figure 7.11   Sales per square foot (£), 1980–85.

North. In effect they were limiting each other's potential by being so similar in positioning. In such circumstances the inevitable outcome is to revert to price promotion. ASDA might be better able to sustain this, lacking the expensive high-street sites in the South of England compared to Tesco.

Tesco's change in strategy had brought it far closer to the Sainsbury/Marks and Spencer dominated sector. Assuming the changes in Tesco's positioning continue, the problem facing Marks and Spencer in the future, in sharing out-of-town locations with Tesco, could be having a retailer with an increasingly up-market image selling at a lower price adjacent to them.

Referring back to Figure 7.1, which shows net profit margin before tax well before the studies discussed here, the most dramatic and sustained improvement in performance has come from Sainsbury. While the general trend has been towards reducing margins they have increased theirs in a decade by about 20 per cent.

Given the circumstances surrounding Tesco's improvement and Marks and Spencer's considerable success with food, it may be that

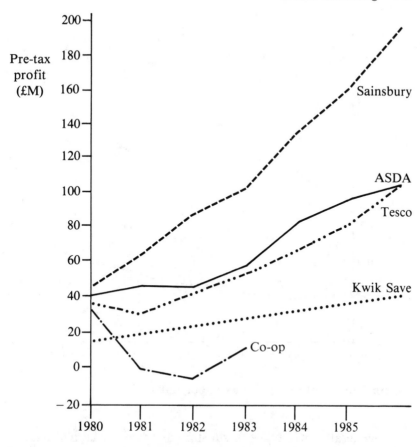

Figure 7.12 Profit before tax (£M), 1980–86.

own-label products are at least important in both positioning strategy and financial success. Sainsbury had increased its sales of own label to some 60 per cent of turnover (although it had announced in 1986 its intention to reduce dependency on own brand). It can be argued that own label encourages store rather than brand loyalty. It removes the normal basis for price comparison for the shopper (the relative price offered by competing retailers on national brands). At the same time it offers the retailer the benefits of the manufacturer's promotional margin to absorb as extra profit, or pass on to the customer as a price reduction. Own label had certainly been used as a price promotional tool (Table 7.4). Generic products (own-label goods in simple wrapping) had been offered at nearly half the price of branded product. Even the better promoted, own-label products

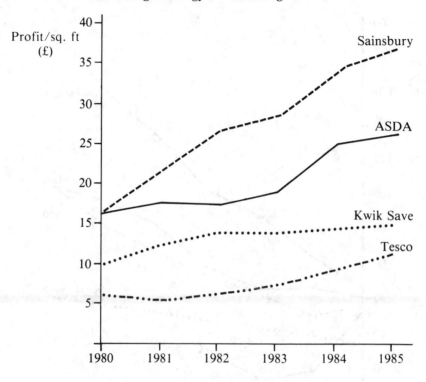

Figure 7.13   Profit (£) per square foot, 1980–85.

were generally offered at a substantial price advantage against brands. It is interesting to compare this approach in using own label to that of Marks and Spencer which seemed to price above the prices charged for brands, at least by shops like Kwik Save.

Earlier in this book it was argued that retailers were, and should be, becoming brands themselves, offering customers the added value they sought and were prepared to pay for. Using own-label products merely to offer substantial price reductions does not seem to be compatible with that concept. Offering high-quality, well-presented, own-label products marginally below brand prices is, on the other hand, totally compatible with image promotion and offers the retailer the potential for excellent margins to boot.

Another component in image building is likely to be advertising. While measured expenditure is not a foolproof measure of advertising's role in business, Figures 7.18 and 7.19 show total advertising expenditure and expenditure as a percentage of sales volume and offer a startling view of the effect advertising can or cannot have.

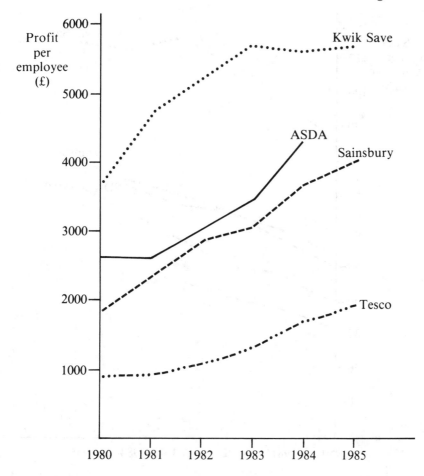

Figure 7.14 Profit (£) per employee, 1980–85.

Marks and Spencer's advertising is not included, partly because of the problems of comparison. If it had been possible to include, it would have been well below all the rest as a percentage of turnover and in total. Sainsbury, the other highly image-led retailer, also spent relatively little on advertising. At the time that Tesco was improving its image, its advertising/sales ratio fell, as did total expenditure. ASDA, the only retailer to lose relative position, can hardly blame this on low advertising expenditure. In short no direct links between advertising expenditure and relative positioning can be argued. In fact a case can be made for the opposite proposition!

It is also interesting to examine the content of the food retailer advertising at the time. ASDA, the Co-op and Kwik Save all majored

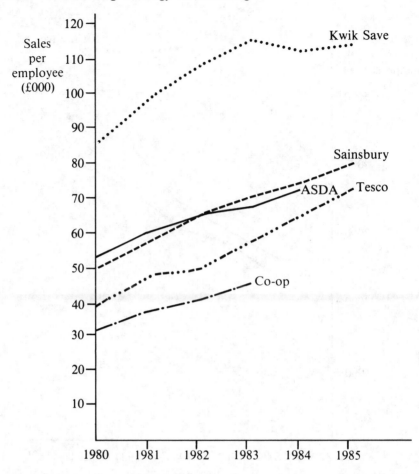

Figure 7.15   Sales (£000) per employee, 1980–85.

on price, while Sainsbury, Marks and Spencer and Tesco featured product quality far more. The latter group either possessed a good image or improved on an existing one.

In examining the causes and effects of positioning on customer behaviour it is also useful to examine the customer flows at this time. One very useful measure is offered by the HISPI service of Harris International Marketing (HIM), who assess the number of people visiting each grocery store and analyse the results in terms of visits per branch in relation to the selling area of each retailer. Their figures show an overall decline in the number of household purchasing trips (HPTs) from 67 million trips per week in 1980 to 64 million per week in 1985, and within this total number a gain

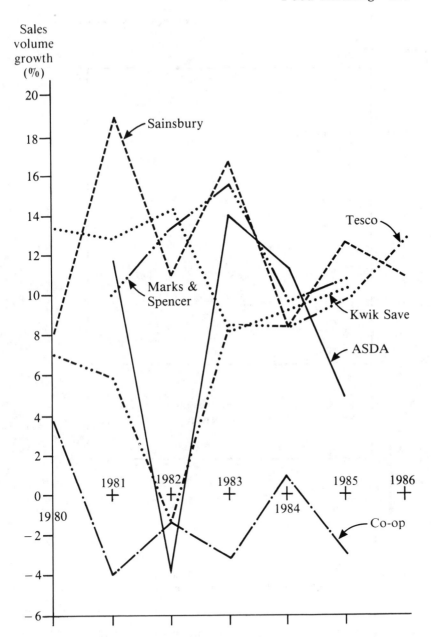

Figure 7.16 Sales volume growth (%), 1980–86.

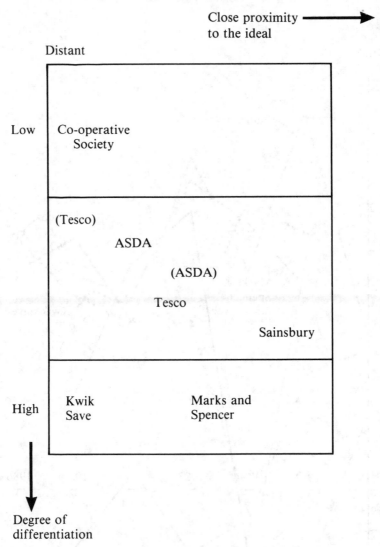

Figure 7.17   Matrix of store images (food retailers). 1983 positions of
ASDA and Tesco are in parentheses.

in share for Tesco and Sainsbury and share losses for ASDA and
Kwik Save. A household purchasing trip represents one visit from
a household. In other words a visit from one member counts the
same as a single visit by the whole family together. Table 7.5
summarizes some of the findings from the survey.

Table 7.4 Price comparison on generics and own labels

Company	No. of products analysed	Generic price	
		% below brand	% below own label
Presto	5	45.9	28.6
Carrefour	13	25.7	—
Fine Fare	13	39.6	17.2
International	14	30.4	—
Tesco	13	45.0	23.4

Source: Financial Times (1982), quoted in Davies, Gilligan and Sutton (1985).

Table 7.5 Summary of findings from HISPI survey (Harris International Marketing, 1985)

Store group	Share of HPTs (Feb. 1984– Mar. 1985)	HPTs per branch (1982–85)	HPTs per sq. ft. (1982–85)
ASDA	Declined from 4.1% to 3.5%	− 30%	− 33%
Tesco	Share rose strongly	+ 86%	+ 10%
Sainsbury	Slight decline, but latest figures show steady rise	Steady over the period	+ 20%

HPT, household purchasing trip.

The trend shown most clearly in Table 7.5 is an increase in the number of shopping trips accounted for by Tesco, apparently at the expense of ASDA. In reality, the change may not be as drastic financially as some of the figures suggest, given that the survey only covered grocery shopping trips (while ASDA and Tesco also sell other merchandise) and took no account of the amount spent per trip. It does, however, indicate that fewer visits were made to ASDA stores and, as Jeff Harris, managing director of HIM, commented, 'every person who comes through the door offers a sales opportunity, but if they don't come in the first place, there'll be no sale'.

Data on average customer spending for 1982 shows a clear difference in shopping behaviour at different stores (Channon, 1985c). The average purchase at ASDA was £14.19 compared with £7.25 at Sainsbury, £5.12 at Tesco, £5.01 at Marks and Spencer and £3.84 at the Co-op. To an extent, the average size of store could

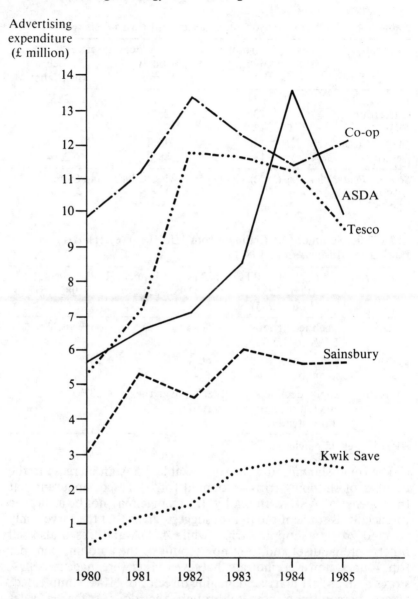

Figure 7.18   Food retailers: advertising expenditure (£ million), 1980–85.

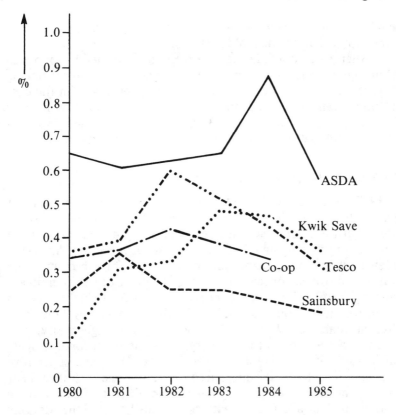

Figure 7.19 Food retailers: advertising as a percentage of sales value, 1980–85.

be expected to influence the level of purchase, with the larger, out-of-town stores being used for less frequent but higher-spend shopping trips. However, Sainsbury's lead over Tesco cannot be explained on this basis, nor can the fact that Marks and Spencer achieved a very similar level of spend to Tesco.

Relating this information to image and positioning, the comparatively high spend for Sainsbury and Marks and Spencer would support the view that a good store image is linked to a higher average spend (of retailers of a comparable size), and the Co-op's poor performance could similarly be linked to its weak image. It is, however, difficult to draw conclusions on the significance of ASDA's high average spend as more up-to-date figures could well show ASDA's lead diminishing as the average store size of competitors increased. A statistic from Sainsbury's 1985 company report would suggest that this is indeed the case as their new larger stores achieved an average spend per visit three times higher than that of their older stores.

We therefore conclude that the available data lend support to the argument that image is linked to average spend. Improvements in store image should be measurable at this level, and in the case of food retailers the authors would predict an improvement in Tesco's average spend from 1983 onwards and a decline in ASDA's position after 1984–85, until their new strategy took effect.

INCREASING CONCENTRATION

By 1987 the structure of food retailing in Britain had changed yet again. The trends identified in the early 1980s continued to some extent but the main news had been made by the Dee and Argyll groups. Argyll had acquired the British arm of the American Safeway chain and had announced plans to refurbish many of its own Presto stores, concentrated in the North-east of Britain, in the Safeway format. The Dee Corporation had been debating how to handle the integration of a number of well-known names, Fine Fare, International, Carrefour and Gateway, into a single entity. The Gateway name looked to be emerging as the main logo, at least outside Scotland. ASDA had divested most of its non-superstore interests in 1987 and announced a very large refurbishment programme and new openings in the South-east. Tesco's move northwards had accelerated with the acquisition of Hillards, one of the few regional chains still existing at the time.

The market share of the leading multiples had continued to grow at the expense of the Co-ops and independents. Figures for 1986 gave the multiples' combined share as 71.4 per cent with the Co-op's at 11.2 per cent and independents at 17.4 per cent (Institute of Grocery Distribution, 1987). Dee and Argyll now held third and fourth places in the turnover league.

We were interested to see how the last two initiatives might affect the market-place. The problem to be addressed in methodological terms was the increased number of retailers to be accommodated in a map, too many in fact to be valid using the method employed in the three studies presented earlier in this chapter.

Figure 7.20 uses the alternative mapping method discussed in Chapter 6 to present the results of an analysis conducted in 1987. The results are based on the data in Figure 7.21 and Table 7.6 but only for those stores included in the earlier studies. Comparing the positions of the stores with the 1985 model in Figure 7.6, and ignoring for a moment the vectors, Tesco is again the main mover,

Table 7.6 Food retailing: store–concept ratings, 1987

	Wide product range	Helpful staff	Interesting place to shop	Basic products	Low prices	Well laid out	Value for money	Good for own label	Good checkout operation	Good for fresh food	Good for specialist food
Tesco	2.33	3.59	2.85	2.07	2.79	2.79	2.44	2.94	2.90	2.68	2.74
ASDA	2.28	3.27	3.24	2.20	2.79	3.27	2.36	2.88	3.30	3.19	3.63
Sainsbury	2.11	2.47	2.69	2.58	3.93	2.74	2.96	1.98	2.84	2.46	2.51
Kwik Save	4.29	4.73	5.13	2.80	2.25	4.17	2.63	5.31	3.98	4.52	5.57
Co-op	3.55	3.40	4.70	3.09	3.16	4.04	3.35	3.98	4.25	4.23	5.00
Marks & Spencer	3.86	1.92	2.57	4.24	5.06	3.58	3.02	1.59	3.01	2.25	3.02
Gateway	3.83	4.09	4.43	2.89	3.58	4.30	2.90	4.11	4.72	5.01	5.20
Safeway	2.95	2.85	3.42	2.21	3.41	3.08	2.89	3.26	3.46	2.61	2.82
Morrisons	2.86	3.63	3.93	2.63	3.08	3.39	3.13	2.98	3.37	3.08	3.62
Waitrose	2.72	2.75	3.24	2.24	3.00	2.62	2.51	3.53	2.44	2.57	3.42
Ideal store	1.68	1.85	2.42	1.82	2.62	2.07	1.55	3.09	1.72	2.00	2.69

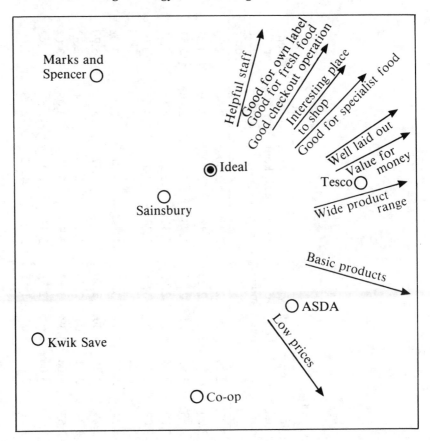

Figure 7.20   Food retailing, 1987.

having gone still further away from the price-led end of the market and at the same time further away from ASDA.

In Figure 7.22 Safeway and Gateway are both included. Despite removing the concepts from the model there were still too many retailers for the market model to include Waitrose and Morrisons successfully. Waitrose, from the data in Figure 7.21 and Table 7.6, is close to Sainsbury in image; Morrisons lies somewhat between Sainsbury and ASDA. As both were smaller regional chains their inclusion in the model would have been something of a luxury, and one which does not alter the main findings.

The first conclusion was that the Safeway image was quite clearly a threat to both Tesco and ASDA. Safeway was seen as making a similar offer to Tesco and ASDA and doing it better than ASDA and at least as well as Tesco. (Its position with respect to the ideal

	Ideal store	Tesco	ASDA	Sainsbury	Kwik Save	Co-op	M & S	Gateway	Safeway	Morrisons	Waitrose
Ideal store	1										
Tesco	3.23	1									
ASDA	3.61	3.07	1								
Sainsbury	2.40	3.18	3.86	1							
Kwik Save	4.92	4.81	4.43	5.27	1						
Co-op	4.57	4.31	3.95	4.95	3.27	1					
M & S	3.41	5.00	5.28	3.41	5.87	5.94	1				
Gateway	4.74	4.09	3.12	4.98	3.50	3.27	5.63	1			
Safeway	3.21	3.21	2.69	2.78	4.32	4.42	4.41	4.35	1		
Morrisons	3.78	3.52	3.52	4.35	4.12	3.72	4.69	3.25	4.00	1	
Waitrose	4.22	4.69	3.78	4.09	4.23	4.15	4.36	3.62	3.48	2.78	1

Figure 7.21   Food retailing: store–store comparisons, 1987. Average ratings: 1 = totally similar, 7 = totally dissimilar.

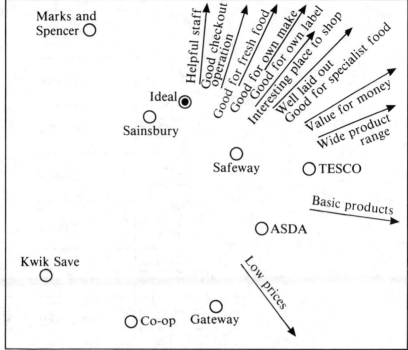

Figure 7.22 Food retailing, including Dee and Argyll, 1987.

in Figure 7.22 is slightly better than the market research results prove.) If that image could be grafted onto all Argyll stores then it placed the company in a strong position to take business from both. Press comment at the time indicated that Presto superstores refurbished and renamed as Safeway showed substantial increases in turnover, higher than might have been expected from a refurbishment alone.

Gateway had very different problems. Their overall image was somewhat away from the ideal and associated with low prices, something that could have been a valid position if the company could apply its considerable size to achieving economies of scale. The problem, however, remained of integrating a number of operations into a cohesive unit, many of which had their own image and market position. The Gateway name appeared to be more associated with the smaller, high-street stores. In Scotland the Fine Fare name had been retained, adding to the complexity of distribution and management of at least own-label lines. Referring to the data in Table 7.6, the vector representation somewhat exaggerates Gateway's price

Table 7.7 Food retailing: store–concept ratings (see Table 7.6) expressed in rank order, 1987

	Wide product range	Helpful staff	Interesting place to shop	Basic products	Low prices	Well laid out	Value for money	Good for own label	Good checkout operation	Good for fresh food	Good for specialist food
Tesco	4	9	4	2	3	3	3	4	4	3	3
ASDA	3	6	5	3	3	6	2	3	6	8	7
Sainsbury	2	3	3	6	10	3	8	2	3	3	2
Kwik Save	11	11	11	8	1	10	5	11	9	11	11
Co-op	8	7	9	10	7	9	11	9	10	9	9
Marks & Spencer	10	2	2	11	11	8	9	1	5	2	5
Gateway	9	10	10	8	9	11	6	10	11	10	10
Safeway	7	5	7	3	8	5	6	7	8	3	4
Morrisons	6	8	8	6	5	7	10	4	6	7	7
Waitrose	5	4	5	3	5	2	4	8	2	3	6
Ideal store	1	1	1	1	2	1	1	6	1	1	1

image but that remained the only concept that customers could associate with the company in 1987.

Table 7.7 represents in rank order the market research data given in Table 7.6. Gateway and the Co-op demonstrate the weakness of their position in that neither rated high against any criterion compared to other retailers at the time. Kwik Save, by comparison, although equally far from the ideal, rated first on low prices and high on value. Safeway rated well on fresh foods and basics and is marginally closer to the ideal than ASDA and Tesco in Figure 7.21.

Argyll was, therefore, better placed in 1987 as a result of its acquisition strategy to take advantage of its increased size. Gateway was yet to find a coherent image. It was perhaps inevitable that 1987 saw a takeover bid for Dee itself from the Barker and Dobson/ Budgen group, headed by an ex-managing director of ASDA. ASDA itself had yet to see the benefit of its refurbishment programme although its good rating against own-label products at an early stage in their development would have been encouraging.

The 1987 model serves to re-emphasize the fast-moving nature of food retailing as a sector, and the importance of image management in operating such organizations. Unfortunately the full 1987 model cannot be linked directly to the earlier ones and the financial data on the newer arrivals would be misleading to present in this context. Nevertheless ASDA would have been relieved to see a gap opening up between itself and Tesco, but both would be concerned about the threat posed by the Safeway name appearing on all Argyll stores.

Finally, one point of interest to retailers outside the UK is the relatively high profitability of British food retailers, especially on margins. This point is developed in Chapter 9 but the one notable point to be made is the level of differentiation between food retailers in Britain at the time. Most of the larger operators had clear points of difference and few relied on price as a major point of differentiation.

KEY POINT SUMMARY

(1)   Food retailing in Britain offers an excellent opportunity to study links between image and commercial performance.

(2)   Sainsbury, the market leaders, had achieved a broad appeal by being close to the average perception of the ideal food retailer and by being differentiated from its competition.

(3) Price-led Kwik Save achieved success despite receiving a relatively poor rating against the average view of the ideal food retailer. It benefited by being clearly associated with low prices.

(4) Tesco showed the largest change in image in the early 1980s and this was associated with a significant improvement in sales volume growth rate.

(5) Tesco's success could have been partly at ASDA's expense. Tesco had improved its image, a change which seemed to stem from closing smaller stores, emphasizing quality rather than price and opening larger, well-laid out stores. ASDA had remained much where it was and had not responded as quickly to the change in people's views on the value of price within the total retail offer. As both competed in the same sector and were, increasingly, competing with each other, there may well have been a switch in customers from ASDA to Tesco at the time.

(6) Marks and Spencer offer an example of a food retailer succeeding by not competing on price. They were differentiated in the market and, while not being closest to the ideal, were associated with a number of image factors.

(7) The Co-op, and apparently Gateway, suffered from the lack of a coherent image. The Co-op had lost its earlier market dominance and was still seeking a point of differentiation.

(8) The British food retail market is highly segmented with a number of retailers seeking and succeeding in defining their own unique market niche. Both price and non-price factors are prominent but between the two extremes of price and image are a number of successful offers.

References

AGB Consumer Panel Data (1986)

Channon, D.F. (1985a) *'J. Sainsbury Plc' Case Study*, Manchester Business School, MBS/SM/85/1.

Channon, D.F. (1985b) *'Kwik Save Discount' Case Study*, Manchester Business School, MBS/SM/85/4.

Channon, D.F. (1985c) *'Associated Dairies Plc' Case Study*, Manchester Business School, MBS/SM/85.

Channon, D.F. (1985d) *'Tesco Plc' Case Study*, Manchester Business School, MBS/SM/85/6.

Christopher, M., Walters, D. and Wills, G. (1978) *Effective Distribution Management*, MCB Publications, Bradford.

Consumer Association, *Which* Reports, October 1976, 1979, 1982.

Davies, K., Gilligan, C. and Sutton, C. (1985) Structural change in grocery retailing: the implications for competition, *International Journal of Physical Distribution and Materials Management*, Vol. 15, no. 2.

Gayfer, A. (1980) Price cuts: why the war must continue in the 80's, *Campaign*, 15 February, p.59.

Harris International Marketing (1985) *Report on Shopping Trip Market*, HIM.

Institute of Grocery Distribution (1987) *Food Retailing 1987*, IGD.

Street, G. (1986) Changes in grocery retailing: the ASDA story, *ADMAP*, December, p.36.

Themistoclik & Associates (1986) *The Secret of the Own Brand.*

Chapter 8

Manchester Department Stores: Changing Attitudes Can Take Time

This chapter examines the effects of a change of positioning strategy in another sector, department store retailing. It also provides the opportunity to illustrate the emotional dimension in the way shoppers perceive stores. While there are few national chains of department stores in Britain, there are a number of important regional chains and even single stores. This study, therefore, was based on one city centre, Manchester, the heart of Britain's third largest conurbation.

A department store has been defined as a large retailing institution that carries 'a wide variety of merchandise lines with a reasonably good selection within each line'; and from an operational standpoint 'most of the basic functions of buying, selling, promoting and servicing are conducted entirely or at least in part at the department level' (Lewison and Delozier, 1986).

An allied sector is that of the variety chain store, which is different, it appears, in that control is centralized often at a head office rather than at store level, and the typical store is smaller with fewer distinct departments. Marks and Spencer, Littlewoods, Woolworth and British Home Stores are generally categorized as variety stores and Debenhams, House of Fraser and the John Lewis Partnership as department stores.

The demise of the department store and its replacement by the variety chain store and even subsequently the hypermarket are often predicted (Knee and Walters, 1985). What is ignored, but what became apparent to us in this study, was that the customer has a rather different perception of what constitutes a department store from those of us who seek to categorize retail operations. In the group discussions held to generate the concepts used to analyse the department store market, it became clear that many shoppers saw Marks and Spencer as their 'ideal' department store. This view was confirmed in the later quantitative research.

Traditional department stores seemed to be losing ground. Between 1978 and 1981, for example, one source claimed the percentage of adults visiting in any one week had fallen 3 per cent to 16 per cent (Robertson, 1984). The high costs of city-centre sites, the lack of convenient car parking and the higher staff costs by comparison to the out-of-town, more streamlined retailers, were cited as the main contributors to decline. However, the 1980s saw a new confidence in the high street and ambitious plans for many of the so-called 'dinosaurs' of retailing to return to former glories.

DEPARTMENT STORES IN MANCHESTER IN THE EARLY 1980s

Manchester's city centre in the early 1980s provided a focal point for the shopping needs of around three million people in the surrounding suburbs and for those who commuted to work each day in the commercial centre. A large covered shopping area, the Arndale Centre, was situated at one end of Market Street, a pedestrian thoroughfare (Figure 8.1). At the other end were two

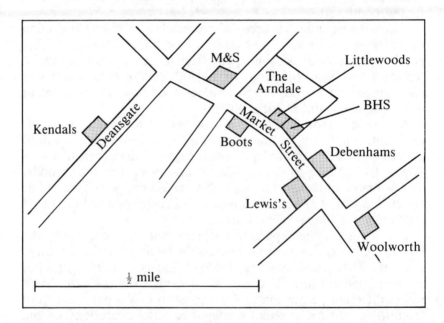

Figure 8.1   Stores in Manchester city centre, 1982–84.

traditional department stores, Debenhams, at the time of the study part of the national chain of 67 outlets, and Lewis's, a provincial chain of 10 stores and part of Sears Holdings. Further out from the centre was the Manchester branch of Woolworths. In 1982 the original American parent, F. W. Woolworth, had sold out its UK interests consisting of 800 high-street and 80 out-of-town Woolco superstores.

Adjacent to the Arndale Centre was the third largest branch of Marks and Spencer, arguably Britain's leading retailer. Walking up Market Street from 'M and S', one would have passed the frontages of British Home Stores (BHS), part of a chain of 125 stores, and Littlewoods, with a somewhat similar offering to BHS in 108 stores. Littlewoods was the retail arm of the Littlewoods Organization, market leaders in football pools and a major mail-order company.

Away from the main shopping centre along Deansgate, which ran at right angles to Market Street, was the Manchester store of the House of Fraser Group, Kendal Milne (Kendals for short). House of Fraser was regarded as a market leader in department store retailing with 102 outlets, the most famous being Harrods of Knightsbridge.

Finally, opposite the Arndale Centre on Market Street was a large branch of Boots. This incorporated many departments not normally associated with 'Boots the Chemists', Britain's largest pharmacy. Boots had developed a number of such large stores carrying a similar merchandise selection to many department and variety chain stores.

Two separate studies are reported and analysed here, one in 1982 and the other in 1984. Because of the attitudes apparent in the preliminary group discussions, the first study incorporated not only the traditional department stores of Lewis's, Debenhams and Kendals, but also Marks and Spencer, Woolworth, Boots and BHS.

THE 1982 AND 1984 SURVEYS

Table 8.1 shows the concepts found to represent the 'ideal' department store and those used to segment this market sector. The concepts generated in the later study are more descriptive than those in the earlier study, and those found to describe the ideal store were more concerned with product attributes. The amount of movement between studies was far less than that observed in the food retailing studies reported in Chapter 7, indicating a less fluid market situation. Woolworth and Boots were both dropped from the analysis in 1984 as they were found to be unassociated by shoppers with the department store sector in the quantitative part of the 1982 work. The matrix data for 1982 in Figure 8.2 include these two stores, but for the sake of clarity, the models presented are those constructed excluding the Boots and Woolworth data.

In 1982 the first significant feature of the market was that two of the traditional department stores, Lewis's and Debenhams, were

Table 8.1 Concepts and retailers used in department store studies

	1982	1984
Stores	Lewis's, Debenhams, Kendals, Woolworth, BHS, Boots, Marks and Spencer	Lewis's, Debenhams, Kendals, Marks and Spencer, BHS
Concepts used	Comfortable Expensive Polite Wide range Traditional	Good for browsing In-store comfort Good for planned shopping Up-market store Specialist departments Competitive prices Wide range of products
Concepts found to describe the ideal department store	Efficient service Courteous Helpful Honest	Reliable products A quality store Efficient staff Knowledgeable staff Good refund policy Satisfaction with previous product

seen as very similar. In fact when the stores are modelled on their own, they are seen as identical (Figure 8.3 and 8.4). The second feature is that Marks and Spencer were seen as the closest to the ideal department store, confirming the views in the earlier group discussions. BHS tended to share the sector dominated by Marks and Spencer but with a weaker image. The BHS image was difficult to define, but being furthest from 'expensive' it was likely to be price led, a conclusion that was confirmed in the second study.

Kendals was well differentiated, had some similarities with Marks and Spencer, but was associated more with the concepts of 'expensive' and 'traditional'. The most similar store to Kendals was Lewis's, sharing with Debenhams the 'wide range' positioning of the traditional department store. Debenhams held the weaker position image-wise, rated slightly further from the ideal by shoppers and less well associated with many of the concepts. (Table 8.2 provides another method of checking on the market research data, using rank order instead of absolute values.)

Retailers which are undifferentiated and therefore appeal equally to the same group of shoppers or to all shoppers for the same type

	Debenhams	Lewis's	Marks & Spencer	Kendals	British Home Stores	Woolworth	Boots	The ideal store	Wide range	Polite	Expensive	Comfortable	Traditional
Debenhams	1												
Lewis's	2.50	1											
Marks & Spencer	4.08	4.29	1										
Kendals	4.13	3.39	4.16	1									
British Home Stores	3.64	4.09	3.21	5.12	1								
Woolworth	4.76	4.80	5.38	6.38	4.17	1							
Boots	4.75	4.65	4.57	5.22	4.12	4.66	1						
The ideal store	3.44	3.15	2.85	3.20	4.36	5.32	3.52	1					
Wide range	2.70	2.22	3.23	2.32	3.67	3.32	3.36	2.00	1				
Polite	3.05	2.52	1.92	2.46	3.07	4.22	2.81	1.97	5.08	1			
Expensive	3.59	3.36	3.34	1.82	4.26	5.11	4.00	4.43	5.01	3.86	1		
Comfortable	3.55	3.35	2.88	2.76	3.73	4.79	3.10	2.09	4.77	3.76	4.06	1	
Traditional	3.81	2.96	3.53	2.25	3.96	3.63	3.68	3.85	4.15	3.14	3.98	3.91	1

Figure 8.2 Manchester department stores, 1982: semi-matrix of arithmetic means. Average ratings: 1 = totally similar, 7 = totally dissimilar.

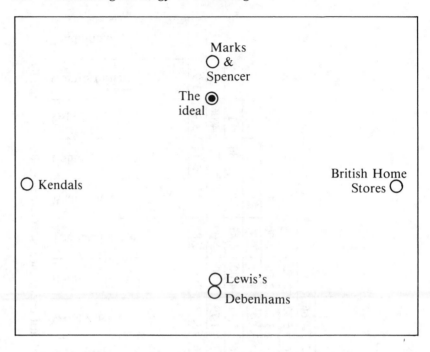

Figure 8.3   Manchester department stores, 1982, stores only.

of purchase, tend to compete on price. Debenhams and Lewis's in the early 1980s provided a classic example of such behaviour. A sale on one side of Market Street was followed by another opposite. Sales and special promotions merged, making a nonsense of the concept of a sale as the cutting of normal price levels for a limited period. British Home Stores, although not as obviously positioned against Marks and Spencer as Debenhams was to Lewis's, also tended to use price as their strategy in following Marks and Spencer. With the exception of lighting, where they held a strong position, BHS had tended to carry a similar but lower-priced product range to Marks and Spencer.

The study was repeated at the end of 1984, this time excluding Boots and Woolworth and including a larger number of concepts. Figures 8.5–8.7 and Table 8.3 present the relevant data and market models. Marks and Spencer again appear to be the best positioned store, close to the ideal yet distant from competition. The model in Figure 8.7 in fact misrepresents somewhat Marks and Spencer's broad appeal across a number of concepts, even ranking second against competitive prices. Marks and Spencer did appear to have slipped slightly in its position with respect to the ideal store. In

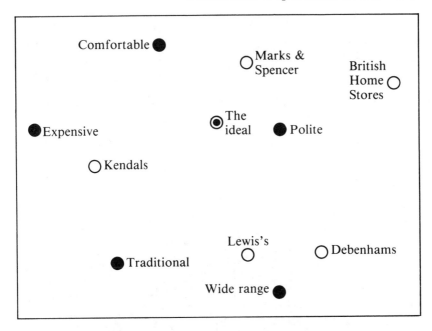

Figure 8.4   Manchester department stores, 1982, stores and concepts.

reality, its average mark against the ideal had marginally improved, but other stores received a better rating implying a relative improvement for them. At the time Marks and Spencer was losing ground nationally in women's fashions, traditionally an area of some strength, to NEXT and the more focused high-street fashion retailers.

Kendals had invested money in remodelling part of their store, and this might explain the slight improvement in their position with respect to the ideal. However, the most significant move had been made by Lewis's, which had managed to improve its overall rating, and to differentiate itself from Debenhams. It had become more closely associated with the concepts describing the traditional department store sector, leaving Debenhams with a more obviously price-led position, itself occupied more convincingly by BHS.

British Home Stores had adopted a price-led image but seemed to have few advantages to support an overall price-led strategy. Marks and Spencer had a policy of concentrating on merchandising British-made products, while many comparable BHS lines were imported. Manning levels also tended to be tighter. Neither factor allowed BHS the same advantages as those obtained, for example, by Kwik Save (see Chapter 7) in positioning itself on an overt price

	Debenhams	Lewis's	Kendals	British Home Stores	Marks & Spencer	The ideal store	Competitive prices	Specialist departments	Wide range of products	Suited to planned shopping	In-store comfort	Up-market store	Good for browsing	Well laid out
Debenhams	1													
Lewis's	2.66	1												
Kendals	3.13	2.89	1											
British Home Stores	4.53	4.92	5.42	1										
Marks & Spencer	4.89	4.68	4.66	3.78	1									
The ideal store	4.19	3.04	3.00	4.80	2.80	1								
Competitive prices	3.24	3.62	4.42	2.87	3.12	1.62	1							
Specialist departments	3.04	2.45	2.55	4.45	3.80	2.00	4.46	1						
Wide range of products	2.84	2.09	2.52	4.16	3.52	1.40	3.63	3.38	1					
Suited to planned shopping	3.38	2.76	2.95	3.95	3.09	1.99	4.23	3.19	3.04	1				
In-store comfort	3.75	2.87	2.61	4.07	3.00	1.74	4.63	3.55	4.02	3.39	1			
Up-market store	4.01	3.02	2.15	5.03	2.82	2.81	5.23	2.96	3.73	3.85	2.17	1		
Good for browsing	3.40	2.64	2.48	3.84	2.84	2.01	4.45	3.00	2.49	3.79	2.46	3.05	1	
Well laid out	4.09	2.75	2.91	3.60	2.77	1.47	4.01	2.90	3.18	2.05	2.75	2.86	2.17	1

Figure 8.5   Manchester department stores, 1985: semi-matrix of arithmetic means. Average ratings: 1 = totally similar, 7 = totally dissimilar.

Table 8.2 Manchester department stores: store rankings, 1982

(a) Stores compared to concepts

Concepts	Stores						
	Debenhams	Lewis's	Marks & Spencer	Kendals	BHS	Woolworth	Boots
Wide range	3	1	4	2	7	5	6
Polite	5	3	1	2	6	7	4
Expensive	4	3	2	1	6	7	5
Comfortable	5	4	2	1	6	7	3
Traditional	6	2	5	1	7	4	3
The ideal	4	2	1	3	6	7	5

(b) Stores compared to stores

Base store	Compared against						
	Debenhams	Lewis's	Marks & Spencer	Kendals	BHS	Woolworth	Boots
Debenhams	—	1	3	4	2	6	5
Lewis's	1	—	4	2	3	6	5
Marks & Spencer	2	4	—	3	1	6	5
Kendals	2	1	3	—	4	6	5
BHS	2	3	1	6	—	5	4
Woolworth	2	3	5	6	1	—	4
Boots	5	3	2	6	1	4	—

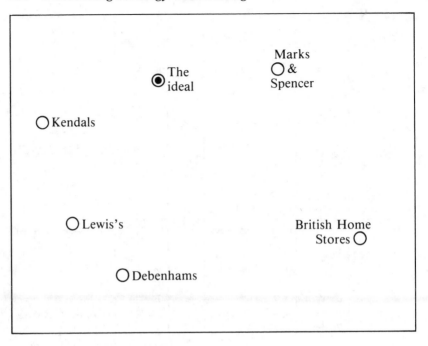

Figure 8.6   Manchester department stores, 1985.

platform in food retailing. However, BHS had differentiated itself from its competition mainly on price.

An easier positioning strategy to adopt was that of Kendals – up-market. The 'Harrods of the North' would always be a valid concept for part of society, but Kendals had probably not been able to invest heavily enough in the more ambience-related factors that would allow it to dominate such a position. In fact Kendals had endeavoured to broaden its appeal partly by advertising, using a theme which explained that Kendals was not as expensive as shoppers might think with the slogan 'Kendals expensive — think again'. Advertising in 1983 and 1984 was measured by MEAL at over half a million pounds each year.

A more significant change had occurred at Lewis's. Under the direction of a new managing director the strategy had been changed from 1982 towards an image based on fashion. By mid-1985 £15.5 million had been spent on refurbishment throughout the chain, including an estimated £1 million on the Manchester store's ground floor alone. The main expenditure was on elegant new fittings, carpets, soft lighting and lowering the ceilings. The quality of merchandise and style of presentation were improved. In the food

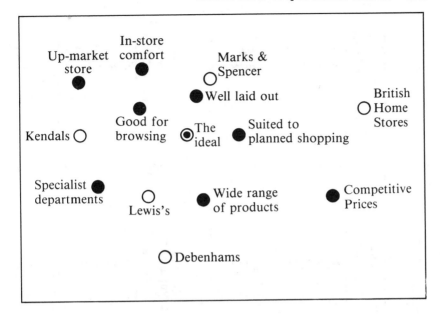

Figure 8.7   Manchester department stores, 1985.

hall, for example, a greater emphasis had been placed on speciality and delicatessen lines. Under the banner of 'The New Lewis's' £3 million was spent promoting the new look. The company's PR emphasized that their aim was to 'become the most fashionable department store group in the country'. Their trading policy explained that 'Lewis's does not intend to be the cheapest in our markets – neither in price or quality'.

A staff training policy was introduced in support of the change in strategy, emphasizing customer service. Staff uniforms were introduced. Some staff, however, found it difficult to adapt to the change and were replaced. The philosophy behind the image change was illustrated by managing director John Begg (1986) in quoting the results of group discussions held to guide the company's rethinking. One woman had said, in describing her use of two department stores: 'When I shop at Store A, I feel like a housewife and a mother. When I shop at Store B I feel like a woman.'

The above quotation illustrates a more general point made by one of the earliest writers on the subject of retail image, Pièrre Martineau, (1958): 'The shopper seeks the store whose image is most congruent with the image she has of herself'. In this instance Lewis's research had revealed that the same shopper can have two or perhaps even more than two images of herself. The keypoint here is: which

Table 8.3 Manchester department stores: store rankings, 1985

(a) Stores, compared to concepts

Concepts	Stores				
	Debenhams	Lewis's	Kendals	BHS	Marks & Spencer
Competitive prices	3	4	5	1	2
Specialist departments	3	1	2	5	4
Wide product range	3	1	2	5	4
Planned shopping	4	1	2	5	3
In-store comfort	4	2	1	5	3
Up-market store	4	3	1	5	2
Good for browsing	4	2	1	5	3
Well laid out	5	1	3	4	2
The ideal	4	3	2	5	1

(b) Stores compared to stores

Base store	Compared against				
	Debenhams	Lewis's	Kendals	BHS	Marks & Spencer
Debenhams	—	1	2	3	4
Lewis's	1	—	2	4	3
Kendals	2	1	—	4	3
British Home Stores	2	3	4	—	1
Marks & Spencer	4	3	2	1	—

mode will it be the more profitable for the retailer to appeal to? The 'housewife' and 'mother' are likely to be more price sensitive than 'the woman' but profit can be made from both.

As an illustration of what can occur, whoever was now attracted to the remodelled and renamed electrical department in Lewis's, Manchester, increased sales there by 49 per cent. Lewis's strategy contrasted somewhat with the changes being made in food retailing (see Chapter 7). National brands rather than own brands were made a key element, accounting for 80 per cent of household goods. Advertising budgets had been increased to £3 million in 1985, significant for a regional chain, but still lower than the £15.5 million spent over three and a half years on refurbishment.

Buying operations at Lewis's had been centralized to ensure more co-ordination between departments. A price pledge, to refund money on a more competitive price on offer elsewhere, was the only concession to the earlier price-led approach. The evolved style was described by Lewis's Managing Director thus: 'Our pricing is competitive, but we are selling on style, flair, quality and service, not price'.

More generally it is interesting to compare some of the background data for the retailers included in this sector. Marketing executives in BHS commented that although BHS achieved a good rate of customer flow through stores, their conversion rate (the proportion making a purchase) was considerably lower than that of Marks and Spencer. Woolworth had also experienced an equally good customer flow (Simmons, 1984) but found that few customers saw Woolworth as a first-choice store and tended to visit after looking elsewhere. The typical dwell time in the store was also low, about 5–10 minutes, and the average spend was also comparatively low.

Under its new management, Woolworth had made significant improvements in performance but was still seeking a credible market position in 1985. Clearly Mancunians at least did not see it as part of the department store sector, nor was it seen as competing with other variety chain stores. It is worth noting that Woolworth's original market position had been genuinely price led, the company having to lock out of its original store on opening day the crowds who were clamouring to take advantage of the low prices. By the 1980s Woolworth was still using a price platform, promoting the 'Wonder of Woolies', but the company had retained no economic advantage to sustain a genuine price-led strategy. The advertising campaign achieved an 86 per cent recall of advertisements. It was hailed as technically brilliant, but did not succeed in arresting a profit fall and did not promote sales of high margin lines (Piercy, 1983).

Following an unsuccessful bid by the Dixons electrical retail group in 1986, Woolworth embarked on a more focused merchandising policy and a refurbishment programme, the long-term success of which will have to be left to the reader to judge. The Manchester store, reduced in size following a fire and now far away from the main shopping centre, had been closed.

The new Woolworth strategy, named Focus, was certainly a radical move on top of an ambitious refurbishment. Merchandise was limited to six market segments and the 20 per cent of floorspace freed by the change was to be used in part at least to enhance store ambience. A target market of younger married women and their families had been identified. By late 1986 profits remained elusive. The Woolworth chain returned a six-month operating loss of £8.6 million although the earlier refurbishment had reportedly lifted expenditure rates per visit from £2 to £2.50.

In the more mainstream department store and variety store sectors, Marks and Spencer had increased the floor area of their Manchester Store in 1984 and on a national basis were experimenting with out-of-town and satellite stores. The company had never relied much on advertising. MEAL recorded a national total of £155,900 in 1982, UK sales in that year being over £2,000 million (and this had been a peak year for M & S advertising). However, in 1985 Marks and Spencer reorganized their head office giving greater emphasis to formal marketing. Fashion leaflets were made available at store level. Advertising expenditure rose modestly to £500,000. More important key stores were refurbished using carpeting, clear walkways and more definite yet still subtle wall colours to offer a warmer atmosphere. The refurbishment programme was projected to cost £500 million over two years. Marks and Spencer began spending substantially on advertising in 1988, majoring on their fashion merchandise.

British Home Stores merged with Habitat Mothercare in 1985 under the Storehouse banner. As such it came under the influence of Sir Terence Conran, founder of the Habitat and Conran chains. A refurbishment programme was already under way but the merger prompted a quick all-round facelift with a new logo, some new merchandise ranges and a general heightening of BHS interiors, building on the company's recognition in 1982 of the 'need to create a more attractive and exciting environment in which to shop' (Belsham, 1982).

In 1985 the Burton Group succeeded in a takeover bid for Debenhams. One of their promises had been to rejuvenate Debenhams' image and by 1987 Group Managing Director Sir Ralph Halpern's team were ready to unveil their new concept in the main

London store. Nationally Debenhams problem in image projection lay with the shop-within-a-shop strategy that had led to a total of over 700 different concessions in Debenhams stores. These had been rationalized to about 100 (Newman, 1984), but providing the shopper with a new but coherent image at a reasonable cost was clearly going to be difficult. A galleria concept, much talked about before the Burton takeover was a potential solution. The concept 'good for browsing' was, at least in Manchester, not associated with Debenhams, the closest concept being 'wide range of products', a positioning not associated with the high-ambience sector. At the end of 1986 Debenhams was still persisting in its main promotion of 'Debenhams, The Sale' at a national level. It seemed unlikely that Burtons could afford to refit each Debenhams store to the same standard as in the Oxford Street site. Concessions had been reduced to 25 per cent of business and much of the buying had been centralized, in particular for 'lifestyle coordinated ranges' (Sharples, 1984).

By the end of 1986 the amount of planned activity in the department store sector was relatively high. However, the main moves in positioning monitored up to 1986 in the Manchester market had come from Lewis's. Others had remained implacably true to the idea of evolution rather than revolution in retailing. Marks and Spencer's Chairman Lord Rayner was quoted at the time, on the topic of focused retailing, as saying his company was 'focused on everything for the family'.

DEPARTMENT STORE IMAGE AND FINANCIAL PERFORMANCE

Table 8.4 cites three financial measures of the companies represented in the models of the Manchester market but at a national level only. They illustrate two main points: the better overall performance of the variety chain stores by comparison to the more traditional department stores, and the pre-eminence of Marks and Spencer. The overall picture seems to fit the concept discussed earlier of a downturn in the traditional department store as it became superseded by the variety chain store. Nevertheless all three traditional stores increased national sales volume growth to 1983–84. However, the most telling figures are those for 'return on capital employed'. BHS and Marks and Spencer stand out, while the traditional stores show unacceptably low levels of profitability on this measure.

None of these figures necessarily relates to the local situation in Manchester. The performance of individual stores could reflect the

Table 8.4 Financial data on department store chains nationally

(a)   Sales per employee (£000)

	1980–81	1981–82	1982–83	1983–84
Marks & Spencer	59	67	70.8	76.6
BHS	15.4	16.9	18.3	20.5
Lewis's	n/a	n/a	n/a	n/a
Debenhams	32.9	37.5	33.5	36.6
House of Fraser	28.58	28.20	26.71	30.5

(b)   Sales volume growth (%)

	1980–81	1981–82	1982–83	1983–84
Marks & Spencer	12.3	17.4	14.0	14.0
BHS	11.9	4.26	6.58	8.49
Lewis's	20.5	− 11.0	5.1	8.51
Debenhams	− 1.61	11.5	4.16	10.87
House of Fraser	24.01	− 6.39	0.0	9.10

(c)   Return on capital employed (%)

	1980–81	1981–82	1982–83	1983–84
Marks & Spencer	28.0	19.9	19.7	21.3
BHS	21.8	21.23	22.58	23.25
Lewis's	− 0.41	− 0.28	0.29	− 0.46
Debenhams	7.98	7.16	5.00	7.85
House of Fraser	6.75	5.36	5.99	6.57

Source: Annual reports and Manchester Business School.

national position, but local trading conditions and local investment in, say, store refurbishment, a pertinent issue here, can modify the national picture substantially.

We managed to obtain local data on all but the Debenhams store. Much of the data were supplied in confidence and cannot be referred to in detail. However, examining the two models the following summary can be gleaned of what changes in financial fortune might be expected and what differences might be expected in overall position.

Lewis's had made the most significant shift in image, becoming better differentiated and closer to the ideal. The improvement in sales volume growth in the company's total figures is compatible with this. The performance of the Manchester store was even more impressive, providing another example of relative improvement in image producing a relative improvement in sales volume growth.

Kendals had shifted towards the ideal. Nationally the performance of House of Fraser is difficult to encapsulate other than to point to a marked change of performance in sales volume between 1981–82 and 1983–84. The Manchester store's performance was better than the parent company's, but below that of Lewis's. Nationally House of Fraser had announced a number of changes in its approach, including the innovation of a marketing department, a big switch into own label and broadening of its appeal to encompass the fashion conscious socioeconomic groups of C1 and C2 (Anon., 1985). This was to be accompanied by a heavy advertising campaign and a £100 million refurbishment programme for its 100 stores.

Marks and Spencer's position nationally was the maintenance of a high standard. Locally the sales performance was compatible with national trends although it is difficult to analyse the precise position because of the expansion in selling area between the two studies.

So far the market positioning and the changes therein are broadly reflected in commercial performance. The one possible anomaly was British Home Stores, which returned the highest sales volume growth of the four stores providing data. This was without the benefit of either the refits then being applied to the BHS chain nationally, or the later facelift following the merger with Habitat–Mothercare. There had been no radical change in BHS positioning in the Manchester market between 1982 and 1984, apart from the close association in the 1984 model with the concept of 'competitive prices', which was not included in the 1982 model. Indeed BHS slipped slightly against the 'ideal' in overall rating, but it increased its differentiation from each of the other retailers (see Figures 8.2 and 8.5). BHS had managed to increase the public's perception of its differences compared to the competition. It can be argued that with everyone else busily moving up-market, this left a major slice of that market served only by BHS. This situation would have been aided still further by the changes in strategy adopted by Littlewoods, first up-market, and then down, which occurred at about this time. It is possible that BHS in Manchester provides an example of the importance of considering what the competition is doing, while at the same time deciding on one's own direction.

The main lesson of this chapter, and one that has not been emphasized so far, is the time and cost involved in the most significant image shift – Lewis's. In the group discussions held for the second survey it was interesting that male shoppers seemed unaware that Lewis's had undergone a major refurbishment. Female shoppers seemed to feel the changes had been far more recent than they actually had been. According to Lewis's management the increase in sales that eventually occurred at the Manchester store seemed to take a long time. Certainly there was no steep change in financial performance. This leads to the conclusion that changing image can be a long-term task. Alternatively an actual change in image will take some time to impress itself on the general public. Having said this, image changes can be effected more quickly, as in the case of NEXT, where such changes are dramatic. Changes in the image of an existing business will, arguably, be akin to changes in the personality of an old friend. It is some time before we acknowledge such a change, and even longer before we modify our attitude and behaviour towards the person as a result.

KEY POINT SUMMARY

(1) The department store label is one that means something different to the shopper and to the retail analyst. The Manchester shopper certainly saw the leading variety chain store, Marks and Spencer, as the ideal department store in the early 1980s.

(2) The department store sector did not appear to change as rapidly in terms of image as the food retailing sector.

(3) Lewis's benefited financially by moving its image away from that of Debenhams. Up until their change in strategy, Lewis's and Debenhams seemed both to concentrate on 'sales' in competing with each other on price, with neither having an obvious economic advantage to sustain price leadership.

(4) Lewis's change in image took some time to achieve. It involved change in advertising, merchandise, staff training, PR and a substantial store refurbishment.

(5) British Home Stores benefited from all its competition moving up-market and leaving it to dominate the price-led sector.

(6) In the department store sector Marks and Spencer were perceived as being differentiated yet close to the ideal – the best position for any retailer. This was at the same time as they held a different image as a food retailer.

(7) No coherent pattern emerges of management action in this sector in response to the various opportunities at the time, other than refurbishment.

References

Anon. (1985) *Marketing Week*, 9 August.

Begg, J. (1986) The New Lewis's, *The Retailing Event Conference*, London, Hay MSL.

Belsham, M. (1982) BHS press release, 30 November.

Knee, D. and Walters, D. (1985) *Strategy in Retailing*, Philip Allan, Oxford, p.44.

Lewison, D. M. and DeLozier, M. W. (1986) *Retailing* (2nd edn), Merrill Publishing, Columbus, Ohio.

Martineau, P. (1958) The personality of the retail store, *Harvard Business Review*, Vol. 36, pp.47-55.

Newman, M. (1984) Debs delight, *Large Mixed Retailing*, Aug./Sept., p.19.

Piercy, N. (1983) What marketing lessons can retailers learn from the recession? *Retail and Distribution Management*, May/June, pp.15-20.

Robertson, P. (1984) Department stores, *Large Mixed Retailing*, April, p.13.

Sharples, S. (1984) From dinosaur to stable of thoroughbreds, *Retail and Distribution Management*, Sept./Oct.

Simmons, G. (1984) The penetration of major retailers in the UK, *Retail and Distribution Management*, May/June.

Chapter 9

West German Department Stores: When Price Promotion Fails

This chapter presents an analysis of West German department store retailing in 1984. As in Chapter 8 the stores were chosen in one geographical location. The results and comparisons with the measures taken of the British/Manchester stores are used to illustrate the consequences of an entire sector using price as its main promotional platform.

As with the Manchester department store study it was considered advisable to focus the German study on one centre, in this case Hagen/Dortmund in the Ruhr area of West Germany. Table 9.1 lists the various stores trading in a department store format and mentioned in the preliminary work with shoppers. The methodology used in the Hagen study differed slightly from that used for the analysis of Manchester department stores in that we were experimenting with an idea that would allow the inclusion of a much larger number of concepts. The concepts used are listed in Table 9.2 translated from the original German.

Table 9.1 West German department stores

Store	Location	Type
Horten	Hagen town centre	Traditional
Kaufhof	Hagen town centre	Traditional
Quelle	Hagen town centre	Specialist in mail order
Karstadt	Dortmund town centre and outskirts	One traditional outlet and two specialist outlets
Kaufhalle	Hagen town centre	Owned by Kaufhof but selling more on price
Plaza	Hagen town outskirts	Self-service

Interestingly, two concepts appear in the ideal rather than as segmenting concepts – 'value for money' and 'wide range of products'. This compares with the Manchester study (see Table 8.1)

Table 9.2 Concepts used in the Hagen study grouped by type

(1) *Merchandise range*	(5) *Store atmosphere*
Stocks well-known brands	Attractive store
Specialist departments	Friendly atmosphere
Good for gifts	Good layout and store signage
	Exciting
(2) *Fashion*	(6) *Post-transaction satisfaction*
Good for everyday wear	Good service policy
	Recommended by friends
(3) *Sales personnel*	(7) *Advertising*
Good sales personnel	Believable advertisements
Sufficient sales personnel	
Fast till service	
(4) *Sales promotions*	(8) *Ideal*
Special offers	Value for money
Good window displays	Wide product range
	High quality
	Well-informed staff
	Polite staff
	Free customer parking
	Free delivery service
	Fast delivery service
	Product guarantees
	Money-back policy
	Good handling of complaints
	Good advice and service

where price and wide range were key discriminators in the market. Other concepts found to represent the ideal in the Manchester study were found potentially to segment the Hagen market, such as the two staff concepts.

Figures 9.1–9.3 present the results of the German study. Three concepts – 'fast till service', 'believable advertisements' and 'good service policy' – were deleted from the analysis in Figure 9.2 as they were found to be largely unassociated with the model. Figure 9.3 presents the data in an alternative form as described in Chapter 6. Despite the introduction of a larger number of concepts, the Hagen market appears to lack differentiation (Figure 9.2). Few concepts appear to be useful in differentiating between stores. Plaza, the self-service outlet, is seen as somewhat differentiated on price, being closest to 'value for money' and 'special offers'. Kardstadt, Kaufhof

	Value for money	Stocks well-known brands	Wide product range	Specialist departments	Good for gift articles	Good for everyday wear	Good sales personnel	Sufficient sales personnel	Fast till service	Special offers	Attractive shop windows	Recommended by friends	Nicely fitted out	Stimulating	In-store signage	Friendly atmosphere	Generous service policy	Believable adverts
Horten	4.24	5.31	5.42	5.55	5.18	5.07	3.73	4.76	5.09	5.04	4.83	4.71	4.97	5.06	5.38	4.65	5.31	4.90
Kaufhof	4.46	5.17	5.25	5.28	4.97	5.13	4.29	4.65	5.00	4.91	4.80	4.58	4.61	4.69	5.22	4.46	4.78	4.78
Quelle	4.72	4.15	4.78	4.51	4.29	4.49	3.87	4.17	4.59	4.59	4.21	4.14	4.02	4.08	4.82	3.91	4.59	4.55
Karstadt	4.29	4.86	4.96	4.97	4.79	4.72	4.38	4.25	4.93	4.65	4.17	4.51	4.82	4.51	4.92	4.42	4.77	4.87
Kaufhalle	4.55	2.80	3.40	3.06	2.90	3.25	3.14	3.60	4.04	4.01	2.73	2.73	2.71	2.90	3.54	2.90	3.69	3.93
Plaza	5.11	4.16	4.51	3.83	3.55	2.90	3.50	3.85	4.40	5.15	2.90	3.98	3.88	3.83	4.52	3.10	4.01	4.59
'Ideal'	6.76	6.43	6.69	6.40	6.28	6.36	6.48	6.25	6.56	6.39	6.11	5.79	6.34	6.31	6.55	6.56	6.65	6.00

Figure 9.1(a)   Store–concept comparisons.

Figure 9.1(b) Store–store comparisons. 1 = totally dissimilar, 7 = totally similar in both tables, reflecting different scale perceptions in Germany.

	Horten	Kaufhof	Quelle	Karstadt	Kaufhalle	Plaza	'Ideal'
Horten	7						
Kaufhof	6.01	7					
Quelle	4.83	4.74	7				
Karstadt	5.19	5.09	4.77	7			
Kaufhalle	3.02	3.11	3.74	3.21	7		
Plaza	3.45	3.48	3.62	3.43	4.20	7	
'Ideal'	5.39	5.11	3.96	4.92	2.70	3.84	7

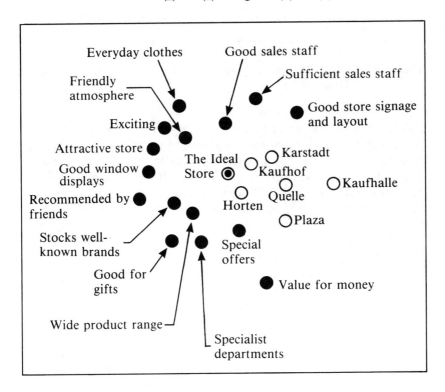

Figure 9.2 West German department stores, Hagen area, 1984.

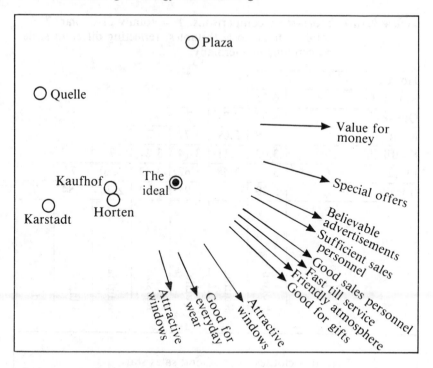

Figure 9.3   West German department stores: vector presentation of Hagen data.

and Horten appear better placed with respect to the ideal, but none can claim to be well associated with any of the more ambience-related concepts, by comparison with their British counterparts. There was some association of Horten with merchandise-related concepts, some of Kaufhof with ambience factors and some of Karstadt with the staff service factors. Horten and Kaufhof were closest to the ideal, indicating they would be preferred to Karstadt, but overall there is little to choose between all three. Quelle and Kaufhalle were weakly associated with the second price concept, 'special offers', but both would probably appeal equally to the shopper preferring Karstadt, Kaufhof and Horten over the more overtly price-led Plaza.

Figure 9.3 tends to confirm the interpretation of Figure 9.2. This kind of representation presents a stores-only model (in this case including the ideal) and superimposes vectors onto the store model. Thus 'value for money', for example, increases from left to right and Plaza can be seen to offer more 'value for money' than Quelle or Karstadt as it is placed further along that vector. The bunching of vectors into the bottom right-hand corner of Figure 9.2 indicates two things: first, that there is a grouping of concepts, many of which are measuring much the same thing, and second that the market-place and the concepts relevant to department store shopping in Hagen are some distance apart in the minds of shoppers. The second point merely confirms the observation from the market representation in Figure 9.2, that the competing retailers lack differentiation along any relevant image dimension.

To check further on this point the matrix data in Figure 9.1 were used in Table 9.3, which displays the rank order of concepts against stores. The concepts could be divided into three groups: those which seemed to measure the same general property because all stores were rated in the same rank order irrespective of concept (group A); a smaller group which had one or two changes in rank order (group B); and a third group where the overall response pattern was markedly different (group C). The group C concepts seem to offer the greatest potential for identifying differences between stores; two of these, 'value for money' and 'special offers', were price based. Interestingly Plaza, which was more associated with these concepts, was a relatively new store. Because it held a strong price-led image, it could be argued that this kind of positioning is easier to establish.

However, price appears to be the main method used by all the West German stores in their positioning. In the group discussions used to generate the concepts, price also appeared to be more important in store choice than in the British surveys. Many Germans claimed to compare prices before making a purchase. The older shoppers in particular referred to the literature sent out by the many stores promoting special offers. Many seemed to plan their shopping trips around the available offers. Retailers in West Germany seemed to make far greater use of direct mailing to promote special offers. Within the stores, much of the selling space near to entrances was given over to price promotions. In Britain in 1984, with the exception of Debenhams, there was a very different orientation. British department stores had been far more successful in segmenting their market-place using non-price factors, despite the fact that the British stores tended to be closer together, geographically speaking, in Manchester.

FINANCIAL ANALYSIS

If competing stores are undifferentiated then, according to both theory and our observations thus far, this should be manifest in a poorer overall commercial performance. No data on the individual West German stores were available to us so we decided to see how

Table 9.3 Rank order of stores against concepts

Concepts	Horten	Kaufhof	Karstadt	Quelle	Plaza	Kaufhalle
Group A						
(1) Wide product range	1	2	3	4	5	6
(2) Specialist departments	1	2	3	4	5	6
(3) Good for gifts	1	2	3	4	5	6
(4) Adequate sales personnel	1	2	3	4	5	6
(5) Fast till service	1	2	3	4	5	6
(6) Recommended by friends	1	2	3	4	5	6
(7) Stimulating	1	2	3	4	5	6
(8) Good store signage	1	2	3	4	5	6
(9) Friendly atmosphere	1	2	3	4	5	6
(10) Generous service policy	1	2	3	4	5	6
Group B						
(1) Stocks well-known brands	1	2	3	4	5	6
(2) Attractive shop windows	1	2	3	4	6	5
(3) Nicely fitted out	1	3	2	4	5	6
Group C						
(1) Value for money	6	4	5	2	1	3
(2) Special offers	2	3	4	5	1	6
(3) Good sales personnel	4	2	1	3	5	6
(4) Good for everyday wear	2	1	3	4	6	5
(5) Believable ads	1	3	2	5	4	6

the various retailers compared at a national level in both countries. It could be argued that British department stores had adopted a more differentiated approach in their positioning strategy compared to their West German counterparts. It should follow that the British stores overall would demonstrate a better overall financial performance.

Table 9.4 presents data for 1980 and 1985 for the British and West German retailers considered in the research. Kaufhof and Kaufhalle were part of the same company. Plaza was a part of a much larger grouping as was Quelle, so it was impractical to separate figures for the retail chains under study. Despite the difficulties of comparison, the following generalizations emerge:

(1) The West German stores exhibited a far lower sales volume growth, showing in fact a decline in volume, even allowing for relative inflation assessed by comparing relative interbank rates (Table 9.5).

(2) Profits in the British stores were rising. In the West German stores they were falling.

(3) Margins tended to be higher in Britain.

(4) Sales per employee in Britain were rising much faster than in West Germany.

(5) Overall profitability, measured by return on capital employed, even allowing for any differences in accounting conventions and bank rate, was often far higher in Britain.

It is difficult, if not impossible, not to link the clear differences in commercial performance to the differences in market structure. The lack of differentiation in the West German market had led to virtually identical strategies based largely on price, but possibly only Plaza had evolved a trading stereotype which could sustain a price-led position. Low margins leave little room for a change in approach towards more image-led strategies, although clearly there were a number of options open to most of the competitors if they had chosen to adopt them.

Some explanations of why West German stores should be so concerned with using price as their main strategy were gleaned from discussions with marketing personnel in the stores. They include the following:

(1) While West German retailers do undertake market research, senior management do not appear to use the data, especially those on image.

Table 9.4 Comparative financial performance of British and West German stores 1980 and 1985

Company	Turnover (million £/DM)		Profit before tax (million £/DM)		Sales area (000 m²)		No. of stores		Employees (FTE*/000)		% Profit on sales		Sales/employee (000s £/DM)		Return on capital employed (%)	
	1980	1985	1980	1985	1980	1985	1980	1985	1980	1985	1980	1985	1980	1985	1980	1985
Britain																
House of Fraser	627	930	37	48	N/A	567	112	105	29	20	5.9	5.2	22	46	12.1	7.8
Debenhams	539	729	16	41	421[1]	401[2]	72	67	21	13	2.9	5.2	26	56	5.2	9.7
Lewis's	113	140	(1.5)	1.4	N/A	N/A	11	11	4[2]	3	(1.3)	1.0	32	42	(2.0)	1.9
Marks & Spencer	1668	3208	170	366	592	670	251	265	30	41	10.2	9.5	52	81	29	22
British Home Stores	366	550	43	61	266[1]	292	115	128	17	16	11.6	11.1	21	35	31	22
West Germany																
Karstadt	9650	8980	77.6	50.4[3]	1248	1280	157	162	64	51	N/A	N/A	163	186	4.2[5]	1.8
Kaufhof	8600	8500	143.5	133.6	977	1037	203	200	57	43[4]	1.6	1.6	151	199	4.4[5]	4.1
Kaufhalle			61.4	60.9												
Horten	3800	3600	74.3	46.9	587	613	57	58	24	18	1.9	1.3	148	182	1.0[5]	1.9

[1] 1981; [2] 1983; [3] Gross profit; [4] Total employees; [5] 1982.   * Full-time equivalents.

(2) The West German shopper, although relatively affluent, had been educated by the retailer to use price as the main point of discrimination.

(3) West German stores tend to have similar architectural styles making differentiation more difficult.

Table 9.5 Comparative interest rates in the UK and West Germany

	West German 3-month interbank rate (mean %)	UK 3-month interbank rate (mean %)
1980	9.8	16.6
1981	12.1	13.9
1982	8.9	12.3
1983	5.8	10.1
1984	6.0	9.9
1985	5.4	12.4

INTERNATIONAL RETAILING

There is a lesson to be learned from this example about international retailing. Many manufacturers have been successful in taking their brands into other markets. Quite often the brands have needed considerable retailoring before they succeeded. There are nevertheless numerous international brands whose marketing has a common theme irrespective of the country where the product is being sold. Many retailers in Britain have looked overseas, arguing that the natural limits to the growth of the larger multiple can become irrelevant if the market-place can be redefined as being the world. Even so, there are relatively few examples of an international retail operation where the retailer can claim to be successful in all or even the majority of markets.

If our analysis is right, a British department store adopting an image-based approach would have a high chance of succeeding in the West German market, at least at the time of these studies. A West German retailer would have little chance in the British market unless it learned how to embrace a more targeted approach. It follows that success due to a particular competitive position in one country is no guarantee of equal success in another market or country, if that same positioning does not offer a comparable advantage. For example, British Home Stores with its largely price-led appeal would have far less chance of succeeding in West Germany than Kendals, Lewis's or Marks and Spencer.

KEY POINT SUMMARY

(1) West German department store shoppers have different ideas from their British counterparts on what constitutes an ideal department store.

(2) West German department stores were not differentiated along any of the image factors identified in the research, other than those associated with price.

(3) West German stores lacked differentiation as a whole and tended to compete with each other on price, despite having no economic advantage over each other.

(4) West German stores performed less well on a national basis than their British equivalents, even allowing for variations in inflation and interest rates. This could be linked to their lack of differentiation.

(5) Conclusions can be drawn as to how a retailer seeking international success might approach its corporate strategy. It is suggested than an image-based retailer (Marks and Spencer, Kendals, Lewis's) would have a better chance of succeeding in West Germany than a price-led West German retailer might have in Britain.

Chapter 10

Furniture Retailing, 1985: Price Promotion Succeeds

In this chapter we analyse one of the few British retail sectors where the market leader majors on a price-led positioning strategy and employs substantial advertising.

Furniture and furnishings were one of the quieter British retail sectors in the 1980s. Total consumer expenditure on household goods rose over 20 per cent from 1980 to 1984, while expenditure on furniture and floor coverings rose less than 12 per cent in the same period (EIU, 1985a) after a 7 per cent fall in 1980. Prices also increased more slowly than for retail sales as a whole. In the typical household, expenditure on furniture and furnishings tended to take second place to the purchase of electrical goods. This was unlike the situation in other European countries, where furniture sales in particular were more buoyant. While the typical British household spent nearly 10 per cent of disposable income on clothing and footwear, and 22 per cent on housing costs, only about 3–4 per cent was allocated for furniture and furnishings.

The furniture market was catered for by a number of different types of retail outlet. Some retailers specialized in furniture and in perhaps only one type of furniture. Others offered some furniture as part of a wider retailing activity, perhaps as a department store, or as a furnishings specialist such as a carpet retailer. The specialists held about two-thirds of the market in 1982 (EIU, 1985b). The furniture market was worth over £2,800 million in 1983. It could be subdivided into four roughly equal sectors by furniture type: bedroom furniture; kitchen furniture; upholstered furniture for the living room; and other living and dining room furniture. Of these, kitchen furniture had shown the most growth.

Import penetration had become significant during the early 1980s, and by 1983 imports accounted for 20 per cent of the furniture market. The British furniture manufacturing sector was highly fragmented and generally suffered from poor profitability. Christie Tyler, the leading manufacturer, held only an estimated 6 per cent share in 1983 (EIU, 1985b), using a large number of subsidiaries and trading names. Hygena was the next largest manufacturer, whose output in the UK was retailed almost solely by MFI.

Furniture retailing and manufacturing are further examples of control over the market-place changing from manufacturer to retailer. As far back as 1976, for example, the total expenditure by furniture manufacturers on advertising had been £5.1 million while the top three furniture retailers alone spent £5.6 million (Fulop, 1986).

In the 1980s one of the few buoyant sectors in the furniture market was self-assembly, sometimes referred to as 'knocked down' or 'KD' products. Most of the KD sales were in bedroom or kitchen products and their growth had been ascribed variously to the price advantage, immediate delivery and to an improved perception of the quality of KD furniture. The price advantages of KD furniture resulted from its relatively low cost of distribution and the fact that assembly was performed by the customer.

Furniture was not a regular household purchase in the early 1980s. In any year, only half of all households would make any purchase. Specific events in life, such as marriage or moving house, tended to be the reason for purchase, although it had become fashionable in the 1980s to replace or install fitted kitchens and bedrooms – with KD furniture benefiting from both trends. By 1982 KD products accounted for 60 per cent of the kitchen furniture market and 11 per cent of bedroom furniture purchases – beds and bedding being unsuited to the KD concept. In occasional furniture KD held roughly half of all sales.

Furniture posed a number of problems to the retailer. Because of the fragmented market, the absence of dominant brands and the wide range of furniture types, large areas of display space were needed. Although unit purchase prices could be high, purchase and customer flow rates were low. All these factors demanded high margins on furniture while the market seemed to be becoming increasingly price conscious.

Furniture retailing had been as fragmented as furniture manufacturing, with the typical retailer having only one or two outlets. However, the larger multiples had been gaining share to achieve some 45 per cent of sales by 1985 (EIU, 1985a). Table 10.1 shows an estimate of furniture outlets by ownership in 1984. However, share of footage would have favoured the newer and out-of-town stores of MFI and Queensway.

Ninety-five per cent of furniture retailers were sited in the high street, accounting for some 80 per cent of floor space, yet two retailers, MFI and Queensway, both out-of-town specialists, held nearly 20 per cent of the market between them. MFI dominated

Table 10.1 Major furniture retailers, 1984

Retailers	No. of stores
Great Universal Stores	440
Harris Queensway Group	256
MFI Furniture Centres	123
Courts	100
Waring and Gillow (inc. Maples)	100
Co-op	93
Wades	68
J. Boardman	67
Cantors	56
Habitat	41
Total	1,344
Total UK furniture retailers (1982)	9,533

Source: EIU, 1985b.

the KD markets for bedroom and kitchen furniture and Queensway offered a wide range of upholstered furniture. Their stores tended to be large with ample car parking.

Great Universal Stores, one of Europe's largest retail groups, owned a number of high-street names including Times and Cavendish Woodhouse, the latter having about four times more outlets than Times. Waring and Gillow operated about 40 shops, under their own name, in the high street. Wades, once part of ASDA until a management buyout, also had fewer than 100 high-street stores.

A rather different offering was available from Habitat. Located in the high street but usually in secondary sites, Habitat was one of the few retailers, along with MFI and Queensway, to have exhibited growth. By 1985 Habitat, together with Heals, was part of the Storehouse group with Mothercare and British Home Stores. Habitat offered a wide product range besides furniture and had pioneered 'lifestyle' retailing in the 1960s. Habitat offered buyers a 'look' as well as furniture and furnishings, and appealed strongly to the younger middle class. Although Habitat held a low overall share of the furniture market it attracted more than twice the traffic of Queensway, for example (see Table 10.2).

THE 1985 STUDY

The analysis presented below is based on data gathered in 1985 from MFI, Queensway, Wades, Cavendish Woodhouse, Waring and Gillow and Habitat. They were chosen to represent the out-of-town

Table 10.2   Retail penetration in furniture, 1983

Retailer	Estimated shoppers during 1983 (million)
Cavendish Woodhouse	0.9
Courts	0.9
Habitat	3.0
Harris Queensway	1.3
MFI	6.8
Times	0.9
VKay	0.4
Waring and Gillow	0.9
Williams	0.4

Source: Simmons, 1984.

and high-street retailers while Habitat, although small in turnover, was added as an example of a different approach to furniture retailing.

The concepts identified with the ideal furniture retailer were found to be 'fast delivery', 'good customer service', 'quality' and 'good value for money'. The market research data and the resulting models are presented in Figures 10.1–10.3 and Table 10.3. One point of interest emerged from the conduct of the research itself. By comparison with the research into other retail sectors, it was difficult to find people who could respond to all the comparisons. People did not have a strong image of all the leading furniture stores.

The market models reveal three distinct sectors. The high-street sector is occupied not surprisingly by Waring and Gillow, Wades and Cavendish Woodhouse. It is not unreasonable to speculate that all other high-street furniture multiples would be similarly placed. However, 'well-trained staff' is the only concept to appear firmly in that sector, although Waring and Gillow were well associated with all concepts, in particular product range and design. They appear to be the best placed of the high-street majors although their strength in positioning will be diluted by the close presence of their competitors. Typically the high-street furniture shopper was likely to opt for Waring and Gillow as first choice but to be attracted by other high-street outlets who, being less well placed image-wise, would be selling more on price to attract custom. Even Waring and Gillow used the slogan 'Unbeatable price promise' in their £2.5 million advertising campaign in 1983 (Manchester Business School, 1985). Throughout the early 1980s their financial performance showed very small profits and some pre-tax losses.

	Wades	Cavendish Woodhouse	Waring & Gillow	Habitat	MFI	Harris Queensway	The ideal	Wide product range	Good product design	Co-ordinated ranges	Well-trained staff	Fashionable	Well laid out	Good displays
Wades	1													
Cavendish Woodhouse	2.77	1												
Waring & Gillow	4.25	4.16	1											
Habitat	5.58	5.36	5.36	1										
MFI	4.91	4.83	5.74	5.49	1									
Harris Queensway	3.89	4.48	4.88	5.70	2.94	1								
The ideal	4.61	4.36	2.84	3.42	4.90	4.68	1							
Wide product range	3.65	3.78	3.00	3.97	3.15	3.18	2.50	1						
Good product design	3.59	3.74	2.42	3.07	4.58	4.88	1.73	4.76	1					
Co-ordinated ranges	3.88	3.96	3.22	2.31	4.40	4.31	2.44	3.59	3.65	1				
Well-trained staff	3.78	3.44	2.27	3.89	4.11	3.98	1.66	5.34	4.92	5.40	1			
Fashionable	4.28	4.28	3.90	1.81	4.64	4.44	2.84	4.73	3.66	3.22	5.51	1		
Well laid out	3.73	3.65	2.50	2.66	3.33	3.69	2.08	4.59	4.45	3.66	4.32	4.36	1	
Good displays	3.63	3.62	2.84	2.73	3.47	3.69	2.16	4.02	3.97	3.26	4.22	3.96	1.74	1

Figure 10.1 Furniture retailers, 1985. Average ratings: 1 = totally similar, 7 = totally dissimilar.

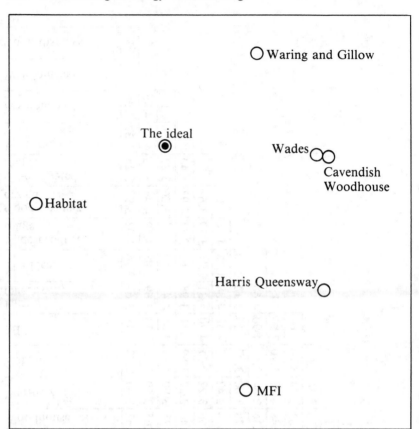

Figure 10.2   Furniture retailers, 1985.

The second grouping consisted of the out-of-town specialists, MFI
and Harris Queensway. MFI and Queensway had a similar rating
against a number of concepts but could be differentiated somewhat
by MFI's better rating for layout and display. Both MFI and
Queensway rated low against every image factor, including the ideal,
apart from 'wide product range'. Habitat, on the other hand, rated
first against four concepts and was highly differentiated in the
'fashionable', 'co-ordinated ranges' and 'good product design'
sectors.

It is difficult to present a valid financial comparison of the main
players in furniture retailing, as they were often part of larger groups,
or themselves had major subsidiaries. However, the possession of
a good image has been linked in earlier chapters to high market
share, good financial performance and to an absence of advertising.

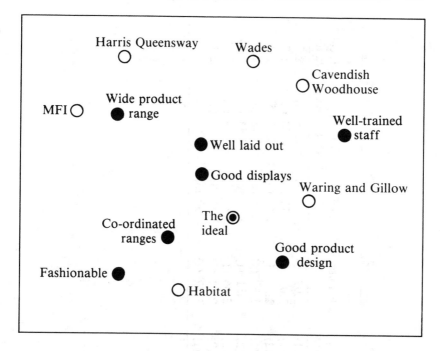

Figure 10.3 Furniture retailers and concepts, 1985.

The company with one of the highest growth rates in any retail sector and certainly with the highest advertising expenditure was MFI. It was also one of the more profitable of all retail organizations, despite being part of a sector suffering generally from low profitability and little growth in real sales value.

On the other hand, Habitat fits the main formula for successful positioning strategy that could be proposed from earlier chapters. Table 10.4 presents advertising as a percentage of sales revenue figures for 1985. Habitat has the lowest. Habitat's sales increased 265 per cent from 1980 to 1985 compared to an increase for the total furniture and floorcoverings market of 36 per cent (Verdict, 1986) and MFI's next best performance of 163 per cent. However, by 1985 MFI's market share was still some five times that of Habitat.

Perhaps the most interesting comparison between MFI and Habitat is on sales per square foot. Habitat achieved £138 per square foot in 1985 compared to £93 at MFI. However, MFI achieved a higher trading margin at 13.4 per cent compared to Habitat's at 11.4 per cent. MFI's return on capital employed – around 35 per cent or more – was also a remarkable figure. While Habitat's excellent performance can be linked to a good image-led positioning

Table 10.3 Ratings and rank orders of stores against concepts

Concepts	Wades	Cavendish Woodhouse	Waring & Gillow	Stores Habitat	MFI	Harris Queensway	Ideal values
Wide product range	3.65 (4)	3.78 (5)	3.00 (1)	3.97 (6)	3.15 (2)	3.18 (3)	2.50
Good product design	3.59 (3)	3.74 (4)	2.42 (1)	3.07 (2)	4.58 (5)	4.88 (6)	1.73
Co-ordinated ranges	3.88 (3)	3.96 (4)	3.22 (2)	2.31 (1)	4.40 (6)	4.31 (5)	2.44
Well-trained staff	3.78 (3)	3.44 (2)	2.27 (1)	3.89 (4)	4.11 (6)	3.98 (5)	1.66
Fashionable	4.28 (3)	4.28 (3)	3.90 (2)	1.81 (1)	4.64 (6)	4.44 (5)	2.84
Well laid out	3.73 (6)	3.65 (4)	2.80 (2)	2.66 (1)	3.33 (3)	3.69 (5)	2.08
Good displays	3.63 (5)	3.62 (4)	2.84 (2)	2.73 (1)	3.47 (3)	3.69 (6)	2.16
The ideal	4.61 (4)	4.36 (3)	2.84 (1)	3.42 (2)	4.90 (6)	4.68 (5)	—

Table 10.4 Advertising as percentage of sales revenue

Retailer	%
Habitat	0.6
MFI	5.3
Queensway	4.1
Waring and Gillow, Maples	2.3
Wades	1.2

Source: Verdict, 1986.

strategy, MFI's apparent lack of image platform had not prevented the company returning impressive financial figures. MFI's positioning, like that of Kwik Save, was based solidly on price promotion and cost reduction.

KD furniture offered intrinsic cost benefits over traditional manufacturing and retailing methods. MFI's relationships with Hygena and other manufacturers allowed an investment in high technology which reduced costs and improved design in mass-produced lines. Noel Lister, Chief Executive of MFI in 1984, gave examples of a standard sink base unit that retailed for £30 in 1976 and £24.95 in 1984, and second, a double wardrobe which was £66 in 1978 and, in a better quality, sold in 1984 at £49.95 (MFI, 1985). MFI's out-of-town sites, originally industrial units or converted buildings, but more recently purpose-built units in modern retail parks, offered a significant cost advantage over the high street. The company owned its own distribution system and had invested heavily in computer systems.

While in many ways Harris Queensway had travelled down a similar road it catered for a different sector, majoring on soft furnishings and upholstered furniture. MFI had little price competition in kitchen and bedroom furniture at the time. MFI's huge advertising expenditure (Table 10.5) was almost entirely price based, promoting what appeared to be a constant sale. Their high

Table 10.5 MFI turnover, advertising and advertising as percentage of sales

	1985	1984	1983	1982	1981	1980
Turnover (£ million)	386	334	301	246	177	191
Advertising (£ million)	18.7	16.4	12.9	10.0	9.6	6.7
Advertising as percentage of turnover	4.8	4.9	4.3	4.1	5.4	3.5

Source: MEAL, MFI reports.

customer flow (Table 10.2) must have been due in part to their advertising strategy. This flow was converted to sales with MFI reaching an estimated 50 per cent market share in self-assembly bedroom furniture in 1983 and 25 per cent of self-assembly kitchens.

Interestingly by 1986 there were a number of signs that MFI was adopting a slightly more image-based approach in response to a flattening of its financial performance. The merger with ASDA had bought an association with Allied Carpets. Carpets were now being carried in more stores, as were soft furnishings and pictures. Colour supplement advertisements featured the Hygena range, mentioning almost incidentally that it was available at MFI. A new tv advertising campaign, carrying the message 'Take a look at us now' underlined a greater emphasis on image, but the company still retained a strong price appeal.

The furniture market offers the examples of successful image and price-based retail positioning in a market where the mainstream traditional retailers were struggling to break even. It emphasizes that retailers can co-exist profitably, even in a static market, if they adopt coherent and differentiated strategies based on either cost or image. The role of advertising in this context is worth considering. MFI certainly considered it an essential part of their price-based approach even though expenditure at measured cost accounted for around 5 per cent of turnover. Habitat, like other successful image-based retailers (NEXT and Marks and Spencer), seemed equally convinced they did not need it. While NEXT and Marks and Spencer normally occupied prime sites and, it can be argued, used their store fronts as their advertising media, Habitat occupied many secondary sites. It must be concluded that word of mouth and reputation may be a vital element in promoting such retailers.

KEY POINT SUMMARY

(1) The furniture market in Britain in the early 1980s was relatively static. People bought furniture infrequently and did not have a strong awareness of competing retailers.

(2) MFI dominated the flatpack or KD sector specializing in self-assembly fitted kitchens and bathrooms. Queensway held a similar market share and out-of-town trading format specializing in lounge furniture and bedding.

(3) The high-street furniture retailers were struggling to be profitable at the time, with the exception of Habitat which had a strong image, based on a lifestyle concept but little advertising.

(4) MFI, unlike other leading retailers in different sectors, spent heavily on advertising. This generated high rates of customer flow. However, its operation was very much a price-led one.

References

EIU (1985a) Furniture shops, *Retail Business*, no. 324, Feb., p.3.

EIU (1985b) Special Report No. 3, Furniture, Part 2, *Retail Business*, no. 329, July, p.31.

Fulop, C. (1986) *Retailer Advertising and Retail Competition in the U.K.*, Advertising Association.

Manchester Business School (1985) *Retail Reference Book 1985*, Part 1, p.170.

MFI (1985) MFI employee newspaper.

Simmons, M. (1984) The penetration of major retailers in the UK, *Retail and Distribution Management*, May/June, p.33.

Verdict (1986) *Verdict on Furniture and Carpet Retailers*, May.

Chapter 11

Electrical and DIY Retailing: Markets Needing Marketing?

In this chapter we present a limited analysis of two markets – electrical and DIY retailing. The purpose is to demonstrate the potential for differentiation between competing retailers, rather than to make specific points on the value of any one positioning strategy. Both sectors are dominated by price-led promotion, but individual retailers do not appear to have any clear economic advantages. This could lead to low overall profitability but in the case of electrical retailing in particular this is not the case.

ELECTRICAL GOODS RETAILING

As we saw in Chapter 10 expenditure on electrical goods has grown to occupy a significant percentage of disposable income. At the same time real price levels have fallen. For example, the prices of radios, televisions and other appliances fell by 1 per cent in 1984 and grew by only 1 per cent in 1985 (EIU, 1985a).

At a time of still significant price inflation it is worth examining why electrical goods prices have not kept pace. Imports constitute the major part of retail sales. In some areas, for example, video recorders, domestic production is almost non-existent. Even in more mainstream product areas such as audio equipment imports account for around 70 per cent of the market. British-manufactured products are strong only in certain specialist areas or when distribution costs form a significant proportion of costs, as in loudspeakers, the larger televisions and many white goods (EIU, 1985b).

The increased value of the pound in the early 1980s, in its role as a near petrocurrency, clearly contributed to the decline in the prices of imported goods. However, the main factor predates even North Sea oil. In the immediate post-war years an automatic Bendix front-loading washing machine, virtually the only such product line available, retailed at about £70. In 1983 an Indesit machine, visually almost identical to the Bendix, retailed at about £70. One of the authors purchased a pocket calculator with a single memory in 1971 for £35; a similar product, with the added benefit of solar power, cost £6.99 in 1987; and a credit card-size version was given for nothing as part of a promotion by a transport company in 1988.

As products move from speciality lines to becoming mass-market items economies of scale can be significant. More significant still is the experience curve effect (see Chapter 2) which is very marked in electrical and electronic products. The experience curve can be a major factor in a price-led strategy. What happens is that each time a company's historical production of a product doubles, the costs it incurs in producing a single item reduce by a constant amount. New ways are being found constantly to reduce manufacturing costs by what can become embarrassingly large amounts. The embarrassment stems from being able to charge lower prices each year for the same product and make higher profits. At the very least this risks dissatisfying the customer who bought last year at a higher price (and who probably does not wish to understand about experience curves).

The British seem to enjoy electrical goods. Ownership of record players and video equipment in Britain is the highest in Europe. Video equipment ownership was more than twice the European average in 1985 (EIU, 1985a).

Branded products were probably more important in electrical goods than in most other retail sectors, and in any one sector the number of major brands can be large. In audio products, for example, the Japanese brands AIWA, JVC, Panasonic and Technics (Matsushita), Hitachi, Pioneer, Sanyo, Sharp, Sony and Toshiba competed with the Dutch-based Philips, Britain's Amstrad, BSR, Fidelity, Binatone, Ultra, HMV, Ferguson (Thorn EMI), West Germany's Grundig and the Danish Bang and Olufsen. Own-brand products were growing in brown goods. Comet sold televisions under the Solarvox name; Dixons sold a range of products as Saisho, or under their own name; Currys (part of Dixons) as Triumph and Matsui. The various electricity boards had traditionally used the Electra label mainly for large white goods. Tandy was the only retailer to sell almost exclusively under its own name. Manufacturers largely managed to fend off the own-label challenge from retailers by supporting brands and by using the device of producing special variants or model numbers for specific retail sectors or individual retailers. In 1985 Dixons were believed to have the largest proportion of sales as of their own house brand, after Tandy.

Electrical retailers in 1985 were not a totally homogeneous group. Some, such as Ladbroke Leisure Group's subsidiary Laskys, specialized in audio, video and computers. Others such as Comet, the discount shop and warehouse subsidiary of Woolworth, carried a much broader range. Currys, a high-street retailer which had edged ahead of Comet in total sales to become the leading retailer in this sector, carried a fairly wide range in its somewhat smaller outlets. The rising star in the sector was Dixons, which bid successfully for the larger Currys in 1984 and narrowly missed acquiring Woolworth in 1986. At the time Dixons also operated a small chain of large units under the Power City name. Dixons' origins were as photographic dealers, but it was now a far more broadly based electrical retailer. Dixons was said by many to be the most profitable of any high-street retailer.

Rumbelows was owned by electrical manufacturers Thorn–EMI but concentrated on white rather than brown goods. It also operated a substantial TV rental business. Tandy was the semi-franchised operation of America's Radio Shack. Finally, the Electricity Board showrooms collectively represented one of the largest retail operations, although each regional board controlled its own retailing. The showrooms doubled as customer service points for the public utility, many people choosing to pay electricity bills directly to their board. Showrooms were used to promote electricity generally and carried some lines, such as electric showers, not carried by most retailers in the sector.

Advertising in this sector was almost totally based on price. Comet, for example, specialized in buying substantial space, mainly in local newspapers, to list its range of products. Price pledges were very common with retailers guaranteeing that they would not be undercut by local competition. Dixons featured 'Dixons deals' in bright red display cards in their windows and stores.

Table 11.1 Concepts describing the ideal electrical retailer

Low prices
Good service
Helpful
Reliable products
Knowledgeable
Not condescending
Wide range
Discount prices
Value for money

In 1985 a study was made of the electrical retail market. Figures 11.1–11.3 and Table 11.2 present the results of the analysis. The ideal electrical retailer was described by the concepts in Table 11.1.

Table 11.2 Rank order of concepts against stores

Concepts	Stores						
	Dixons	Laskys	Comet	Currys	Rumb-elows	Tandy	Electricity Board
Stylish	2	1	5	4	3	6	7
Good display	3	1	2	4	5	6	7
Well laid out	4	1	2	3	5	6	7
Wide selection	4	5	1	3	2	6	7
Good for browsing	3	1	4	2	6	5	7
Competitive	2	4	1	5	3	6	7
The ideal	1	2	3	4	5	6	7

The list is unusual in a number of respects. First, it is very long, a fact which may not be notable but could indicate, when the market models are examined, considerable dissatisfaction with the typical electrical retailer. Second, the list contains three price-linked concepts and both 'low prices' and 'value for money'. In all other markets we have studied to date, none has been so overtly price orientated and in none have low prices and value been so closely associated. It is almost as if electrical retailing had become a commodity market dominated by price. Finally, the concept 'not condescending' reflected a strongly held view by female members of the group discussions that women were not made to feel at ease, especially in those outlets selling electronic products. Typical comments included the observation, 'They (the shop assistants) assume that because you are a woman you don't understand even the basics of hi-fi. Their voices noticeably change to a patronizing tone when they switch from talking to your husband to talking to you.'

The market model in Figure 11.3 is unusual in that the retailers are positioned further from the 'ideal' than the concepts. It is again unusual to see no retailer, rated on a one to seven scale, closer to a mark of one than Dixons with an average of 3.60 against the ideal (Figure 11.1). None of the retailers is very well associated with any of the concepts which tend to form a cluster on their own well away from the retailers. Laskys was the best rated against the more ambience-related concepts. Tandy and the Electricity Board did not really appear to be part of the same market as the rest. Dixons was rated closest to the ideal with a similar profile to Currys, which was less well rated against 'stylish' and 'competitive'.

Because of the nature of the companies being modelled, most being part of larger interests, few commercial data were available to us about individual concerns. Using the available financial

	Comet	Currys	Dixons	Electricity Board	Rumbelows	Laskys	Tandy	The ideal	Stylish	Good display	Well laid out	Wide selection	Good for browsing	Competitive
Comet	1													
Currys	3.97	1												
Dixons	4.50	3.43	1											
Electricity Board	4.88	4.50	4.94	1										
Rumbelows	4.22	3.51	3.91	4.30	1									
Laskys	4.32	3.95	3.61	5.23	4.32	1								
Tandy	5.31	4.62	4.06	4.93	4.59	4.23	1							
The ideal electrical retailer	3.83	3.92	3.60	4.75	3.93	3.74	4.25	1						
Stylish	4.27	3.95	3.64	4.43	3.77	3.57	4.38	2.97	1					
Good display	3.39	3.54	3.44	4.17	3.67	3.28	4.05	2.27	3.46	1				
Well laid out	3.29	3.42	3.77	4.04	3.93	3.21	3.98	2.10	3.18	2.38	1			
Wide selection	2.74	3.18	3.31	4.09	3.10	3.65	3.73	2.06	4.35	3.18	3.36	1		
Good for browsing	3.54	3.43	3.53	4.26	3.67	3.32	3.56	2.47	3.83	2.50	2.46	3.52	1	
Competitive	2.42	3.45	2.80	4.24	3.16	3.21	3.53	1.70	4.56	4.16	4.05	3.52	4.04	1

Figure 11.1 Electrical retailers, 1985. Average ratings: 1 = totally similar, 7 = totally dissimilar.

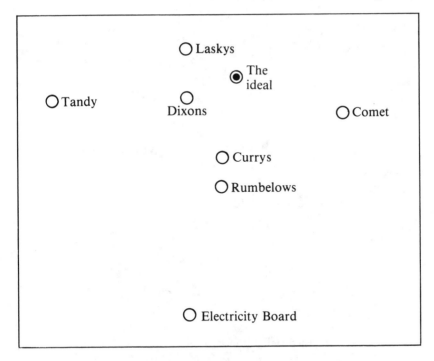

Figure 11.2 Electrical retailers, 1985: stores only.

information Dixons seemed to lead the field. Sales per employee were nearly double those of Rumbelows and Currys. Comet had the best net margin, and only Rumbelows was out of step, with half the net margin of Currys and Dixons.

Tandy's figures were not available. Although the retailer's position must be seen as well differentiated, it had no concept closely associated with it, implying no clear positioning in the sector. The Electricity Board was the surprise; it was rated the lowest against each of the concepts, and as seemingly unwilling to profit from its captive custom and an early position in own-label goods. Laskys was rumoured to be not returning the profits looked for by Ladbrokes. Despite being well rated against four concepts it had somehow failed to profit from being the most ambience-led retailer in the sector. Despite its strong image, it had few exclusive lines and offered many prices that could be matched by the discounters. Its image and its delivery were possibly at variance. However, its low traffic flow (Table 11.3) indicated that, together with Tandy, its more specialist image linked to a perceived narrow product range limited its appeal. An absence of prime sites meant little casual trade.

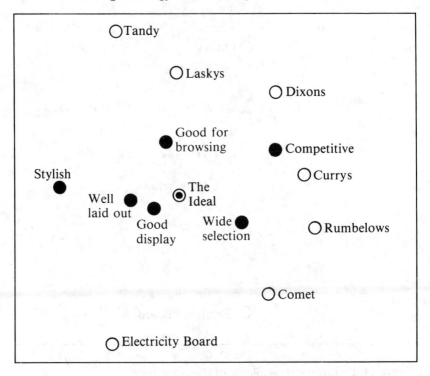

Figure 11.3   Electrical retailers, 1985: stores and concepts.

Table 11.3   Shoppers at electrical retail outlets, 1983

Retailer	No. of shoppers (million)
Currys	10.2
Dixons	6.4
Electricity Board	11.1
Laskys	0.4
Rumbelows	4.7
Tandy	0.9

Source: Simmons, 1984.

DIY RETAILING

Do-it-yourself was a growth area in Britain in the 1970s and 1980s, and was constantly tipped for even higher growth. However, few companies found that they could make it pay well, and in the 1970s DIY retailers seemed to be constantly changing hands. Historically DIY products such as paint, wallpaper, spare parts and timber products were sold in a variety of outlets, ranging from builders' merchants specializing in supplying trade customers, to retailers specializing in the sale of limited product areas such as paint and wallpaper, or car spares and accessories.

From the 1960s onwards there had been a growth in the larger multipurpose DIY outlet, often situated out of town. The high-street specialist remained although there were few large chains. One exception was A. G. Stanley's Fads. In 1984 Fads had 204 mostly high-street sites, compared with 212 in 1983. Fads had also dropped an experiment started in 1982 under the name of Bargain Wallpapers. Fads remained the largest of the non-superstore operators and by far the largest specialist paint and wallpaper retailer of its type. They were regarded as aggressive in pricing and carried a range of own-label products.

By 1985 there were a number of DIY superstore operators. B & Q (Black and Quayle), founded in 1960, had belonged to Woolworth since 1980; by 1985 they had 175 stores. New store openings were of a minimum of 30,000 sq. ft. The Homecharm Group, trading under the names Texas Homecare and Bulk DIY, had over 100 outlets, 32 of which were under the Texas name. Payless DIY, at the time a division of Marley, were the third largest and had tended to follow the Bulk DIY arm of Homecharm into the heavier end of the market, likely to appeal more to the professional. The 60 or so Payless stores were concentrated in the South of England, as was Homebase, operator of the largest of the out-of-town DIY stores and owned by Sainsbury. Homebase had a more up-market positioning emphasized by the unusual and stylish design of its stores and through concessions to, for example, Laura Ashley.

The fourth largest DIY multiple with around 50 stores at the time of the study was Do-It-All, owned by newsagent multiple W. H. Smith. Do-It-All tended to carry a wide product range in its larger than average outlets. It was perhaps best known for its highly effective, price-led advertising which included the theme 'How do Do-It-All do it?'

There were a number of other chains involved in DIY. Many department stores carried DIY products and grocery multiples were estimated to hold 7 per cent of the market. At a local level there were a number of prominent regional outlets. Although DIY retailing was growing, it was still at an early stage in its evolution, especially in the out-of-town developments. Own branding was relatively underdeveloped and tended to concentrate on staples such as white gloss paint, woodchip paper and similar products usually sold at a heavy price advantage alongside nationally known brands.

Most retailers could not trade legally on a Sunday in England

and Wales at the time of the study. DIY retailers were to the fore in lobbying for Sunday trading. They argued strongly that limiting their opening hours, especially over weekends, restricted their business more than most, because the weekend was when the DIY enthusiast would be most interested in buying.

Advertising as a percentage of turnover was relatively high, especially among the out-of-town operators; Do-It-All in 1984 spent 4.2 per cent, Texas 3.8 per cent and B & Q 1.3 per cent of turnover. Fads spent only 0.6 per cent and with its relatively low turnover this, measured by MEAL at £359,000, represented an expenditure that would have been lost in the coverage purchased by its competitors. Even so Fads had the advantage of being in the high street and consequently of being more in the public view.

While Fads' turnover remained constant between 1981 and 1984, B & Q, Texas and Do-It-All doubled their sales volume or more. The market certainly seemed to be shifting in favour of the out-of-town operators.

In 1985 we conducted a study on DIY retailing in the Greater Manchester area. The study was made a local one for a number of reasons, the most relevant here being the regionality of many of the leading retailers. We were also interested in examining the effect of the clustering that seemed prevalent in the geographical position of the DIY multiples.

In south Manchester, for example, two companies, Do-It-All and Texas, backed onto one another in a retail park that only they occupied together with MFI. B & Q were only about 3 km away. The results of the exercise are shown in Figures 11.4 and 11.5 and Tables 11.4 and 11.5. The concepts describing the ideal DIY retailer

Table 11.4   Concepts describing the ideal DIY retailer in Greater Manchester

Convenient
Knowledgeable staff
Willing to exchange goods
Essential products stocked
One-stop shopping
High availability of goods
Saves you money
Not aggressive

were found to be those in Table 11.4. As with electrical retailing, the list is rather long, with price implicitly although not totally

	B & Q	Do-It-All	Texas	Fads	The ideal DIY store	Stocks quality products	Wide range	Good display	Easy shopping	Efficient checkouts	Pleasant surroundings	Helpful advice
B & Q	1											
Do-It-All	3.02	1										
Texas	3.27	4.12	1									
Fads	5.19	5.13	5.15	1								
The ideal DIY store	3.28	3.35	3.85	5.29	1							
Stocks quality products	2.88	3.52	3.49	3.87	2.12	1						
Wide range	2.50	2.78	3.29	4.49	2.22	3.49	1					
Good display	2.60	2.89	2.98	3.53	2.31	3.80	3.13	1				
Easy shopping	2.50	2.69	2.96	3.83	2.06	3.78	3.36	3.27	1			
Efficient checkouts	3.50	3.17	3.67	3.77	2.07	3.88	4.14	4.36	2.42	1		
Pleasant surroundings	3.00	3.26	3.27	3.91	2.58	3.90	4.19	2.95	3.52	4.48	1	
Helpful advice	4.00	3.52	4.00	3.60	2.13	3.49	3.89	3.90	3.21	4.13	4.34	1

Figure 11.4 DIY retailing in Manchester, 1985. Average ratings: 1 = totally similar, 7 = totally dissimilar.

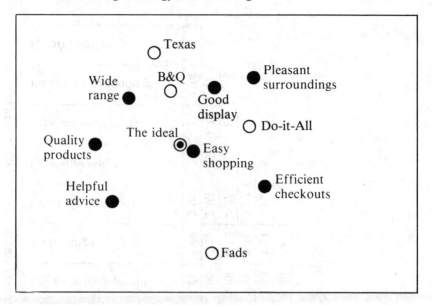

Figure 11.5   DIY retailers in Manchester, 1985.

Table 11.5   DIY retailing in Manchester, 1985: rank order against concepts

Concepts	B & Q	Do-It-All	Texas	Fads
Quality product	1	3	2	4
Wide range	1	2	3	4
Good display	1	2	3	4
Easy shopping	1	2	3	4
Effective layouts	2	1	3	4
Pleasant surroundings	1	2	3	4
Helpful advice	3	1	3	2

included in the idea of 'saves you money'. The overall impression in the group discussions, for example, was that DIY was intrinsically concerned with saving money, and low prices were only part of the way a retailer could help. Stocking everything you needed and offering advice were valued just as much in this context.

The market model and the market research data show the three DIY superstore operators somewhat clustered, with B & Q best placed against five of the seven concepts and the ideal. Yet again the concepts were each closer to the ideal than the stores themselves (something not obvious from the model but apparent in the matrix).

Texas was least well placed, being seen as similar to B & Q but not as well rated against any concept. Do-It-All was differentiated somewhat on 'efficient checkouts' and 'helpful advice', two concepts which are not totally unrelated in that the people factor is common to both.

Fads was differentiated but unassociated with any concept other than 'helpful advice'. Fads and Do-It-All had different ways of offering advice, Fads by being well staffed, and Do-It-All by pioneering, at least in Manchester, display boards alongside merchandise containing practical tips for the DIY customer. Interestingly Do-It-All, perhaps majoring more than the rest in price promotion, had a poor score against 'quality products'. None rated highly on advice or on efficient checkouts, Do-It-All's main points of difference.

In 1985 the DIY superstores were winning the battle against the high-street competition if Fads' position is anything to go by. The superstores' problem was each other. A lack of differentiation means that while any store with a better image will benefit, the competition will inevitably react on price, reducing margins. Siting outlets near or even next to one another adds to the problem, as it makes the consumer's job in comparing prices easier and makes the retailer more conscious of price comparisons. While their customers may not complain, their shareholders may take a different view.

THE IMAGE AND PRICE FACTORS

In 1985 DIY and electrical retailing were similar in that they both appeared to be immature in their use of image. Both sets of competitors tended to employ price as their main marketing weapon, with the limitation that few held any real economic advantage allowing them to base their strategies on a real cost advantage in the longer term.

Both sectors held some advantages at the time, which could have allowed them to sustain a collective price-led approach. The electrical retailers had segmented the market to some extent on the basis of product type. They also had the benefit of a genuine fall in the real cost of much of the equipment they retailed, due to the experience curve effect at the manufacturer. As Japanese electronic companies in particular were finding increasingly cost-effective methods to produce ever-larger volumes, prices could be held in store during times of inflation, or cut during times of minimal inflation, giving the consumer the impression of price benefits.

The DIY superstore retailers had benefited from the lower costs of out-of-town locations and larger units. In particular they could discount staple products such as white gloss paint at levels unattainable by the smaller high-street independent.

However, by concentrating on these price advantages the competing companies seemed to have ignored the potential for building an offer based on image. In electrical retailing, for example, there was a huge gap in the market for a stylish, well-laid out retailer with good displays. Some independent chains retailing more up-market products had recognized this, but the larger groups had not. There was some evidence that Dixons had been improving its image against the concepts identified as representing the ideal electrical retailer. The DIY retailers were in a worse position. Every aspect of the operation was seemingly geared to encouraging the shopper to buy on the basis of price. There were fewer opportunities to promote on any clear point of differentiation, although in 1985 the areas of 'quality products,' 'helpful advice' and 'easy shopping' could have been considered.

The main conclusion from both studies is that neither sector appeared to be adopting a true market orientation towards its customers at the strategic level. It is difficult to accept that none of these firms was so unsophisticated as to be unaware of the opportunities. However, virtually all the competing retailers seemed to be relying on their relative price to attract custom, rather than focusing their offers on different market sectors based on image. In DIY retailing this had already resulted in low profits. It is tempting to suggest that electrical retailers could find similar problems when the falling prices for electrical goods or less innovation in new products produces a flatter market.

These two brief studies have been included in the same chapter to illustrate the potential for clearer positioning. Our arguments may not be too convincing in electrical retailing, given the profitability of many of the stores, but time may tell. From our experience of other sectors, price leadership as the basis for all competitors in a market is no basis for profitability for all concerned. Unless the competitors can differentiate one from the other and become clearly associated with one or more image factors, the inevitable could be for one or more to fail.

KEY POINT SUMMARY

(1)   British electrical and DIY retailing in 1985 are two sectors where retailers did not position themselves on the available concepts in the market-place. The electrical retailers fared better than the West German department store retailers by differentiating,

largely on the basis of product type. All, however, were some distance from the customer's ideal store. The DIY superstores were far too close in customers' perception in 1985.

(2)   In both sectors retailers might have improved their commercial situation by changing their image, de-emphasizing cost as the basis of competition and seeking to emphasize other points of difference.

References

EIU (1985a) Audio products, Part 2, *Retail Business*, no. 323, January.
EIU (1985b) Domestic appliances and sound equipment, *Retail Business*, no. 332, October.
Simmons, M. (1984) The penetration of major retailers in the UK, *Retail and Distribution Management*, May/June.

Chapter 12

Health Food Retailing: The Problems of the Small Retailer

Every retailer, no matter how small, has an image. This image may be known to only a few shoppers, but even so the smallest retailer can still use positioning strategy as a keypoint for its business. In this chapter we analyse the health food market in 1987, and in particular the fortunes of an independent chain trading at the time in the north-west of England under the name of the Happy Nut House. The smaller retailer must avoid price competition with the larger multiples which have the price advantage from economies in purchasing and operation.

THE HEALTH FOOD MARKET

Concern about a healthy diet has grown rapidly in the latter half of the twentieth century. In the 1950s the emphasis had been on 'proper' meals. In the 1960s dieting to keep slim became fashionable. In the 1970s lack of dietary fibre and a propensity to consume too much sugar, salt and hard fats were being blamed for a wide range of health problems from heart disease to varicose veins. In the 1980s artificial colourants and additives became the targets of nutritionists and popular press alike.

The greater publicity given to dietary issues was having its effects on consumption patterns. Between 1981 and 1984 sales of whole-wheat or wholemeal bread tripled. Consumption of fresh fruit and vegetables was on the increase, while sales of full cream milk and meat were falling. Farmers were looking more and more to organically grown crops. By 1987 over 2 million of Britain's population were said to be wholly and partially vegetarian. Within this environment sales of health foods were booming, while total food sales remained somewhat flat. Table 12.1 identifies the estimated growth in market size in the early 1980s, a performance that was projected to continue at least until 1990.

The market for health foods was divided between a number of distinct sectors (Table 12.2), with the specialist stores estimated to hold the largest single slice in 1984. This sector was, however, largely

Table 12.1 Size and growth of the health food market

	£ million (RSP)	% change
1982	200	
1983	230	15
1984	260	13
1985	300	15
1986 est.	350	15

Source: Mintel (1987).

Table 12.2 Shares of turnover in health foods, 1984

	% Share
Specialists	30
Grocery multiples	25
Chemists	20
Boots	15
Wholefood and grain outlets	10

Source: Euromonitor.

fragmented with a predominance of small, family-run stores (Table 12.3). Holland and Barrett, the single largest chain, contained a number of franchises and was part of the large Booker McConnell group. The same group included Brewhurst Wholesale, a distributor of health foods which supplied an estimated 60 per cent of the total market, including 83 per cent of Holland and Barrett products. Other associated interests included Allinsons and Prewitts. The next largest chain was Lifecycle, based solely in the South of England. A voluntary association of independents, Realfare, had attracted some 550 members. By 1987 the Happy Nut House, with 17 retail outlets located in the north-west of England, was the third largest chain.

Table 12.3 Health food stores, 1987

	No. of stores
Estimated total number of stores	1700
Holland and Barrett	160
Lifecycle	35
Happy Nut House	17

Source: Booker Health Foods, Mintel (1987).

The typical health food shop carried a varied range of products. Table 12.4 presents one view of the type of product mix that could be expected. Gross margins on many lines were relatively high at around 27–33 per cent compared to the margins expected by most mainstream food retailers for packaged groceries. Some independents trading in a typical 450–800 sq. ft store might achieve £8,000 per week turnover. Others might be only marginally profitable and offer their owners more satisfaction in retailing health food products than in financial returns.

Table 12.4   Selected products through specialist stores

Product	% of turnover by value
Vitamin and dietary supplements	36
Cereals	18
Pulses	11
Nuts	11
Snacks	9
Other foods	15

Source: Mintel.

Other types of retail outlet had traditionally competed for some of the same market as the health food shop. Vitamin products, for example, were well within the territory of the chemist. The leading chemist at the time was Boots. More recently the public's changing attitudes to food had attracted the attentions of the food multiples. Tesco had evolved an approach to nutritional labelling of their own-label foodstuffs that was to be copied by the manufacturers of national brands, and had used 'healthy eating' as a main plank in their promotion. Certain products that only 10 years earlier had been seen as unusual or even faddish had become major sellers for the multiples. Muesli was a typical example. By 1987 only 15 per cent of muesli was sold through health food shops. Other products such as bottled spring water became difficult to offer at a reasonable price by the independents, given the purchasing power and discount policies of the food multiples.

Less well-known products such as lecithin, carob and mung beans were still the preserve of the specialist health food store, which could offer advice to the uninitiated. However, only some 20 per cent of high-street shoppers had ventured into a health food store. Many regarded them as cranky and over-priced.

THE MARKET MODEL

To create a market model it was decided to select three health food specialists, Happy Nut House (HNH), Holland and Barrett and the 'independent health food shop'. The use of the latter term to represent the large number of independents was something of an experiment in that customers would have possibly rather different views on individual independents. Despite this, in practice the results were good enough to be of use.

To represent the larger multiples, Boots was selected as an example of a chemist, and Tesco as a grocer. The interviews were all conducted in areas served by HNH. The resulting research results and models are shown in Figures 12.1 and 12.2. The ideal store was described as 'the ideal health food and product shop', a clumsy phrase perhaps but one which we hoped would make it clearer to respondents to the market research that Boots and Tesco, in particular, were to be compared on their health products alone.

The ideal store itself is described by the long list of concepts shown in Table 12.5. A number are the same or similar to concepts describing the ideal food store (see Table 7.3). Others, however, such as those relating to staff (well-presented staff, well-trained staff, gives advice), were either segmenting concepts in mainstream retailing, or not relevant at all. It emphasized the extra advice sought in speciality shopping. The inclusion of vitamins and supplements emphasized a major area of business for health food shops (Table 12.4).

In the model itself the specialists were seen as having a different image from the mainstream Tesco and Boots, who were in turn more associated with the concept of being 'good for staple items'. The specialists were associated more with staff, underlining the points made earlier.

The problem facing the specialist in a market where the larger multiples have identified a significant trend, is to avoid price competition. Table 12.6 presents the results of a price comparison and stocking survey conducted in 1987 on a range of typical health shop products. Well-known brands and widely used health products such as decaffeinated coffee, honey and mineral water were generally cheaper in the larger stores. The specialist shop tended to stock more obscure and specialist products, but even these were often stocked by multiples in their own specialist sections.

To minimize any damaging price comparison HNH decided to substitute own-label products wherever possible in areas where the multiples had begun to dominate such as muesli, spring water and honey. In some product areas, for example honey, HNH stocked

	Happy Nut House	Holland and Barrett	Independent health food shop	Tesco	Boots	Good for staple items	Friendly approachable staff	Good for own label	Family orientated	Easy to shop at	Good for slimming products	Nice smelling	Good for takeaway food	The ideal shop
Happy Nut House	1													
Holland and Barrett	2.15	1												
Independent health food shop	3.57	2.72	1											
Tesco	5.35	4.14	6.87	1										
Boots	5.22	3.90	5.30	2.41	1									
Good for staple items	3.40	3.56	3.58	2.53	3.86	1								
Friendly approachable staff	2.72	3.28	2.68	4.40	3.31	3.63	1							
Good for own label	3.30	3.58	4.83	2.52	2.48	2.89	4.35	1						
Family orientated	3.91	3.89	4.11	2.78	2.61	3.03	3.06	3.88	1					
Easy to shop at	2.97	3.25	3.14	2.43	2.36	2.84	2.97	3.46	2.52	1				
Good for slimming products	2.96	3.04	3.44	4.01	2.02	2.84	4.24	3.79	4.70	4.32	1			
Nice smelling	2.98	3.27	3.07	4.43	3.32	4.94	3.93	4.59	3.93	3.99	4.86	1		
Good for takeaway food	2.82	3.61	4.51	6.04	5.14	3.82	3.93	4.34	4.05	3.18	4.96	3.19	1	
The ideal shop (health foods)	3.19	3.05	3.24	4.97	4.32	2.32	4.56	2.84	2.98	1.68	3.19	1.93	2.95	1

Figure 12.1   Health food retailing, 1985.

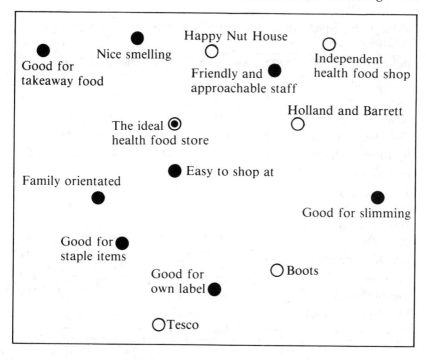

Figure 12.2 Health food retailing, 1985.

Table 12.5 Concepts describing the ideal health food store

Hygienic
Well-presented staff
Value for money
Wide range
More for women
Convenient
Good for vitamins and supplements
Well laid out
Good for natural products
Well-trained staff
Good choice
Gives advice

a wide selection of speciality lines. HNH offered honeys from many different countries and in a number of different types. HNH also sought new and even more specialist lines to replace those 'lost' to

Table 12.6 Selling prices (pence) of the same or similar products in various outlets

Product	ASDA	Sainsbury	Tesco	Superdrug	Boots	HNH
Orange juice 1-litre pack	45	42	45	42	—	54
Bran (500 g)	37	38	—	39	—	38
Café Hag (100 g)	178	178	178	188	188	199
Wholemeal flour	51	—	54	—	—	63
Perrier water	53	47	—	49	—	59
Jordans Health Bar (multipack)	—	75	75	69	62	78
Honey (1 lb) own label	—	62	69	69	—	79
Lecithin granules	—	—	—	—	255	255
Ginseng	—	—	—	—	447	469
Vecon (large)	—	—	—	—	159	159
Multivitamins (30) own label	—	125	125	50	—	119

the larger multiples. However, the problem remained that its competition was not just limited to the multiples. Holland and Barrett had the advantages both of economy of scale, and of controlling the major wholesaler in the market.

By 1987 HNH had grown to a chain of seventeen stores and a turnover of over £3 million a year from modest beginnings in 1976. It had benefited from the high growth rate in health products but was, by 1987, feeling the price pressure of the larger multiples and other specialist competition. The owners recognized the need to innovate and evolve the 'health food shop of the 1990s' but lacked the profits to experiment with their more radical ideas. Ultimately the business was sold to Holland and Barrett, who were themselves struggling to generate reasonable profits, but who were better placed to finance the necessary changes to maintain a specialist image.

The problem for the smaller independent who has probably grown on the back of rising sales for a specialist product or service, is that this success is the source of failure when the multiples are attracted into the market. However, as this study indicates, as long as the independent can avoid price competition, the major threat can be limited to the other specialists in the market.

KEY POINT SUMMARY

(1) Positioning strategy is relevant to the specialist retailer, especially in identifying the main non-price points of differentiation from the larger competition.

(2) In the example of health food retailing, the specialist stores had to move away from many products which had been their traditional preserve. A major point of difference for them in retailing their more speciality products was customer service, in that shoppers looked for advice. While this would mean extra cost, it would justify the higher selling price inherent in speciality retailing.

(3) In this example the main threat to one specialist proved, in the end, to be another, larger specialist which was better able to exploit the market.

References

Mintel (1987) *Market Intelligence: Health Food Shops*, January.

Chapter 13

The Elements of Image

In this chapter we assess some of the points which have emerged in earlier chapters about the image of a retail store together with some of the ideas on retail image presented by other authors. Our purpose in this chapter is to offer the reader an overview of what retail image really is, as a precursor of the final chapter where the various ways of developing a successful positioning strategy are discussed.

A major theme in this book is that retailing strategy can draw not only from corporate strategy but quite often from ideas and concepts in consumer marketing. The various maps that have been presented demonstrate that shoppers are perfectly able to pigeonhole something as complex as a retail organization, and to differentiate between competing retailers using often quite simple measures. There is clear evidence from the various models and the related financial analyses that having a 'good' image is a determinant of commercial success. A 'good' image appears to be one which differentiates the store from its competitors or one which positions it close to the general view of the ideal retailer in a given sector. Companies such as Marks and Spencer in the department store sector, and Sainsbury in food retailing, have managed to combine both approaches, being simultaneously close to the ideal and differentiated from competition.

What causes shoppers to differentiate a store is, by definition, the image of that store. The simplest approach is likely to be based solely on price. Kwik Save offers an excellent example of price-led retailing to the point where price advantage is not only its main corporate platform but also its main image factor. MFI offers a similar example of a genuine price-led strategy being successful, because the retailer has a real economic advantage on which to base the strategy.

In the previous chapters a good deal of evidence is presented to confirm the view that it is not good enough to evolve a coherent image for a retailer, but that image must be different from others on offer in the market place. Lewis's succeeded by moving away from Debenhams. Asda suffered because Tesco moved closer to their position in the market. All West German department stores, most British menswear retailers (in the early 1980s) and the larger DIY retailers suffered from a lack of differentiation. Among electrical retailers there appeared to be a need to move away from mere price promotion, as few seemed to have a real economic advantage to sustain a long-term, price-led strategy. There was no shortage of image-led options.

An obvious but none the less important point to emerge from all the image studies is the value of a hypothetical 'ideal' store in each market sector. The position of the ideal store acts as a marker or reference point in each model. However, the facts that some image factors can be included in the ideal, and that some are more useful in segmenting the market, need further comment.

In the food retailing example, the composition of the factors describing the ideal store changed over the three years. 'Value for money' and 'good for fresh foods' both joined the ideal. It has been argued that customers had come to expect different things from their food retailer, and that these factors would have to be offered by all mainstream food retailers. Ideal factors do not offer the retailer any basis for differentiation other than by being placed closest to them, or possibly by deliberately differentiating from some of them. A position closest to the ideal is not easy to achieve, given that all retailers will have to encompass some of the ideal factors to compete at all in the same sector. Deliberate differentiation from the ideal is a dangerous approach to take, given that being placed too far from the ideal, which is after all the average view of what constitutes a good place to shop, will limit the size of the market segment to which the retailer can appeal. Kendals, for example, was well differentiated in the department store model, but by being associated with concepts that were some distance from the ideal and which might only appeal to a minority.

It is also important for a retailer to be associated with at least one relevant concept in positioning strategy. Both the Co-op in food retailing, and Woolworth in department and variety chain retailing, suffered by not being associated with a clear position. They were each different from their competitors but neither had a clear point of differentiation. Differentiation can, therefore, only be valid where the reason for difference is both clear to, and valued by, the customer.

All the empirical work presented in this book is based on the measurement of customer perception. How customers perceive retail stores is clearly important. Here we begin to examine the various ideas that have been put forward to explain retail image, and the various theoretical concepts associated with image, such as perception itself. We have produced a model of buyer behaviour in retailing. So, based on what was said briefly in Chapter 3 about such models, can some theoretical concepts be used to expand on the ideas from our empirical results?

THEORIES ABOUT PERCEPTION

There is no shortage of academic theory that endeavours to explain human behaviour. Unfortunately no single theory explains all behaviour to the satisfaction of all academics, but certain theoretical approaches have been more successful than others in explaining certain specific areas of behaviour. We attempt, therefore, to abstract a number of ideas from social and psychological thought which, we feel, will help one to understand how customers build and receive images of retail organizations.

It is generally agreed that human beings strive to make sense of their environment. Because we cannot understand everything in detail but equally because we need to place everything we experience into some kind of framework, we tend to simplify the complexity around us. As pointed out in Chapter 3, there are two main theories on how we achieve this, the so-called behavioural and cognitive approaches. A typical behavioural approach describes human behaviour by arguing that the human will react in a learned or predetermined way to a given set of stimuli. The cognitive approach argues that we have a pattern in our minds which we use to assess any new situation. When the situation matches the pattern of what are now internal cues, we make a judgement about what we are experiencing. On average people will share many of the same patterns and will behave in similar ways in similar circumstances.

The two approaches differ in many ways. One could argue, from the behaviourist model, that it should be relatively easy to get customers to absorb a retail image once the key stimuli have been identified. The cognitive approach implies that image formation is more complex and more difficult to affect in practice because it involves identifying what the typical customer's cognitive map looks like in any retailing situation.

In many ways our results tend to support the idea of a cognitive explanation of retail image, in that the MDS models can be regarded as representing the average structure which customers perceive a market to have. They seem to represent some inherent model that the typical customer holds of competing retailers. However, the idea that there are a number of key external stimuli that will cause customers to form or modify their image and behaviour towards a retail outlet could still be of value and will not be discarded yet.

To concentrate first on the cognitive view of perception and behaviour, the idea of the customer dealing with the complexity of making choices within a retail market-place based on a simplified model of that situation could have value. Figure 13.1 presents the idea in diagrammatic form. The human being picks up data via his or her senses. The data are processed by the brain. The pattern in

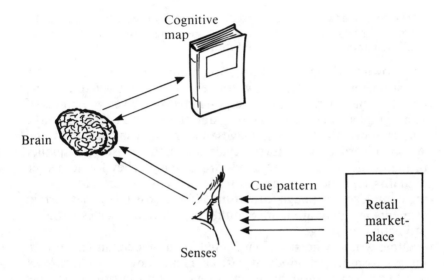

Figure 13.1   A cognitive model of perception.

the data is compared to a cognitive map formed by the individual and informed by experience. A need to purchase will be referred to the individual's cognitive map which will determine which outlets to visit in the expectation of satisfying that need.

The model can be used to explain why shoppers react against retail outlets which lack a clear and coherent image. The typical shopper receives a confused set of cues or messages about the store. This confusion is passed to the brain to be sorted into some logical pattern. The brain refers to this cognitive map, but the data cannot be matched against the individual's cognitive map. The individual may experience what Leon Festinger (1957) described as 'cognitive dissonance' – that feeling of unease when what is perceived cannot be rationalized. The object causing the dissonance could well be labelled with a number of negative feelings and associations, or it could be rejected from the individual's map as the individual seeks 'cognitive consonance', a rationale, at all costs. In either case the retailer will not be included when a shopping decision is to be made, evoking the typical response, 'Well I never thought to visit them for that!' or, because the in-store offer is confused or confusing, 'You can never get what you are after there!'

Other authors have argued similarly for a cognitive explanation of the way store image is formed. Mazursky and Jacoby (1985, 1986) describe their view of image formation thus:

> The consumer extracts and perceives certain features from... reality and forms beliefs and/or affects which are congruent with his or her idiosyncratic cognitive configuration.

Their own work on image formation modelled the situation where a customer is faced with a new store either by being new to an area, or following a new opening. Respondents were given portfolios of photographs and data on 'stores', and the research centred on the data shoppers used to form images of stores in what Mazursky and Jacoby regarded as the three key areas: quality of service, quality of merchandise and pleasantness of shopping. They found people used different cues to assess a store for a given property, underlying the complexity of image formation and the possibility that certain elements in the retailing mix could be predicted to be essential in projecting an image.

Other writers who have contributed to our understanding of how images form in the minds of customers and how customers react as a result, have thought of retail image as an 'attitude' or have described it in such a way as to imply that label. An attitude is a predisposition to react in a certain way to a certain stimulus. As such, an attitudinal explanation for image is more compatible with a behavioural model of store image and customer action, in that a given set of circumstances may trigger a given response in the shopper. Many of the more anecdotal statements about store image contain the explicit or implicit assumption that a shopper's image of a store is akin to an attitude.

Pierre Martineau is, quite rightly, often quoted in reviews of early work on retail image. His 1958 paper contained the statement cited in Chapter 8: 'The shopper seeks the store whose image is most congruent with the image she has of herself'. Martineau defined store image as: 'the way in which the store is defined in the shopper's mind, partly by its functional qualities and partly by an aura of psychological attributes'. Thus Martineau explains store patronage by arguing that certain types of shopper will frequent the stores they see as being for them. That is not to say that shoppers can be expected in the model to frequent only one type of store. In the research work conducted by Lewis's (see in Chapter 8) one shopper explained how she felt 'like a housewife and mother' when shopping at one store and 'like a woman' when shopping at another. This implies that a store can choose to appeal to a person in a particular state of mind and that a single customer can have a number of such 'states'.

The idea of market segmentation based on attitudes rather than demographic factors was mentioned in Chapter 3. Demographic and attitudinal factors have been successfully used to position different retail chains within the same retail organization, for example, Burtons. In its corporate advertising in 1986 Burtons described its various offerings (Table 13.1) using a mixture of demographic (the young market, the teenage market, etc.) and psychographic (the style market, the Knightsbridge market) labels (see, for example, *The Observer*, 23 November 1986, p. 9). Clearly even 'the young market' can be taken to include the 'young at heart' as well as those of limited age. A shopper could well patronize more than one Burton outlet, seeking different satisfactions each time. Other Burton chains such as Evans are targeted at tighter, demographic groups.

Table 13.1   Positioning of different Burton outlets, 1986

Dorothy Perkins	The young market
Principles	The style market
Top Shop/Top Man	The teenage market
Evans	The larger market
Burton	The men's market
Harvey Nichols	The Knightsbridge market
Debenhams	The family market

To summarize the contribution that formal theory can make to an understanding of retail image, the behaviourists' approach of conditioning seems more useful in describing behaviour once the shopper has entered the store, and how shoppers form images of stores. Certain stimuli may affect our perception of a given store. The cognitive approach is more useful in explaining how shoppers differentiate between stores, by using something akin to a map of competing stores, to decide where to shop.

One of the problems with approaching retail image from the more fundamental perspectives of the social sciences is that it is sometimes difficult to see direct links between theory and practice. Martineau's definition of image could, for example, be compatible with both cognitive and behavioural theory. While an academic understanding of retail image, even an imperfect one, can be more useful, it is probably more valuable to bypass basic theory and try to identify lists of factors, possibly through market research, which might be of practical use in projecting image. The next section examines some of the work and ideas that stem from a pragmatic approach to the issue of retail image.

EMPIRICAL STUDIES ON RETAIL IMAGE

There has been much research on retail image. While this has been based on many different sectors and sometimes individual stores, there may be some general truths to be gleaned by examining some of these studies.

One of the potentially more valuable pieces of work on retail image was by J.D. Lindquist, who in 1974 published a review of a number of earlier works on the subject. He tried to assess what seemed to be important in store image, by listing all the areas covered in earlier studies and by identifying those areas used most often to measure image. Table 13.2 lists the nine attribute areas identified

Table 13.2   Lindquist's summary of attributes

(1)	Merchandise
(2)	Service
(3)	Clientele
(4)	Physical facilities
(5)	Convenience
(6)	Promotion
(7)	Atmosphere
(8)	Institutional factors
(9)	Post-transaction satisfaction

by Lindquist and dealt with in greater detail in Chapter 6. Table 13.3 lists the areas he found to be most often mentioned by earlier researchers. Two points emerge: the long list of individual factors, and the dominance of merchandise factors in earlier work.

L.L. Berry (1969), concentrating on department stores, cited twelve image criteria which he showed accounted for 99 per cent of the responses made by shoppers in his studies of actual stores (Table 13.4). There are some overlaps with Lindquist's listings.

The work of both Lindquist and Berry is compatible with the idea of a retail mix (see Chapter 3), the idea that a number of factors

Table 13.3 Research frequency of image areas (from Lindquist, 1974)

Area	Scholar mentions (%)
Merchandise selection/assortment	42
Merchandise quality	38
Merchandise pricing	38
Locational convenience	35
Merchandise styling/fashion	27
Service, general	27
Sales clerk service	27

Table 13.4 Berry's 12 image criteria

(1)	Price of merchandise
(2)	Quality of merchandise
(3)	Assortment of merchandise
(4)	Fashion of merchandise
(5)	Sales personnel
(6)	Location convenience
(7)	Other convenience factors
(8)	Services
(9)	Sales promotions
(10)	Advertising
(11)	Store atmosphere
(12)	Reputation on adjustments

blend to form a store image, and that there are various key factors. Another idea, that stores and specific customer groups could be linked, has been taken up in a number of studies. Weale (1961), for example, proposed that customers might ask themselves four questions about a store:

(1) Who are the other shoppers?
(2) How will the sales clerks treat me?
(3) What are the price ranges?
(4) Do I fit in that store?

The hypothesis is that a certain 'type' of person would shop at a certain 'type' of store, in many ways the basis of market segmentation. But three of Weale's four questions emphasize one point not stressed so far: the importance of personal interaction with other shoppers and sales assistants in retail patronage.

Rich and Portis (1964) studied nine stores and found they could be classified into three 'appeal' groups: high fashion, price appeal and broad appeal. They found that the price appeal stores had few other image components in their portfolio. Each group appealed more strongly to different shopper groups, with high-income, high fashion-conscious women at one extreme, and lower-income groups at the other. This more traditional view of market segmentation, with socioeconomic group playing a key role, contrasts with studies where attitude is claimed to be more important. In two of the authors' studies reported earlier, two clearly price-led retailers, MFI and Kwik Save, both claimed a broad cross-section of partonage when measured by socioeconomic group.

Leon Arons (1961) used customer type and behaviour to explain patronage. His work established that while the majority of people shopped in various stores in a given sector, they did not shop equally at each store. He found the store shopped at most frequently was seen by its patrons as having the better image. This introduces the idea of a 'first choice store' which a shopper might select to visit from all the stores seen as having a similar offer.

After reviewing previous research into store loyalty, Bellinger *et al*. (1976) claimed that such research showed socioeconomic and demographic variables were generally of limited use in explaining store patronage. Their own work tended to confirm this view and to lend support to the congruence theory of compatibility between a shopper's self-image and the image of the preferred store, as first explained by Martineau (1958).

In summary, empirical studies on store image allow us to draw a number of conclusions:

(1)   A number of studies show that store image and customer behaviour are linked. This complements the results of our work which did not measure patronage, but sought instead to establish direct links to overall financial performance.

(2)   Image is complex and can have a long list of contributing elements. However, merchandise, service and location seem to be the three most important elements.

(3)   Store image and customer type appear to be linked and both demographic and psychographic measures *can* be useful in defining customer type, although the same customers will often patronize very different stores at different times.

On the surface there are no unequivocal links between the more theoretical, behavioural and the more empirical studies. One of the problems is that what might be true in one retail sector in one country at one period in time may not hold true for all sectors at all times. The one pointer that does emerge, however, is the presence of a few key groups of factors. Whatever behavioural model one accepts and whatever general truth there may be from any one empirical study, it seems fair to assume that shoppers form store images which determine behaviour and that a limited number of factors hold the key to image formation.

Of these factors our own work would certainly support the inclusion of merchandise and service, but we would query the inclusion of location as a prime factor in *image*. High-image stores such as Habitat trade from secondary locations, and the only apparent point of differentiation for the Co-op was convenience, a location factor which did not appear to be highly valued. However, the DIY and furniture retailer markets appear to segment around the high street and out of town.

In a minority of circumstances, where location affects the trading method, location will have an effect on image. For example, if location were more relevant to image, Tie Rack's location in mainline stations would be an image issue. Location nevertheless affects the number of customers who are able to sample the retailer's offer and thus the overall turnover. We are arguing that location is not so effective in forming of store image. Concepts related to location were notably absent from any of the models apart from 'convenience', which was found to be a poor discriminator in food retailing.

Finally, why are price and advertising not included among our key areas in image formation? First, what of price in retail image?

THE ROLE OF PRICE IN IMAGE

Throughout this book it has been argued that price is a strategic option to be used only with an economic advantage. The retailer's cost advantage, where it is real, must be perceived and valued by the customer as it is with MFI and Kwik Save. However, it is also clear that while retailers generally feature price in their promotions, many as a major theme, it is not the most successful of strategies, and does not generally contribute positively to a retailer's overall image. Customers seem to need reassurance on price, or probably on value for money, rather than just the image of price competitiveness, unless the retailer has a genuine advantage to offer them.

Further information on the role of price in retail positioning can be gleaned from the multidimensional scaling (MDS) models and from a proposition by Doyle and Fenwick (1974–75) in another MDS study on retailing.

In introducing the technique of MDS we emphasized that the traditional x and y axes had no real meaning. While this is true at one level, in that the concepts define a series of discrete points and distances in any direction from them have equal value, Doyle and Fenwick (1974–75) point out that the x and y axes do represent the two directions of maximum variance in an MDS map. They argue that the axes must, therefore, have some meaning and have attempted to label them.

The reader is invited to do the same in each of the models presented in this book by the authors. In many of the models it is possible to argue that either the x or y axis represents 'price' and that the other represents 'ambience'. For example, in the Manchester department store models a horizontal axis could well represent price with Kendals at the high end and BHS at the low end. The vertical axis could represent ambience with Kendals and Marks and Spencer in the high-ambience half and Debenhams in the low-ambience half. Similar observations can be made in the food retailer model, this time with price being the vertical axis, but it is less clear whether there is a useful horizontal axis. In other models, a label for the price axis does not appear to be present, for example in DIY retailing where 'saves you money' appears instead, as a concept within the ideal.

If price is generally present as an axis in most MDS models, it could be evidence that price contributes the image of most retailers (although only those on the extremes of the price axis would be using it successfully as the basis for positioning strategy). This compromise between the view that price should be avoided entirely in retail positioning strategy unless the retailer has as economic advantage, and the view that price promotion is relevant in all retailing, means that retailers can use an element of price appeal, even when this cannot form the main positioning platform, as long as there is another non-price factor which can be used truly to differentiate the store. It follows that the weaker this non-price factor, the stronger the price claim would have to be and vice versa.

Reversing the logic for a moment, those retailers trading in circumstances where their costs make a strong price claim difficult, could be advised to seek a strong non-price basis for positioning, even if this involves raising their cost structure. The reader is referred to the difference in commercial performance between British and West German department stores. The West German stores competed largely on price and remained largely undifferentiated, while the British stores sought to segment their market-place and were generally seeking non-price niches. Indeed the next development in Debenhams was heavy investment to move away from a dependence on a largely price-led position.

THE ROLE OF ADVERTISING IN STORE IMAGE

Advertising is central to the development of an image for a consumer product. In retailing, any such direct links between advertising and image are less obvious, if they exist at all.

The absence of such a link in menswear retailing (Chapter 5) tended to be confirmed in the studies on food retailing. In the department store model, Lewis's used a substantial campaign to support their change of image but other uses of advertising in retailing seem more relevant. For example, the out-of-town retailers, MFI, ASDA and the larger DIY retailers, all appear to rely heavily on advertising. However, until ASDA's change of strategy in 1985-86, all these retailers majored on a price message in their advertising.

Christina Fulop produced a detailed analysis of British retailer advertising in 1986. She pointed to the rapid rise in retailer advertising, linked in the case of food retailing by Davies, Gilligan and Sutton (1985) to the change in power between retailer and manufacturer. Fulop (1986) enlarged on the theme of changing power by observing that economists have argued that a distributive system dominated by retailers and their brands is likely to be more efficient because total advertising costs can be reduced as retailers can promote in their shop windows and in-store displays. Fulop further commented that retailer advertising tends to be more informative than persuasive in its objectives, concentrating on imparting data on prices and availability. Manufacturer advertising contains higher levels of imagery and promotion.

Retailers rely less on television advertising. In 1985 in Britain it accounted for a mere 6 per cent of expenditure while 21 per cent of budgets was spent on press advertising. Fulop argues that the kind of message retailers need to communicate is better done in the press. Retail advertising also dominates radio advertising.

Fulop (1986) claims that an absence of advertising expenditure by some leading retailers, Marks and Spencer, John Lewis and BHS for example, can be explained by a strong high-street presence and in the case of Marks and Spencer, an image of service. Some of the least successful retailers are also to be found among the heaviest advertisers, for example the Co-op and Woolworth. Woolworth offers an even stronger example of the lack of linkage between advertising, image and commercial performance in retailing. Woolworth advertising has often been highly successful in advertising terms, with arguably limited effect on long-term commercial performance. As mentioned in Chapter

8, 'The Wonder of Woolies' campaign achieved a reported 86 per cent recall rate (Piercy, 1983) in the 1970s, but Woolworth's commercial measures did not seem to respond.

We are somewhat at a loss to explain why advertising can affect product image but not retailer image. Other elements in the retail mix appear to be far more effective. Perhaps one practitioner's comment on retail advertising in general is relevant: 'Diabolical is the word you are looking at when you talk about retail advertising' (Sturges, 1986). The implication was that retailers had still to discover effective image-building advertising that worked for them. Perhaps this is true, and advertising agencies should be concentrating on developing effective image-promoting campaigns for retailers. A good summary of the role of advertising in retailing can be found in Lowe's (1983) book on retailer advertising. He claims that advertising is 'no more than a tool, a means by which you create store traffic' and that 'all stores occupy a position somewhere in the marketplace. It is therefore important that the store's advertising matches that position.' Lowe regards advertising as an operational factor encouraging visits to the store and explaining positioning, rather than a strategic factor creating that positioning. This is a totally different role for advertising from that in most product marketing where advertising is often the main platform for positioning. This view of retailer advertising is given further support by Ornstein (1976) in his book based on a series of interviews with retailers in the 1970s. Ornstein found that advertising budgets were often allocated to individual stores rather than being spent centrally for corporate purposes.

For the time being it is not possible to link advertising and image promotion, except where the image platform is price. Retailers positioning on non-price factors must be very wary of using advertising to communicate their strategy to customers. It is likely that a retail image cannot be built through advertising alone.

REFURBISHMENT AND IMAGE

The 1980s saw a boom and then a slight decline in the fortunes of the store designer in Britain. By 1985 Mintel were estimating the size of the market for design services at £20 million. The lifespan of a retail design was being estimated at between three and five years for a fashion store and between five and seven years in less volatile retail sectors (Mintel, 1985). Burton's Ralph Halpern (1985) was claiming that 'Change is constant. Innovation and specialisation with authority the Key'.

Mintel surveyed 44 retailers in 1984 on their experiences of design changes. Table 13.5 shows part of their findings. Design changes appear to be effective, if somewhat costly. Fashion stores tended to spend at the rate of £50 per square foot. Woolworth reportedly spent £30-35 per square foot in its change to the general store concept which yielded an increase in average sales per customer from £2 to £2.50. Estimates for the more ambitious changes, such as the introduction of a galleria concept into Debenhams department store, ranged up to £130 per square foot.

Table 13.5 Success rating of retail design (%, 44 respondents)

	Change of image (%)	Increased store traffic (%)	Increased average spend (%)
Better than expected	25	15	9
As good as expected	43	61	56
Not so good as expected	11	5	7
Don't know	14	14	23
Not an objective	7	5	5

Source: British Market Research Bureau (BMRB)/No. 14 Mintel Retail Design, Summer 1985.

NEXT, as we saw in Chapter 5, was launched with a mere £140,000 spent on advertising but with around £70,000 per shop on refitting. Turnover in such outlets jumped from £10,000 to £30,000 a week, but a new trading format had been introduced as well as a new image.

Refurbishment and the implementation of a new design concept can, it seems, pay handsomely. New concepts do not always succeed, but a refit appears to be one of the more cost effective ways of changing image or implementing an image change. Why then does it not appear more clearly in much of the published work cited earlier in this chapter? Ambience factors are certainly apparent in many of the MDS models, with concepts such as 'comfortable' and 'good for browsing', for example, in the department store models. There could be two explanations. Ambience factors are less easy to articulate, and can therefore be difficult to include in market research. Many ambience factors are effective only at the subconscious level and serve to enhance other, more obvious elements such as merchandise. Certainly many refurbishments in the 1980s concentrated on creating more space, and resulted in less stock on the shop-floor than was previously felt advisable. Merchandise could, therefore, be far better displayed.

The real explanation could be simpler and more direct. We have argued that a store image is active at the psychological level. It is intrinsically complex and difficult to tie down. The successful retail image-makers are seen by their peers as having the same 'feel' for their work as the successful marketers of brands. There is a limit to the extent to which the intangible qualities of a successful brand or retail operation can be formally defined. Flair is easily observed, but less easily codified. While it can be straightforward to identify gaps in markets and to identify the general direction in which a retail company should move to reposition itself more advantageously, translating a positioning statement into practice is unlikely to be achieved without a deal of creativity.

By definition a retail image must appeal at a level that makes it difficult to describe precisely; members of the public are not likely to describe a retailer's image by using words like 'well thought out design concept'. They will be happier to use merchandise-related terms or at best to talk about 'ambience'.

THE ROLE OF OWN-LABEL AND OWN-BRAND PRODUCTS

As the balance of power shifted from manufacturer to retailer in the latter quarter of this century, it is easy to forget that the forerunners of the modern retailer were far less concerned with national brands than were retailers in the 1960s. Traditionally retailers provided a packeting service to customers, buying loose bulk and retailing in usable quantities. What is different about today's retailers is the way they have learned to use own-label products to promote source loyalty and to promote image in an era when the typical shopper is far more mobile and is faced with a greater choice of where to shop.

There are a number of economic reasons why own-label products have become more important. In certain sectors, such as food (Davies, Gilligan and Sutton, 1985), over-capacity in the manufacturing sector has been a major factor. Manufacturers often start offering own-label products by marginally costing their excess capacity to offer a lower price. Some smaller manufacturers gave up trying to compete with the leading brands and chose instead to cut promotional budgets and concentrate on own-label products.

The second economic reason for the growth of the own brand is the high level of promotional expenditure, consumer advertising and trade marketing costs, comprising about 15 per cent of product selling price. An own-label product does not need such a high promotional margin. With an own brand, the retailer can make a higher margin and still sell at a lower price compared to a national brand. A third economic factor is the increased concentration in retail buying power. Retail chains have become increasingly larger and the advantage of centralization as part of the shift towards systems retailing has further concentrated buying expertise. One leading British food retailer can now afford to have a buyer spend all his or her time on white bread rolls, such is the purchase volume involved.

Taking food as an example, by the end of 1986 six retailers – Sainsbury, Tesco, ASDA, Dee, Argyll and Kwik Save – accounted for some 68.5 per cent of UK packaged grocery sales (NMRA, 1986) out of a total share for all multiples of nearly 78 per cent. In 1983 the average for own-label sales as a percentage of all sales was estimated at 27 per cent, with a range from 53 per cent (Sainsbury) to 7 per cent (ASDA) and 0 per cent (Kwik Save). Kwik Save's market positioning was to major on brands but by 1986 ASDA was racing to increase its sales of own brand.

Early policies by most food retailers seemed to be to use own label to cut prices. The price advantages for what came to be called 'generics' (see Table 7.4) were often quite staggering at up to 45 per cent below brand prices. Such tactics seemed compatible with the price-led promotional strategies of the 1970s and could be justified by the economic climate. However, when retailers began to examine the market they had created, the typical own-label buyer was more likely to be the middle-class housewife rather than the unemployed or retired person. Various theories have been put forward to explain this, ranging from the fact that the working-class housewives are generally more avid watchers of commercial television and therefore of brand advertising, to the possibility that the middle-class housewife can afford to make a mistake if the own-label product is poor quality while the working-class housewife cannot, and therefore buys the security of a national brand.

Certainly British food retailers in the 1980s made great strides to improve the real and perceived quality of their own-label lines. Out went the brash labels with the retailer's name being prominent, in came the quality control departments, the designers and nutritional labelling – often somewhat ahead of what the branded goods manufacturers were achieving. Soon it became possible to talk of own-brand, own-label and generic products as three distinct sectors. Generic products sold purely on price in utilitarian packaging: own label sold mainly on price, but own-brand products sold only marginally below brand prices. Marks and Spencer and Sainsbury were the major exponents of own branding in the 1970s, but in the 1980s it became the norm throughout the food sector.

In the fashion sectors own branding had been widespread for longer. Retailers such as Dutch-based C & A offered their clothes under various different labels but nearly all lines were exclusive to them. Marks and Spencer, NEXT, Principles and Dorothy Perkins all majored on their own-name lines. In the British electrical retail market in the early 1980s own labelling was just beginning, with marks like Saisho in Dixons and Solarvox in Comet. Manufacturers talked about 'stencil' models, meaning models they made especially for a given retailer with cosmetic differences, to allow the retailer to claim an exclusive price.

In the furniture study own branding was less prominent. However, the link between MFI and the Hygena brand was close enough for many customers to assume they were the same company. In 1987 MFI bought Hygena as part of a management buyout from ASDA. The department store study offered what appears to be an almost unique example of a retailer, Lewis's, using an increase in national brands as an element in its promotional strategy. Others, such as the House of Fraser, were moving in the other direction.

Own label or own brand is, therefore, a growth area and the potential in almost all product areas is often ignored. How soon will it be, for example, before the own-label car makes its appearance? The European car industry was suffering from gross over-capacity throughout the 1970s and 1980s. Promotional margins on cars were high (figures of £500 per car were quoted). ASDA entered the car retailing market in 1986 although they withdrew in 1987. Halfords were well positioned in the DIY car maintenance business. In France, the Fiat Carrefour was being marketed. While few would argue that national brands will disappear entirely it is not unreasonable to expect that the trend to own label will continue to include such areas as the motor car sooner or later.

A good deal is talked about home shopping. The potential exists for every household to have a computer linked to local retailers who would each have their various offerings listed on computer files. The household could order via the computer system and it is easy to envisage software packages that select the retailer offering the best combination of prices for the routine needs of the household. But this is only possible when the computer or its owner can compare prices directly. National brands can be price compared far more easily than can a retailer's own brand, where the household's perception of the retailer's price/quality relationship will be important if not vital. While we await this technological revolution, retailers are already realizing the advantages of moving into own label to promote source loyalty and avoid price competition. The emphasis, as was implied earlier, is on quality own-label rather than cheap own-label products.

The final advantage of own label lies in control. Fashion retailing offers a good example of the advantages for retailers of controlling their products from production to shop. Both Benetton and Jaeger are as much manufacturers as retailers. Benetton in particular relies on a policy of low stockholding costs with a rapid response to trends in consumer purchasing. Many fashion manufacturers hold stock of unfinished products, for example undyed cottonwear, to be dyed to the shade which their computerized information system tells them is moving well at the point of sale.

In some instances, quality control can be a weakness in own label. The retailer who sees such products as being important cannot afford poor or variable quality. The responsibility for such factors may seem to be with the manufacturer but ultimately it is retailers who must accept that role if their name is on the product. The large number of technologists employed by Marks and Spencer indicates one of the consequences of taking own label seriously.

Finally, the responsibility for product innovation is likely to shift towards the retailer who produces own-label goods. Manufacturers cannot be expected to produce as many new ideas for national brands, if demands for own label or near copies follow any successes they might have. While this may be a disbenefit, for the retailer it offers the potential to develop new products or variants which are more compatible with their own position in the market-place. In other words own label offers potential advantage over brands in positioning and differentiation. Fashion and other retailers talk in terms of lifestyle marketing, producing and offering a range of products compatible with an orientation on life. The major exponents of this approach in Britain are shops like NEXT, Habitat and Laura Ashley where a certain look co-ordinates a mixed range of merchandise. Whether customers are attracted because the lifestyle is that which they perceive to be theirs, or whether the co-ordination of products by the retailer merely makes selection easier for the shopper, is less relevant than the fact that a strict control of merchandise under a common theme is clearly advantageous in offering a coherent image.

THEORY VERSUS PRACTICE IN EXPLAINING IMAGE

A theoretical view of retail image provides us with the idea of a shopper responding to an organized presentation of competing retail images, with certain factors being more likely to form the basis of the way the shopper perceives what is presented. The various empirical studies start with the presumption of some mechanism linking the retail offer to purchasing behaviour, but the studies are almost confusing in the variety and range of factors which they identify as most important in image formation. Merchandise, ambience, service factors and the reaction between shoppers and retail personnel are common themes and ones which have often proved relevant in the MDS models presented in this book. From our work price and ambience do appear to be significant factors, with service and merchandise factors being supporters of these two major themes. Of the two major themes, price is the more often tried by retailers.

Empirical studies offer a good picture of how a retailer can successfully project an image. Without much doubt store design is the most successful method of image formation. Advertising, on the other hand, is unlikely to do more than inform the public about an image. Its ability to create one is, at best, unproven. Finally, own labelling is an obvious way of achieving a desired position on the price dimension in any market, and at the same time offers the retailer a way of controlling image. Where the retailer is keen to major on price, discounting national brands is a credible approach as we see in Europe and the USA.

Before moving on to the final chapter, which identifies how retailers can create the best possible image for themselves, there is one other area of empirical work to be considered: the interaction between individual departments within a store and between individual stores within a chain in projecting an image.

DEPARTMENT, STORE AND CHAIN IMAGES

Earlier in this chapter we commented that people are capable of rationalizing complex things such as a retail operation, and dealing with them in terms of a number of simple factors. But several studies indicate that shoppers can also hold separate images of individual departments within stores, indicating that the overall image can have a number of contributing elements. Further, it is clear from the department store and other surveys that shoppers can hold images both of local stores and national chains.

Work by Cardozo (1974–75) on the additive nature of store image showed that a customer's perception of a store could actually change depending on the product being sought. The different image of Marks and Spencer in the food and department store models is a clear example of this, with Marks and Spencer seen as the specialist in food, but as the ideal department store. McGoldrick (1979), in analysing the Manchester Marks and Spencer store, showed that certain departments could play a more important role in defining image at store level. But perhaps the study that reveals best the effects on store image of what happens in individual departments came from Robert Myers (1960). Myers reported the result of a 'walkout' study of shoppers leaving a midwestern American department store given the pseudonym of Brants. Brants' management perceived their store to be a 'quality, prestige' department store. Myers methodology was to interview only those people leaving the store who had *not* made a purchase. Some 2,654 people not carrying a Brant package were stopped, 1,260 of whom had not made any purchase.

Myers' interviewers determined which departments the shoppers had visited and compared the proportion of walkouts each department accounted for, with the proportion of daily transactions in the same department. Myers proposed that departments exhibiting a higher percentage of walkouts than transactions were potentially problem departments. For example 'main store dresses' accounted for 15.3 per cent of walkouts but only 2.7 per cent of transactions. Figures for sportswear were 5.2 per cent walkouts and 1.8 per cent transactions respectively. Brants' management subsequently changed the merchandise on offer in the problem departments. In dresses sales increased by just short of 100 per cent. Sportswear sales increased by some 150 per cent. In total the store increased sales by twice the local average over the study period.

The inference from Myers' work is that customers were drawn to the store with a certain expectation stemming from their image of Brants. The merchandise or its presentation in certain departments was not compatible with, or did not live up to, the store image. The solution was to change the merchandise in departments or the way it was displayed, to promote greater coherence between department and store image.

Myers' approach was used by one of the authors in two walkout studies of the Manchester House of Fraser department store, Kendals (Brooks, 1988). Transaction data were not available to duplicate fully Myers work, but a number of conclusions were identical to those from Myers' work and a number of new elements were identified.

Kendals operated on seven floors including a basement. Thirty-five per cent of those interviewed had visited the ground floor. The two fashion floors accounted for some 23 per cent. Some 70 per cent shopped only between the basement and second floor. The typical respondent had visited an average of 2.12 departments. High walkout rates were recorded in certain departments, in particular in fashion goods, perfumery and stationery. The fashion goods findings were similar to those of Myers.

In the second of the two Kendals surveys, data were gathered on shoppers' opinions of departments. They were asked to name 'best' and 'worst' departments. The numbers of both types of comment were tabulated against each department. Ladies fashions, the food hall, menswear and perfumery each achieved relatively high levels of comment. The first three accounted for almost half of all consumer comments and most remarks centred on merchandise range. Some departments received little or no comment. It was possible to categorize departments from very high to very low profile in terms of the number of mentions made by shoppers.

The survey led to the conclusion that the high-profile departments were more likely to be important in determining store image than the low-profile departments. Clearly those departments with the high walkout rate by comparison to their contribution to transactions, which were also high profile, should be first for management action.

In the more homogeneous retail outlets there is still evidence that shoppers perceive different sections or departments in the same way as in other retailers. The fresh food department of a grocery outlet could well be a high profile department that should have a low walkout rate.

This is not to say that there is any such thing as an ideal walkout rate. Simmons (1972) showed that rates varied between 77 per cent in a boutique to 16 per cent in a department store, with considerable variations in shoppers' intentions to purchase on entering. Only 54 per cent expected to buy when entering the boutique, emphasizing the unplanned nature of many retail purchases. In a bookseller/newsagent, for example, 79 per cent expected to buy and 76 per cent did so. The browsing rate was, as might be expected, much lower and the walkout rate lower in that type of retailing. A walkout survey was conducted on the independent health food retailer examined in Chapter 12. The walkout rate was very low, at about 20 per cent, and indeed could be argued to be too low. It might have been better if there had been more casual shoppers entering the store to be converted by the assistants into health product users.

The ideas and data presented in this section led us to propose a model that describes how department, store and chain images interact in establishing an overall image for a retailer. The model (Figure 13.2) draws from the idea of a Venn diagram.

In Figure 13.2*a* the retailer is projecting a rather different image for the chain as a whole, the individual store and department being considered. The inner cusp, where all three images overlap, is small. Customers entering the department because of the chain or store image are likely to leave without purchasing. This lack of coherence could well describe Woolworth's problem at the time of the first department store model. It is interesting to note the quite fundamental changes in product policy, store design and personnel policies used from the middle 1980s to reposition the store and provide a more coherent offer.

In Figure 13.2*b* there is a good deal of coherence at store level but the national image is somewhat out of step. This could well describe Tesco in its transition from 'pile it high, sell it cheap' to its later quality platform. The larger Tesco stores would have been easier to make compatible with the new image. Smaller shops may well have been coherent within themselves but incompatible with the new image and hence were sold.

In Figure 13.2*c* the degree of overlap is high. The company is presenting the same, coherent image at all levels and the example here could be Marks and Spencer. Taking the latter's success in food as a case in point, while other variety chain stores were moving out of food in the 1970s and 1980s, Marks and Spencer were busily making food a more profitable operation than many of their other mainstream business areas. However, both the selection of food lines and the service level offered were made compatible with the M & S image. The emphasis was placed on quality and value for money in a selective way, rather than on price and offering a full product range. The food department, very much against the expectations of many, became an integral part of the company's overall offering.

In some ways this view of the need for coherence, because of the danger at store level of underperforming departments, conflicts with the work of Cardozo (1974-75) and McGoldrick (1979) in identifying the importance of key departments. If stores have highly successful sections or departments and if this is an important way of projecting a favourable image, then by definition there will be other departments that perform less well. These

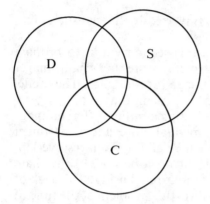

(a) Little coherence between
chain, store and department
image

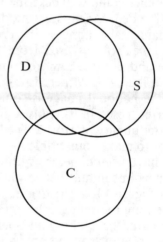

(b) Little compatibility
between national and
local image

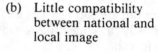

(c) The ideal situation
coherence of image

Figure 13.2 Department, store and chain images. D, department image;
S, store image; C, chain image.

departments may be important in providing the customer with a full range or a complete offer. The answer to this apparent anomaly lies in the way the store allocates space. If underperforming departments, identified from a walkout analysis, cannot be improved, then the space they occupy must be reduced to allow the key departments to expand or to allow new sections to be introduced. The key departments will always exist; the challenge is to match their success elsewhere in the store.

IMAGE AND THE BOTTOM LINE

From a practitioner's perspective perhaps the only valid way to examine image is to assess its effect on company profitability. In Chapter 5 there were apparent links between market positioning and a number of measures of commercial performance in menswear, ranging from gross margins to return on capital employed. In Chapter 7 a more comprehensive analysis of commercial performance and changes in positioning strategy in food retailing identified the rate of growth in sales volume as being the most likely financial measure to be affected by a change in relative image or positioning.

In Chapter 8 an analysis of department stores tended to support the link between sales volume growth and changing image. The comparison between British and West German department stores in Chapter 9 indicated that a whole retail sector could be more profitable if the competitors adopted a differentiated approach to their overall strategy, rather than each competing on price with no real cost advantage on which to base a choice.

These conclusions are compatible with much of the theory, ideas and analysis presented in the earlier chapters on marketing and corporate strategy, and especially with many of Porter's ideas on competitive strategy.

Figure 13.3 explains the way in which a retail image affects the company's financial performance. A better image will mean greater customer flow, fewer walkouts and therefore more customers spending more each time they visit. The first major commercial indicator to be affected will, therefore, be sales volume, explaining why sales volume growth seem to be closely linked to an improvement in relative image. Assuming costs do not rise as fast as sales volume, the next indicator to show an improvement will be net margin (the difference between turnover and the total costs involved in achieving that turnover). It is also likely that a better image will allow the sale of higher margin lines or allow the retailer to increase margin, thus affecting gross margin (the difference between buying and selling prices) as well as net margin, thus increasing profitability. The ultimate measure of commercial performance, the profit or return made as a percentage of the investment in the business (ROCE), will also rise as long as the company does not need to increase assets in order to achieve the desired change in image.

In Chapter 14 we examine how a company can define or select a suitable image, and how best to implement an image change. Changing image can be expensive in terms of capital and operating costs. Logically its effect on return on capital employed may not be as noticeable as the effect on sales volume growth. The way a company manages its assets could well change for other reasons, clouding the effect of an image change. However, in almost every circumstance that we have examined there are clear links between the main commercial criteria in operating a retail business and that business's relative position in the market-place.

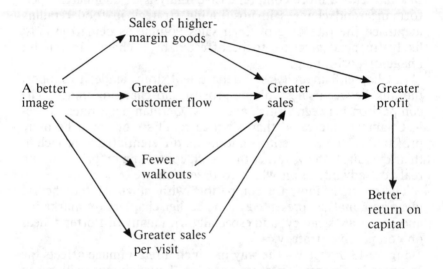

Figure 13.3 The way in which image affects financial performance.

KEY POINT SUMMARY

(1) The two main theoretical approaches to human behaviour, behavioural and cognitive, can each help explain some aspects of how shoppers form and use images of retail stores. The behavioural approach supports the idea of a limited

number of stimuli that evoke a conditioned response from shoppers. The cognitive approach supports the idea of shoppers having a series of reference points, particularly of competing stores.

(2) Empirical studies of the images of actual stores often identify a similar set of factors that affect store image. Merchandise, service, ambience and personnel appear to be key elements. However, the authors would argue that the use of price and ambience are the factors that seem, in practice, to be more generally relevant in differentiation between stores.

(3) The authors argue for coherence between department, store and chain image. If the three images do not overlap considerably customers will 'walk out' or not visit the store.

(4) Image is linked to commercial performance by improving customer flow, expenditure and propensity to purchase higher-margin goods.

References

Arons, L. (1961) Does television viewing influence store image and shopping frequency? *Journal of Retailing*, Vol. 37, pp. 1–13.

Bellinger, D.N. *et al.* (1976) The congruence of store image and self image, *Journal of Retailing*, Vol. 52, pp. 17–32.

Berry, L.L. (1969) The components of department store image: a theoretical and empirical analysis, *Journal of Retailing*, Vol. 45, p.3.

Brooks, J. (1988) Ph.D. Thesis, Manchester Polytechnic.

Cardozo, R.N. (1974–75) How images vary by product class, *Journal of Retailing*, Vol. 50, pp. 85–98.

Davies, K., Gilligan, C. and Sutton, C. (1985) Structural change in grocery retailing: the implications for competition, *International Journal of Physical Distribution and Materials Management*, Vol. 15, pp. 3–48.

Doyle, P. and Fenwick, I. (1974–75) How store image affects shopping behaviour in grocery chains, *Journal of Retailing*, Vol. 50, pp. 39–52.

Festinger, L. (1957) *A Theory of Cognitive Dissonance*, Stanford University Press.

Fulop, C. (1986) *Retailer Advertising and Retail Competition in the U.K.*, Advertising Association.

Halpern, R. (1985) Retail strategy for the eighties, IIR Conference, May 1985.

Lindquist, J.D. (1974) Meaning of image, *Journal of Retailing*, Vol. 50, p. 29.

Lowe, E. (1983) *Successful Retailing Through Advertising*, McGraw Hill, London.

Martineau, P. (1958) The personality of the retail store, *Harvard Business Review*, Vol. 36, Jan./Feb.

Mazursky, D. and Jacoby, J. (1985) Forming impressions of merchandise and service quality, in J. Jacoby and J.C. Olson (eds.) *Perceived Quality*, Institute of Retail Management, Lexington Books, New York.

Mazursky, D. and Jacoby, J. (1986) Exploring the development of store images, *Journal of Retailing*, Vol. 62, no. 2.

McGoldrick, P.J. (1979) Store image: how departmental images differ in a variety chain, *Retail and Distribution Management*, Sept./Oct., pp. 21-24.

Mintel (1985) *Market Intelligence: Retail Design*,

Myers, R.H. (1960) Shaping your store image, *Journal of Retailing*, Vol. 36, pp. 129-137.

NMRA (1986) Retail Audit.

Ornstein, E. (1976) *The Retailers*, Associated Business Programmes Ltd.

Piercy, N. (1983) What marketing lessons can retailers learn from the recession? *Retail and Distribution Management*, May/June, p. 15.

Rich, S.U. and Portis, B.D. (1964) The imageries of department stores, *Journal of Marketing*, Vol. 28, pp. 10-15.

Simmons, M. (1972) *Journal of Market Research Society*, Vol. 15.

Sturges, J. (1986) What's the matter with retail ads? *Marketing Week*, 18 July.

Weale, W.B. (1961) Measuring the customers image of a department store, *Journal of Retailing*, Vol. 37, pp. 40-48.

Chapter 14

Managing Positioning Strategy

In this final chapter we distil the contents of this book into a series of guidelines on how to manage the positioning or repositioning of a retail operation. We started with the assertion that for a retailer, managing strategy and marketing are akin to managing and marketing a branded consumer product. In other words, a retailer offers to the customer far more than the functional benefit of being a purveyor of products and services, but the retailer's offer can be reduced to a single concept or group of associated concepts. There are likely to be certain, less tangible benefits that a retailer can use to promote source loyalty.

In the chapter on corporate strategy we identified the advantages of evolving a clear statement on the direction any company wishes to take. The basic alternative strategies open to retailers were identified as being based on cost or differentiation/segmentation. The key to success, it was argued, lay not only in identifying a coherent strategy but in ensuring that such a strategy differentiated the company from its rivals. The practical studies have demonstrated the advantages of differentiation, and that price is one dimension along which a retailer may choose to differentiate itself. Non-price or image factors have been linked partly to ambience factors but not totally; indeed price itself has been shown to be as much of an image factor as any ambience-related concept.

Before applying the main points arising from earlier chapters, it is worth looking at the statements of retail practitioners and their advisers on some of the main issues covered earlier. The quotations are the equivalent of the anecdotal evidence used in the 1960s by many of the earlier writers on business policy in general, but these were made solely about retail businesses.

> It becomes even more important for the retailer to differentiate himself from his competitor by creating a personality or image which is different and which is his own.

(Peter Davis of J. Sainsbury (*Retail and Distribution Management,*

Sept./Oct. 1982) commenting on the consequences of the major food retailers operating with similar cost structures.)

> Choose products that will appeal to the customer identified as our target; thus giving the collection a homogeneity that is not found in those shops that try to offer a little of everything to everybody.

(Terence Conran, Storehouse. The first of eight principles drawn up to guide the development of Habitat in the 1960s.)

> Good management is making complicated things simple. The first thing you have to decide is what business you're in. A high percentage of organisations are in decline because the original business purpose is no longer relevant to the future. Marketing is crucial.

and

> Change is always on the agenda. No store is allowed to go more than 4–5 years without complete modernisation ... only the most visionary retailers recognise the need to change a successful formula while it is still working.

(Ralph Halpern of Burtons, commenting on the need to be prepared to change.)

> Twenty years ago we would identify shops by their functional offering. So there would be the baker and the grocer, the tailor and the sports goods shop, cosmetics and health food shops. Today, these have been truncated somewhat into what we call functional lifestyle shops. So Sainsbury subsumes the baker and the grocer – and the butcher and fishmonger; NEXT accounts for both the tailor and sports clothes; Boots has health food alongside the traditional sectors. In 15 years we might get a further truncation, with food, clothes and cosmetics being incorporated into a personal appearance shop – the true lifestyle offering.

(Bob Tyrrell of the Henley Centre for Forecasting, 1986.)

> *Making a Statement* is one of the latest buzzwords in retailing, generally used to describe a designer's new line or a best selling department. In the retailing business itself, it is the speciality stores – The Limited, Benetton, The Banana Republic, Crazy Eddie – that have made the most noticeable statements in recent years.

(Isadore Barmash, *New York Times*, 21 September 1986.)

High achievement retailers have above average clarity in projecting a market position to consumers. They focus marketing variables to create dominance at the point of attack.

(Cyrus C. Wilson and Thomas I. Rukel of Management Horizons, a leading consultancy specializing in retailing, reporting the results of an analysis of the common characteristics of the top twenty retail companies in the USA.)

but

If we have a corporate strategy it hasn't been communicated to us.

(A regular comment found in a survey of managers in fifteen leading retailers by Arthur Young, *Retail and Distribution Management*, May/June 1985.)

If the reader accepts that we have not been over-selective in our choice of quotation, this anecdotal evidence on operating a retail organization underlines the idea that a clearly enunciated positioning strategy is central to achieving success in retailing. If this is so, how have organizations devised and implemented such strategies successfully? Merely by adopting what appears to be a clear market position is not, it must be emphasized, a guarantee of such success.

DIFFERENTIATION

From thinking on business strategy, from marketing theory and from the empirical evidence presented in this book and elsewhere, the key to successful retail strategy is differentiation. Differentiation is only valid if the differences are perceived by the customer. It is not necessary for the whole market to value the point of difference or to rate it above other attributes. Differentiation mainly or solely on the grounds of price, as with MFI and Kwik Save, is no guarantee of being seen as closest to the image that shoppers choose to label as their ideal. Kendals was seen as 'expensive' by the typical department store shopper, but this did not prevent the store from finding a valid position in that market. It is necessary for a section or segment of customers to value the chosen point or points of difference, either as their main reason for shopping or as a good enough reason to visit when in a particular mood.

We have argued that most traditional methods of segmentation are less than adequate in forming the basis for retail strategy. We suggest rather that such methods are used to profile the most typical customer who will, or who already does, patronize the store. What is more important is that the store makes a unique offer which attracts a reasonable number of shoppers for a reasonable proportion of their shopping trips. As it becomes more difficult to identify more than just tendencies in groups of shoppers, and impossible to specify a description of the typical shopper which will include the majority of regular customers and exclude the rest, so segmentation will become less and less useful as the basis for retail strategy. We believe that segmentation can be an aid to communicating differentiation but is rarely the basis for differentiation.

The first question to be answered by management seeking a differentiated position is: 'Different from whom?' Woolworth was found to be 'different' in the first Manchester department store sector study, but was not seen by customers as competing in that market. Marks and Spencer, however, was perceived to be not only a department store, but the best. Shoppers seem to think of relatively tight groups of stores when identifying competing offers. Identifying the sector in which the retailer really competes is not as straightforward as it seems. Marks and Spencer were also well positioned in the food sector, not this time as a broad-appeal store but with much more of a niche strategy. Shoppers had little problem seeing Marks and Spencer in their two roles and would presumably have been equally capable of positioning them in the shoe market or any other sector where the company had a strong image and a major presence. What may appear anomalous is that the same company can have a seemingly different image in a number of markets. Marks and Spencer did not have as broad an appeal in food as in general retailing. This raises the issue of the real coherence between their department and store images. The answer seems to be that different labels can be attached to the retailer who competes in more than one sector without losing a central image. This allows Marks and Spencer to enter almost any retail market with customer credibility.

Marks and Spencer had a broad appeal as a department store but a narrower appeal as a food retailer, where Sainsbury had the nearest offer to one that appealed to most shoppers. The advantages of being a broad-appeal retailer are clear enough. The disadvantages include the presence of many would-be imitators, each attacking on a narrower front and each able to concentrate on improving on the broad-appeal store in its own specialist area.

Consequently, the second question to be answered is whether to be a specialist or a generalist in the chosen sector. Being the generalist, the broad-appeal competitor is in many ways an easier road to follow: you merely identify what concepts describe the shoppers' ideal store. The problem is that most if not all retailers in the same sector will be seeking to achieve the same position, or at least a reasonable position with respect to the ideal. This will limit the potential differentiation. The alternative is to aim for a narrower appeal, one that is different from existing competition and closely associated with a concept that is seen as ideal by a substantial group of customers for a substantial proportion of their purchases. This involves research, flair, intuition, guesswork – anything that identifies and emphasizes differentiation. Too many business people are followers rather than initiators, always asking what the competition is doing with the idea of copying, rather than with the objective of differentiating.

The penalties for copying can be severe. Copying an innovative market leader will condemn the follower to what marketers have labelled a 'me too' position, always seen as a pale copy of the real thing. A successful copying strategy will hardly prove more successful in that two identical retail concepts will be reduced, inevitably, to competing on price. If neither holds an economic advantage then both retailers will suffer. This was the case with the majority of menswear retailers and with Debenhams and Lewis's in the department store sector.

Profiling

Instead of segmenting a retail market we argue that differentiation is in effect its own source of segmentation. First, the retailer has to decide which other retailers form the closest competition, in other words in which sector the retailer will compete. The key to success will then be the degree of differentiation that the retailer can sustain and the retailer's proximity to the average perception of the ideal retail outlet within that sector. Other factors such as location, opening hours and parking will affect the ability of customers to shop at any particular store. However, such things being equal, the retailer's market positioning (rather than geographical positioning) will determine the number of visits the individual retailer receives and the propensity of customers to purchase once in the store.

Those people who value the concepts that differentiate a particular retailer from the retail sector being considered, form the target market for the given retailer. It may be possible to profile the typical customer using one or more of the methods of segmentation listed in Chapter 13. Even if the profiling cannot be used to estimate market share, it should be possible to be more specific about the various elements of the retail mix in order to maximize the attraction to the typical customer of the retail offer.

SOURCES OF DIFFERENTIATION

We have identified two types of concept which can be used to attract the customer. One type describes the collective view of the ideal retail outlet. The second type is relevant to the market but attractive to a minority. The first type, the ideal concepts or store attributes such as 'hygienic' in food retailing, 'wide range' in menswear and 'courteous' in department store retailing, can be regarded as core concepts. Every retailer must aim to maximize its appeal to its customers on these factors, as they are clearly important to every shopper. However, as a group of concepts they do not offer an easy basis for differentiation unless the retailer wishes to adopt a broad-appeal strategy. Broad-appeal retailers such as Marks and Spencer and Sainsbury were rated highly by the majority of customers shopping in their respective sectors, and this formed the source of their differentiation.

The second type of concept or store attribute offers a more direct source of differentiation, because it appeals only to a minority. In menswear retailing Dunns chose 'well-trained staff', in department store retailing Kendals chose 'up-market store', in health food retailing the Happy Nut House chose 'good for takeaway food'. Perhaps using the word 'chose' implies a greater proactivity on the retailers' side than really existed. But the lesson is there for those who are seeking a segmented approach, a narrower and more specialist appeal. They must identify retailing concepts that do not appeal to all but do appeal to enough people to ensure a viable business.

Price was found to provide a clear source of differentiation in department store, food and furniture retailing. It is probable that a price dimension exists in most retail sectors, although the electrical study, and to an extent the DIY sector study, might imply that this is not a totally watertight generalization. Price is probably the most obvious source of differentiation, and only in the electrical retail study did price appear as a core concept, although it is close to being so in the West German department store sector. In other UK studies a price appeal was attractive to a sector of the market.

Price and non-price factors in differentiation

While price is an obvious source of differentiation it is not the easiest to sustain. All retailers seek to offer value for money and most interpret this as managing their costs. Cost-reduction tactics include: moving to larger out-of-town premises, using part-time staff, centralizing distribution, bulk purchasing, EPOS, and controlling and evaluating key expenditure areas. Because such tactics are widely used they are unlikely to provide a source of differentiation or, in Porter's terminology, differential advantage. More fundamental factors have to be added to these routine ones before a retailer can rely on cost reduction to produce a sustainable price advantage. Kwik Save used a streamlined, limited-line approach in food retailing but their real economic advantage probably lay in their low labour costs. MFI pioneered out-of-town 'shed' retailing for furniture in Britain and was one of the first to computerize its point of sale. But its real advantage came from the flatpack products, the relationship with Hygena and the economy of scale the operation generated.

A true economic advantage can disappear, as the Co-op discovered after the lifting of resale price maintenance removed the economic advantage which stemmed from having its own manufacturing and a strong own label. Some cost advantages can be transitory. The change to own-label and centralized distribution by retailers saw the move of key personnel from one company to another taking with them their expertise and their previous employer's cost advantages.

Non-price or image factors are more difficult to identify but can offer a better approach to differentiation, in that being copied does not mean that the innovators lose their competitive advantage because of the 'me too' effect. The wheel of retailing theory implies that successful retailers begin with a price advantage that helps them expand, become more image based and, as a result, eventually fall prey to a new price-led formula.

The fate of department stores is often used to illustrate this theory. The same theory cannot account for the rise of NEXT, based on an image platform, or the 100 years of success for Marks and Spencer which, although begun with an economic advantage ('don't ask the price it's a penny') sustained by its innovative relationship with suppliers in its middle years, has moved progressively in the past 20 years. The wheel theory does not seem to apply to Marks and Spencer, and it is less than relevant to NEXT.

As the West German department store and the British electrical studies demonstrated, there are often many opportunities in the market which retailers ignore. The consequences were spelled out by the West German study and reinforced when the financial performance of that sector was compared to the equivalent in Britain. There can be little doubt that competing retailers should seek non-price methods in positioning to maximize the differentiation in their sector. As disposable incomes continue to rise, at least for those in employment, the importance of non-price factors can only grow. Retailers must recognize the opportunities that such trends present.

KEY FACTORS IN AN IMAGE-LED STRATEGY

Much of this book has been concerned with trying to identify what creates a good image. It appears that retail image is not formed by advertising, and there could be a large number of factors that have to be co-ordinated to produce a strong image. Theories of buyer behaviour and previous empirical work do not offer a clear view of what areas a retailer should concentrate on to project its chosen positioning. That said, three groups of factors appeal to us:

(1)   Design.
(2)   Service.
(3)   Merchandise.

Furthermore we would suggest this list in rank order of importance.

Design

Fitch and Wondhuysen (1987), writing about the strategic significance of design in retailing, claim that 'a good designer will deliver a working, exciting store that directly conveys his clients' management philosophy'. While retailers whose positioning is overtly price based neither need nor can afford the expense of store and interior design, the image-led retailers must express the differences inherent in their offer through the design of the store. The narrower the appeal, the more important the relevance of the design concept. It was no accident that the change from Hepworth to NEXT was based on design. Even in the apparently more prosaic area of food retailing, ASDA's improvement against Tesco was based partly on a major redesign of its stores (Fig. 7.22, pp. 116).

In the models presented earlier in this book concepts such as 'well laid out', 'good for browsing', 'comfortable', 'traditional', 'easy to shop at', 'pleasant surroundings', 'stylish' and 'good display' could all be conveyed to shoppers by a good design, from a well-judged shopfront topped with a relevant logo, to the interior store layout and merchandise presentation.

Service

Many of the core and segmenting concepts identified in the various sector models are concerned with the level and quality of staff and the service policies of their employees. 'Helpful staff', 'good checkout operation', 'well-trained staff', 'courteous', 'efficient staff', 'not aggressive', 'helpful advice', and 'not condescending' illustrate what shoppers feel are relevant concepts. But because shoppers vary in the level of service they require and how much they will pay, service level provides a basis for differentiation. In turn the number, demeanour, physical appearance and sheer quality of staff will project an image for the company.

The quality and demeanour of staff are largely determined by the calibre of staff who can be recruited and the quality of their training. Training in customer service was much in vogue in Britain in the 1980s. In companies such as Woolworth staff selection and training had become a cornerstone of corporate policy (Rose, 1988). Store personnel present an image because of their age, apparent social class and fashion consciousness. Marks and Spencer became conscious that the average age of their predominantly female shop assistants was increasing. On the surface this could be regarded as a compliment to their staff policies, and be seen as a benefit given the high costs of recruitment and staff training. The potential disbenefit, however, is that customers see the assistant as part of the retail offer. The same assistant who could help sell miniskirts in her twenties in the 1960s might be unable to do the same for her daughter's generation in the 1980s. In the USA, The Limited, a concept similar to NEXT, reportedly approached the problem by changing their merchandise to suit the ageing profile of both customers and assistants, and introduced a new chain to appeal to the same age-group at which the original concept had been aimed some years earlier.

It follows from examples that the physical look of an assistant can be as important as the design of the store in projecting an image. This raises all sorts of issues in recruitment and selection, including the fairness and legality of seeking a visual stereotype for employees. Staff training in customer care is an obvious follow up to careful recruitment.

Merchandise

It may be a surprise to see merchandise as the last of the three factors recommended for attention in image management. Readers will be familiar with stories of identical merchandise selling for very different prices in different stores to what appears to be the same clientele. What are important are the manner and the context in which the merchandise is presented, rather than just the merchandise itself. Nevertheless, of course merchandise quality, design and range will affect the image presented by the retailer.

An important area to consider here is the role of own label. In food retailing the emphasis on own label has changed from a component of a price-led approach to one of image. In non-food retailing the image potential of own label has been recognized for some time by companies like Benetton, Laura Ashley and Habitat. The presence of a house brand name appears to be less important than the impression of value for money and the contribution the retailer's own-label range makes to the overall image. Own label offers a unique advantage to retailers in conveying to the customers what is different about them. In practice many retailers seem to copy each other's own-label products. They seek out the same own-label manufacturer and often demand the same product as that supplied to their rivals.

What should be happening is that retailers should be insisting on differences in their own-label lines and emphasizing those differences in their packaging and presentation. This in turn implies a greater involvement in design and product technology than most retailers have been used to. Senker (1987) has studied the involvement of food retailers in technology. The extent of involvement, assessed by the number of technologists the retailer employed and what they were employed to do, varied substantially. Significantly the food retailers with the largest number of technologists tended to be those with high sales of own label and, subjectively, those whose own label was used to support the image rather than the price component of the retailer's positioning.

IMPLEMENTING THE CHOSEN POSITIONING

A number of ideas emerge from studying those retailers who have managed to change their positioning. In the studies presented in this book, Tesco and ASDA in food, and Lewis's in department store retailing are the three major examples. All three used design, personnel and merchandise as part of their overall strategy (interestingly only Lewis's used national brands in the merchandise). All three represent changes to existing operations. In Lewis's case the change took time, not only to implement, but also for the perception of the general public to alter significantly. In both food examples the changes were more rapid but no change was dramatic; indeed all could be described as incremental. More dramatic changes, and the example of NEXT has been cited frequently, seem to rely on a total change of operation.

The management of change is a substantial topic in its own right and cannot be surveyed here, except to point to two factors that appear to be important in any organizational change. The first is the presence of one or more strong personalities who will act as the agents or champions of the change. The second is the need for clarity both in describing what changes are to be made and in the expression of what is to be achieved. From our own work, we identify three issues in implementing a positioning strategy in a retail business: organization, clarity and external promotion.

Organization

Apart from the presence of a key individual, retail organizations which have managed change successfully over a long period of time appear to have organized themselves to cope with long-term trends. Gilligan and Sutton (1987) point to the short-term nature of planning in many retail companies and have described strategic planning in retail businesses in general as being 'relatively underdeveloped' by comparison with the norms in other sectors. Some retailers have nevertheless had strong corporate planning sections for many years (e.g. Marks and Spencer and Tesco). While the presence of such a function is no guarantee of successful planning, it is interesting to compare the approaches of other retailers who may have a marketing department concerned with more short-term changes, or no organizational function apart from the board of directors who are clearly associated with future strategy. The West German department store study observed that while research on image was conducted by companies it was not, apparently, used strategically.

Clarity

The clarity of a company's positioning has a number of facets. The concept's chosen image must be clear to the shopper. An ASDA director frequently used the phrase 'making an offer with authority' during a presentation on ASDA's repositioning (Dowling, 1987), thus encapsulating this point. Woolworth's decision to 'focus' on a limited number of key merchandise areas is a similar move towards clarity and simplification. In the earlier studies, both Woolworth and the Co-op seemed to suffer because, being seen as different, they had no association with relevant concepts; in other words they had no clear points of differentiation.

The authors have added the notion of coherence when referring to the need for compatibility between department, store and chain images. Debenhams in the early 1970s found some disbenefits in changing the names of stores to the Debenhams standard

(Ornstein, 1976), because shoppers reacted unfavourably in some stores but favourably in others. Overall there is a general consensus in favour of defining and maintaining retail image centrally and controlling a standardized offer through the systems retailing approach. Most important of all, employees must be informed of the company's positioning strategy.

Promotion

A considerable amount of data has been presented on the role of advertising in retail image. There seem to be advantages to the price-led retailer in advertising such a proposition. It also seems that advertising can be used to inform about a positioning strategy. MFI offer a good example of a company who have used advertising to do both. Until the late 1980s their positioning and advertising were based solely on price. In 1987 the advertising changed to announce a lower emphasis on price and a greater one on product design, with their 'Take a look at us now' campaign. Kendals were equally successful in informing people that their prices were not as high as might be perceived from their overall image. Lewis's used advertising extensively to promote their image change. In 1988 Marks and Spencer launched their first image-based advertising campaign. However, together with British Home Stores, John Lewis, Waitrose and NEXT, Marks and Spencer remain a good example of a company with a strong image which had not relied on advertising in its formation.

The examples in food retailing add further weight to the view that advertising can help communicate an image but cannot create one. This view is supported by the arguably unsuccessful use of advertising by Woolworth and the Co-op during our studies, and the successful use of public relations by NEXT and Marks and Spencer, where the emphasis can only be on communication. Yet the impression still persists that advertising offers the key to image issues in retailing. In March 1988, *Marketing* ran a headline entitled 'Sainsbury tries a smile' over an article claiming that Sainsbury would increase its advertising expenditure with more emphasis on television to combat 'an austere image' and give the company 'a friendlier face', following the results of market research. Whether Sainsbury would have concurred with the article or not is less relevant than the apparent belief that advertising would be the answer to an image issue. It seems that the only way advertising can be used is to inform about what is reality in the store. It cannot change that reality, and any attempt to do so will merely add to the walkout rate experienced by the retailer.

MONITORING AND CONTROL

After the positioning strategy has been defined and implemented, the company's success or otherwise has to be assessed. A good position can be clearly linked to financial performance, as we have demonstrated. A good image enhances customer flow and expenditure per visit. A change to a better image should be measurable by improvements in both statistics. One further measure worth taking is a walkout survey, in order to identify whether certain departments have an image that is incompatible within the overall image. Regular measures of comparable performance on a battery of factors, with the emphasis on assessing positive differentiation, are vital, in our opinion.

The Burton group believes that the life of an image could be limited to a few years. In this case image needs measuring on a regular basis to ensure that the customer agrees with the retailer on the value of the chosen image. Most important of all is to ensure that the image remains differentiated. Markets and perceptions change but the actions of other retailers are probably the most threatening, given the tendency to copy rather than innovate in some sectors. In many ways positioning strategy with respect to competition is like driving a car. Drivers must be aware of what is happening around them and be prepared to take evasive action if appropriate. The main threat to the business may not be whether or not you can manage your own progress; it could be the fool behind you who, quite literally, is not looking where he or she is going.

CONCLUSION

Retailing faces many challenges. British retailing is comparatively profitable at the time of writing. This profitablity is associated with a high degree of differentiation between competing companies in key markets, but it could be threatened by the very success of the multiple operators as they continually seek new sites. A recent survey of American retailing (Cornell University, 1988) indicated that the profitability of American food chains, measured by percentage profit before tax, was less than half that of the leading British food retailers. Sales per square foot were measured at just over half the British rate. This was linked by the commentator to the alleged over-footing of the American retail market.

At the time of writing planning applications for new retail space in the Greater Manchester area, for example, would nearly double the existing retail footage. Such developments have been greeted with grave misgivings, but even if all were successful, the footage per head of population in Manchester would only match that in the East Coast city of Philadelphia. Current trends point to a significant increase in UK footage and to the dangers of a price-led response by British operators, as seen in the USA. The alternative is for retailers to seek to minimize direct price competition and concentrate largely on non-price differentiation.

A further challenge is the trend towards internationalization among retail companies. To date the experiences of retailers operating internationally have been mixed (Mitton, 1987) and it seems that retailers are generally more successful in their home base. Highly targeted retailers, such as Benetton, appear to travel better, possibly because their relatively narrow appeal will generally find a large enough niche in any developed country.

The retailer is now faced with the same problems that once faced the manufacturers of brands who had to learn to reposition their products to suit individual markets or to develop truly international brands. The retailer faces a more substantial challenge in positioning in a foreign market, because the positioning cannot be established as easily by advertising. In addition the operational aspects of the retail business may have to be changed, unless the new market contains an unoccupied segment similar to the one in the retailer's home market. The retailer will need to assess first, in what market sector its basic offer is seen as competing. An evaluation of the probably quite different concepts seen as comprising the ideal retail offer in that sector, and how closely this can be matched, will be essential. Providing these to the customer is, in reality, the cost of entering that market. Finally, the retailer will need to assess how well it can deliver those factors which will differentiate it from existing competition.

As the British domestic market becomes more competitive for British multiples, the temptation will be to move abroad in the search for growth. Positioning will be the key to success or failure at home and abroad.

References

Cornell University (1988) Study cited in *Retailing World*, no. 33, Jan.
Dowling, P. (1987) The ASDA story, IGD Seminar, Manchester 1987.
Fitch, R. and Wondhuysen, J. (1987) The strategic significance of design, in E. McFadyen (ed.) *The Changing Face of British Retailing*, Newman Books, London.

Gilligan, C. and Sutton, C. (1987) Strategic planning in grocery and DIY retailing, in G. Johnson (ed.) *Business Strategy and Retailing*, Wiley.

Mitton, A.E. (1987) Foreign retail companies operating in the UK: strategy and performance, *Retail and Distribution Management*, Jan./Feb.

Ornstein, E. (1976) *The Retailers*, Associated Business Programmes Ltd.

Rose, D. (1988) Changing attitudes, case study of Woolworth presented at Cortco Case Study Conference, Co-op College, Loughborough, January 1988.

Senker, J. (1987) Technological cooperation between manufacturers and retailers to meet market demand, *Food Marketing*, Vol. 2, no. 3, p 38.

Index